TROUBLEMAKER

TROUBLEMAKER

Surviving Hollywood and Scientology

LEAH REMINI

with Rebecca Paley

BALLANTINE BOOKS | NEW YORK

Published in the United States by Ballantine Books, an imprint of Random House, a division of Penguin Random House LLC, New York.

BALLANTINE and the HOUSE colophon are registered trademarks of Penguin Random House LLC.

ISBN 978-1-101-88696-0
eBook ISBN 978-1-101-88697-7

Printed in the United States of America on acid-free paper

randomhousebooks.com

2 4 6 8 9 7 5 3 1

First Edition

Book design by Susan Turner

To my family and friends, for your undying support.
I dedicate this book to you.

And to my fellow nonconformists, aka troublemakers.
May you always continue to speak the truth.

In a time of universal deceit—telling the truth is a revolutionary act.

Let me start with this:

I am an apostate.

I have lied. I have cheated. I have done things in my life that I am not proud of, including but not limited to:

- falling in love with a married man nineteen years ago
- being selfish and self-centered
- fighting with virtually everyone I have ever known (via hateful emails, texts, and spoken words)
- physically threatening people (from parking ticket meter maids to parents who hit their kids in public)
- not showing up at funerals of people I loved (because I don't deal well with death)
- being, on occasion, a horrible daughter, mother, sister, aunt, stepmother, wife (this list goes on and on).

The same goes for every single person in my family:

- My husband, also a serial cheater, sold drugs when he was young.
- My mother was a self-admitted slut in her younger days (we're talking the 1960s, before she got married).
- My dad sold cocaine (and committed various other crimes), and then served time at Rikers Island.

Why am I revealing all this? Because after the Church of Scientology gets hold of this book, it may well spend an obscene amount of money running ads, creating websites, and trotting out celebrities to make public statements that their religious beliefs are being attacked—all in an attempt to discredit me by disparaging my reputation and that of anyone close to me. So let me save them some money. There is no shortage of people who would be willing to say "Leah can be an asshole"—my own mother can attest to that. And if I am all these things the church may claim, then isn't it also accurate to say that in the end, thirty-plus years of dedication, millions of dollars spent, and countless hours of study and training didn't really "fix" me? Perhaps Scientology doesn't work.

SINCE I LEFT THE CHURCH of Scientology in 2013, I am often asked the question "How does someone like you get involved with an organization like Scientology?" Or some people may phrase it more like "How the fuck did you get into some crazy shit like this?"

Describing Scientology is no easy undertaking for anyone. There are plenty of people (many of whom are smarter than I am and have more formal education) who have worked to define and examine the church and the sway it holds over its members. This book, written from my heart and based on personal knowledge, is my attempt to portray my experience within Scientology and the repercussions I endured as a result.

So while I may not be able to say in a few brief sentences why I became involved in Scientology and remained a member for decades, I can tell you that whether you were raised in the organization or came to it after falling out with your own religion, traditions, or family, the central tenet of Scientology, as stated by its founder, L. Ron Hubbard (LRH), is incredibly alluring. Scientology offers a clearly laid out scientific process that helps you to overcome your limitations and realize your full potential for greatness. It is presented as a well-defined path to achieving total spiritual freedom and enlightenment and a full understanding of yourself and others. LRH wrote that the aims of Scientology are *"a civilization without insanity, without criminals and without war, where the able can prosper and honest beings can have rights, and where Man is free to rise to greater heights."*

He went on to state:

"What is true for you is what you have observed yourself. And when you lose that, you have lost everything."

As well as:

"Don't take my word that Scientology works or doesn't work, use it and see for yourself. Take what works and throw away the rest."

I, along with many others, found these approaches to be hugely empowering. I was taken with the idea that a deep, systematic, and straightforward wisdom on how to live the best life for myself (and the planet) could be presented before me in a direct, tangible, and comprehensive way. Through rigorous study and regular counseling (called "auditing" in Scientology), I could work toward the ultimate goal of "going Clear," meaning I would no longer be affected by the part of my mind ruled by pain and irrationality. This promise of a higher living and way of thinking drew me in, along with thousands of others who were looking for an alternative to therapy or more traditional self-help.

I, like many current Scientologists, was a second-generation practitioner (meaning you were either born into Scientology or brought in by your parents as a child). When you are raised in the church, your whole life—each and every day—becomes all about the church. Unlike members of other churches or synagogues, who attend Sunday Mass or Shabbat dinner once a week, as a Scientologist you are expected to spend a minimum of two and a half hours a day, every day, seven days a week, at church, studying and/or in counseling. The same goes for your family, friends, and business associates. It's no wonder the indoctrination quickly sets up an "us against them" mentality. To leave, to question it, would mean leaving anything and everything you have ever known. And because you were raised in the church, your world consists almost exclusively of Scientologists.

For those who are not born into the church or brought in as children, the attraction to join is most definitely there. Imagine you are struggling in your life, in your career, or you are maybe an actor with little or no fame. You walk into a Scientology church or a Celebrity Centre (a Scientology church that caters specifically to artists), having been enticed by an ad you read in a magazine about improving your life or career. You are impressed with the beautiful building, and the welcoming people there. They offer you food, listen to what you have to say. Maybe you talk about how your parents are not supportive of your endeavors, and they respond, "Wow, that is not cool. You *can* achieve your goals in life. Maybe you need to step away from your parents' negativity for a bit and do a course here that will help you to reach your goals." You feel vindicated. *This person understands me. He or she is my ally. This group believes in me.* In the real world you may feel like you are nothing, but here you are treated with respect.

The other aspect of Scientology that draws people in is the recognition the church bestows on its members for their donations. Let's say you are a successful businessperson. Where else would you be pulled up onstage with crowds cheering in admiration for the million(s) you have donated? You are doted on by the church at this level, recognized, and made to feel special. Very enticing. Or what if you are someone who earns $45,000 a year? You're now going to be celebrated and acknowledged for your $2,000 contribution (even if you have no money the church will find a way for you to borrow it) with a framed certificate in calligraphy certifying your donation. This in turn, again, makes you feel special. You believe you are doing great things for not only yourself, but for all of mankind. This type of celebration and recognition works on members of all levels.

During my thirty-plus years in Scientology I spent close to

$2 million for services and training, and donated roughly $3 million to church causes. Most members, regardless of their income, over a lifetime in the church spend upwards of $500,000 to get to the highest levels, which often takes more than twenty years. During this time, they are required to purchase roughly 300 books, 3000 lectures, and 100 courses.

Scientologists funnel their hard work, money, and emotional capital right back into the church, often to the detriment of their own lives. They may sacrifice relationships with family members, contact with friends, and their life savings to move up through the assigned spiritual levels that are dictated by the church's principles. They do this because they're indoctrinated with the belief that Scientology has the answers not only to their own ills but to the ills of all humankind.

I HAVE NO DOUBT THAT when this book comes out, Scientologists will scream about religious intolerance, say that I am a liar, that I was kicked out of the church, and call *Troublemaker* the work of a hateful bigot or a self-absorbed person with an "insatiable craving for attention." (That last part might not be totally untrue; I am an actress, after all.) What they will likely not do, however, is actually read this book, because that would be going against one of the basic tenets of Scientology. A member should not read or watch anything generated by someone whom the church has declared a Suppressive Person, or SP, someone who in the church's eyes and by LRH's policy is found to be a threat to Scientology. Once the church has labeled you an SP, you are "Declared," and as a result, you are cut off from all practicing Scientologists.

So I have been declared by the church to be a Suppressive Person because I questioned, spoke out against, and refused to abide by the hypocrisy that had become my life. The church has lashed out at me in the press and will continue to do so, but the reality is that the church has benefited from me, my money, my time, my celebrity status, and my family. Everything I had dedicated myself to for all those years was taken away in an instant when I was declared an SP. I was the one left with the heartbreak of feeling that the unraveling of my faith and fate, and life as I knew it, was primarily influenced by two people: Tom Cruise, the church's most coveted, celebrated, and protected celebrity member, and David Miscavige, the tyrannical leader and current head of the church. Ironically, for me and for most other people who have left the church and spoken out against it, the very qualities that we've been penalized for—defying, questioning, thinking independently—are the same qualities that made us prime candidates for Scientology in the first place.

According to church policy, since I have been declared a Suppressive Person, all church members, including dozens of my closest friends and family must "disconnect" from me, meaning cutting any and all ties (though thankfully my mother, stepfather, sister, and brother-in-law have stood by me). No more contact. Ever.

I am not the first to leave and speak out against Scientology. Many, like me, have questioned a faith that erratically labels its followers, constantly encourages its parishioners to donate their life savings (and beyond) to its coffers, kicks its followers out of a religion they have believed in and dedicated themselves to. It is to the Church of Scientology that I say this: I wrote this book because I feel an urgency and responsibility to reveal the injustices and hypocrisy that were perpetrated against those who left and spoke out before me. Those who again and again have been harassed and bullied into silence. This book is also a personal act of defiance—against intolerance, which I have witnessed, lived with, and been part of for far too long.

TROUBLEMAKER

Chapter One

As far back as I can remember, I was always performing and trying to make people laugh. I grew up on *I Love Lucy, Welcome Back, Kotter, Happy Days, Gilligan's Island, Three's Company, Sanford and Son, All in the Family, Good Times* . . . You get the idea. Watching all of these shows always made me *feel* something. I knew early on that *I* wanted to make people feel this same way.

As a kid I was always putting on shows—re-creating skits from *The Carol Burnett Show* and singing Donny and Marie songs in the living room. My older sister, Nicole, reluctantly played my sidekick; although she never had any enthusiasm for these skits and performances, she obliged. I also took to giving her notes like "Nic, Donny loves Marie, so when we do 'I'm a Little Bit Country,' you gotta look at me like he looks at Marie, with a smile and maybe a wink." She would respond with "Or how about I just punch you in the face?" Okay, we all make choices as performers.

When I was nine years old, I heard that the Broadway musical *Annie* was holding open auditions for the lead role. I didn't let the fact that I had no singing talent or acting experience deter me. My mom supported me, believing that I would one day be an actress, and she got a playwright friend to teach me the song "Tomorrow" and take me to the group audition. Her boyfriend at the time photographed me for my "headshots," in which I wore my very best *Little House on the Prairie* shirt. When I got the pictures back, I was seriously floored at how beautiful I looked. Clearly, the *Annie* people would see this little gem from Brooklyn and want to hire me on the spot—but I was still willing to sing for them if need be.

The audition was a cattle call, which meant everyone was assigned a number and sat in the audience section of a huge theater until that number was called. The image running through my mind was that of a front-page headline in the *New York Post:* "Brooklyn Girl with No Experience Nabs *Annie* Role." Whatever I lacked in terms of dancing or singing, someone could teach me. I had the chutzpah to land the part. And as for my long, straight brown hair— well, that's what wigs were for. And with that, I was off to hand the director my picture.

But as soon as my name was called and I got onstage, facing the director and all those people sitting in the darkened theater, I went blind with panic.

The pianist hit a key and I started to sing immediately. "The—"

"No. That's for the key," the director interrupted.

"Okay. Well, maybe you should tell people . . . Do you want me to start again?" I said.

"That's okay. Go home to Mommy," the director said as he looked down at his clipboard.

I burst into tears before I had even gotten off the stage. I was crying the way kids do when they can't catch their breath. My mom's friend, the one who taught me the song, who had brought me to the audition, took me for a slice of pizza and an Italian ice, over which we discussed how that director would regret not hiring me and how *Annie* would bomb without me. The Broadway show *Annie* would suffer and suffer big without me in it!

WHEN I WASN'T ACTING OUT my favorite TV shows, Nicole and I could be found hanging out on Eighty-sixth Street, near Bay Parkway, where loud music thumped from the cars to get girls' attention, even though the guys in their gold chains, Old Spice, and gelled hair acted like they were too cool to care. I aspired to be one of those girls whose attention the guys sought—tight Jordache and Sergio Valente jeans with a brush jammed in the back pocket, lots of makeup and Aqua Net, and even more attitude. All they ever seemed to do was hang out on the corner—like a hooker, but not—and I wanted in. I vowed that when I was older—maybe twelve or thirteen—I would be just like them.

This was Bensonhurst, Brooklyn, circa 1980. We talked tough, but ultimately it was a protective neighborhood for those who belonged. When a car alarm went off, there would be five Joeys and Frankies out on the street with bats within two minutes. There was no such thing as minding your own business. If a boyfriend was fighting with his girlfriend, another guy would start yelling at him: "Yo, don't fuckin' talk to a girl like that." 'Nuff said.

When we were kids, our neighborhood—basically consisting of a bakery, a pizzeria, a bagel store, a Baskin-Robbins, a Chock full o'Nuts, a Te-Amo, and an Optima—was our whole universe.

While Manhattan, just a quick train ride away, was foreign to Nicole and me, places like Long Island and New Jersey were another planet. When our mom took us to the Poconos for vacation (a rarity), we met a group of girls who asked us if we wanted to help "collect things for a collage." First we had to clear up what a collage was, because my sister and I didn't speak French. When it rained, these kids stayed inside and played Atari, unlike us Brooklyn kids, who were used to hanging out in front of the candy store come rain, sleet, or mini-hurricane.

Our regular neighborhood haunt was the local Te-Amo convenience store, near the D train. We could also be found at other people's houses, where it seemed there were always better toys and better food than at ours. I spent a lot of time at my friend's place above our apartment on Bay Parkway. She had a Barbie Dreamhouse, which back then, to little girls, was pretty much the equivalent of crack. That's where I was playing one day when my mom called Nicole and me down to share some news.

"I've got to tell you girls something," Mom said. "Your dad and I are separating. I don't want you to be upset. I'm okay, and we're going to be okay."

I sat there basically without expression and looked at my sister, wondering if I should try to fake being more upset.

George, my dad, was the classic *paesan* of Sicilian origin who used hairspray on his remaining three hairs, wore a rope chain and pinky ring, got his nails done, and kept his car—a Cadillac, of course—perfectly clean and smelling good with one of those scented trees that hang from the rearview mirror. And I was scared shitless of the man.

He never hit me. (Nicole, on the other hand, would get smacked. "You are older. You should know better," he used to say to my sister, as if she were going to college already, though she was just a year older than me.) What terrified me was the way my dad could annihilate you when he spoke, throwing around words like "idiot," "retard," "moron" at the drop of a hat.

One time when we were little and pretending to make soup in the bathroom sink out of his Old Spice, Contac cold capsules, and most of the other contents of the medicine cabinet, I saw my dad at the end of the hallway. When he asked, "What the fuck are you's doing?" I got hot all over and couldn't say a word. After Nicole answered, "We are making a soup," he spanked her. For some reason I always laughed when my sister got hit. I'm sure it was a defense against more complicated emotions. Or I was just evil as a kid and liked her getting hit.

"Idiots," he said. "Get into your room."

He was only raising us the way he had been raised, but anytime he was around, I was tense—even when he was trying to be kind. For example, one time when I came to the dinner table, I found a paper bag on my chair, so I didn't sit down.

"What are you going to do, stand there?" he asked, looking at me.

What's the right answer?

I didn't want to say the wrong thing, so I didn't say anything.

"Pick up the bag, idiot," my dad said.

Thinking this was some kind of a trick, I nervously picked up the bag and opened it. Inside was a doll. By the time I realized what it was, however, I was so wound up that I had started to cry.

"What's with you?" Dad started yelling. "Someone tries to give you a gift and you're crying?"

I couldn't catch my breath to explain.

I remember once when I carelessly shoved a box of cookies into the kitchen cabinet. My dad walked by, saw what I was doing, and said, "What kind of fucking animal puts cookies back this way?!" He grabbed the box and threw the cookies across the room.

I responded by giving him the cold shoulder. An hour later I went into the living room to get a blanket, and there was my dad, sitting on the couch watching TV. He smiled at me and gave me a nod. Again, I ignored him.

"What, you mad at me? You're mad at Daddy? You're not talking to me? Come sit down and watch a movie with me."

Before long my resolve melted and I sat down and cuddled up next to him. I fell for it every time.

When he wasn't yelling and calling us names, my dad could be charming, loving, protective, everything you would want a dad to be. Everything that would draw me in. He had a big personality, and when he was around, he would take over the room and everyone else would seem to disappear. Try as I might to resist him, time and time again I couldn't.

When it was just my mom, it was like a different world. Vicki was a fun, free spirit, kind of like a hippie. She didn't believe in sugar, and she wore her hair parted down the middle with barrettes holding it back on the sides. But she always had a look, like she was a little bit of trouble. There were not a whole lot of rules with her.

She was an only child, and her mother and father, who were Jewish, died when she was very young. So she was sent to live with an aunt, who made it very clear that she hated my mother. Because Mom didn't have structure or a traditional mother in her own childhood, she never learned that role. Nor did she want to.

Although she was a stay-at-home mom, she wasn't a big cook. She didn't make her own sauce like the Italian moms did, or rice and beans like the moms of my Puerto Rican friends. Dinner at our house was anything you could coat in egg and 4C Bread Crumbs and fry. That and salad with way too much vinegar.

No one wanted to come to my house after school because we didn't have Twinkies, Devil Dogs, Oreos, or anything else good to eat. Once, after playing Charlie's Angels on the playground at school, I invited my friends over. But when they got there all I could say was, "Hey, anyone up for Wheat Thins? No? We have Tab . . . No? Okay."

That's about when someone would suggest that we move on to hang out at my friend Roberta's house.

I didn't blame them. Roberta's apartment was everything that a household should look like, smell like, and essentially be. It came complete with plastic slipcovers over the furniture to protect it and a special case to house her mother's Norman Rockwell figurines. I was convinced that this was what a home was supposed to be like. And this was definitely not how we were rolling.

When I asked my mom why we didn't have plastic on our furniture like Roberta did, she said, "You want your ass to stick to the couch?"

Yes, and I wanted her to have the lemony smell of Pledge in the house. That's right, the wood cleaner. All my friends had to Pledge all the wood furniture in their houses on the weekends, and I wanted to do the same. I also wanted my mom to iron my clothes for school, putting a crease down the middle of my pants like the other girls' pants had. Instead, Mom showed me where the iron was, told me how to use it.

I was obsessed with how I thought things should be and appear. I think on some level every kid wants what other kids have, but I was particularly status-conscious. It was in my DNA to constantly scan my surroundings, always observing, always making mental notes of the details that would make me "the right kind of person."

And if I couldn't be this right kind of person, with the right kind of things, I would be quick to criticize myself before anyone else could. And I would often bark out to my mother, "Why don't we have this?" and "Why don't we have that?"

Collecting things, creases in my pants, plastic covers, Pledged dining room tables—*this is how you are accepted*, I thought. But I was never able to achieve or find the normalcy I craved. I felt subpar to all my friends. Even those friends who lived in the projects had moms who spent their days at home cooking delicious vats of rice and beans while I was left to eat a two-day-old bagel.

Because of my obsession with appearances, I was skeptical at first of my mom's boyfriend Dennis, whom she brought home when I was seven years old, after she had divorced my dad. In comparison to my dad, Dennis was a bit of a geek, with his glasses, pants belted high up on his waist, and mustache. But he was also very sweet and didn't make me feel tense when he was around, like my dad did. Dennis immediately put Nic and me at ease when he gave us the speech: "I'm not trying to be your dad. You already have one of those. Look at me as a friend. I love your mother, and I will love you." My sister and I liked his spirit, but we were going to have to work on his look, starting with getting a little Dippity-do into that hair.

Dennis was easygoing and playful, just like my mom. They would do things like have water fights where they'd run into our room to use Nic and me as human shields while they tried to throw cupfuls of water at each other.

Even though he was Italian, Dennis wasn't anything like any of the other guys we knew. He didn't seem to have man hang-ups or the macho mentality that most of the men I grew up with had. He was a waiter, and a great cook, and he always made us food whenever he was home. "Your mother's not going to cook a decent meal, ever, for you girls," he joked, "so you better be nice to me."

He didn't dismiss us or try to shoo us away like everyone else in the neighborhood did; instead, he looked us right in the eye and took everything we said seriously, even though we were just kids. Mom said it was because he was a Scientologist. I didn't know what that meant—some kind of scientist, maybe—and I didn't really care either. At least, not until my mother started going to the city by herself and not coming back until late at night.

"Where do you go, Ma?" I asked one night over chicken cutlets at the kitchen table when it seemed like it had been forever since she'd been home for dinner.

"I go to this church," she said.

"But aren't you Jewish?" I asked.

The only church I knew of was the Catholic one, that we often attended with my grandmother, my father's mother, who lived in Little Italy.

"This is the Church of Scientology. This church isn't about God and saints. It is about helping you to live your life better. Like the course I'm doing now. I'm learning that if you do something bad, even if it's little, if you're a good person you feel bad about it. And what happens is that in your mind, that little thing becomes a big thing. And that leads you to feel bad about yourself, which then leads to doing more bad things. All these bad things, no matter how small, are called overts. And if you don't get these overts 'off,' you will do worse things.

"But if you tell the truth about what you've done," she continued, "you kind of clear the slate, and then you don't feel like you have to do more bad things. This is what's called in Scientology 'getting off your overts.' Like confessing your sins, but more practical."

"That's why you should tell me anything you girls have done that I don't know about."

As soon as my mom said that, I thought about the operation I had come up with to feed my leg warmer addiction. After seeing *Flashdance,* I decided I needed leg warmers in every color (I was always about quantity rather than quality). I told the neighborhood boys I'd give a hickey to anyone who stole leg warmers for me from the Chinese vendors. At that time, hickeys were a big deal. It was a sign that you were up to some stuff. We practiced them on ourselves on our upper arms. (This way you could just pull down your sleeves and nobody would know you'd been practicing on yourself.) When it came to my trading hickeys for leg warmers, I was very specific about just what it was going to take to get me to put my lips on a boy's neck—we're talking a minimum of three pairs, preferably purple, purple with glitter, and light purple. It was a brilliant idea, if I do say so myself.

So here I was, at the dinner table, wanting to do what my mom was asking—tell the truth. But if I did that, she was no doubt going to kill me.

"Ma," I said, "I didn't personally steal anything . . ."

"Leah. What did you do?"

"I might have said I would give someone a hickey if they got me leg warmers from the Chinese shop."

"Ewwwww," Nicole said.

Normally I would have told Nicole to shut up, but I was steeling myself for the more important reaction from my mom. The reaction of most moms I knew would be a crack on the mouth. Who tells their mother the truth? No one, that's who! All kids know this. I assumed I'd be punished in some serious way for the leg warmer–hickey racket. This was the test.

"Thank you for telling me," my mom said.

I waited for the catch, but there was none. Instead, she showed me the precepts about stealing and said, "I know you know the difference between right and wrong, and I just want you to make better decisions for yourself."

What is this magic happening before me? I looked at her, looked at my sister, back to my chicken cutlet, back to my mom, back to my plate, hoping the carrots disappeared, but they didn't . . . That was okay. A miracle was still occurring.

It was like the clouds parted and a ray of light came shining down on me. Even for someone as lenient as my mom, this was unheard of. On top of not receiving any kind of punishment for the leg warmer fence, I suddenly felt like I went from being a kid to being someone capable of making my own decisions. The sense of power and superiority was exciting. No, I did not have sugar cereals or arroz con pollo on the stove, but damn it, I had acquired some grown-up power!

"Nicole is making out with boys when you're not here," I added.

"I am going to kick your ass," Nicole yelled at me.

"Well, you're not giving anything up. You have to be honest. I'm just saying."

"Okay, Leah," my mom said, "you don't need to give up other people's transgressions. And stop with the bread. Eat your carrots."

I liked a religion where I didn't get in trouble for stealing leg warmers, but I didn't like that my mom was hardly ever home because she was at the church.

"Does that book say anything about kids being home alone? About you leaving early in the morning for the church and not coming home until late?" I said.

"Well," Mom said, "if you don't want to be here by yourself, come meet me in the city after school and check out the church."

She didn't have to ask my sister and me twice. The next day Nicole and I met at the subway and took the B train into the city for the first time by ourselves. As we walked up the stairs to the elevated subway track, I was fearful. But I was comforted by having my sister at my side.

On the train, I felt less secure. Graffiti was everywhere, and a guy was slumped in the corner. Everything was filthy. We hadn't even arrived in the city yet, and already it was so different from Bensonhurst. There were no friends here, no Joeys or Frankies. Nobody was looking out for us.

We got off at Times Square, which back then was basically the worst place in the world for two young girls. But we were headed to the New York Org, the main place where people studied and did other activities central to Scientology and where my mom was working on staff. By the time we arrived at the building on Forty-sixth Street between Sixth and Seventh avenues, we had passed so many leering men and XXX-rated places that the big building, which looked like a bank or theater and had a hanging metal awning that read, "Church of Scientology of New York," really did seem like a church or a refuge.

Despite how freaked out we were about going into the city that first time, Nic and I started going all the time: after school, on weekends, and all summer. We were "on course" at the New York Org, which meant we were doing one of the twenty Scientology Life Improvement Courses that deal with all parts of life, from finance to family. We were told that L. Ron Hubbard, the founder of Scientology, developed "discoveries of existence," which give you "the knowhow to overcome ups and downs, to know who you can trust, to organize your life, to achieve your goals and much more."

My sister and I were twinning, which meant we took all our introductory courses together and teamed up for the drills you have to do on the course—and one of our first was a cornerstone of Scientology, the Success Through Communication Course. The point of the course was straightforward enough. It was going to teach us how to talk to people better. I was all for that. My mouth was always getting me in trouble. The drills that we did in a room with other kids and adults on all different courses were called "Training Routines," or TRs. During the first one, OT TR-0, Operating Thetan Confronting ("thetan" in Scientology means "spirit"), Nic and I had to keep our eyes closed and sit there across from each other. We often used that as a chance to get a nap in, but our supervisor came over and told us that wasn't the purpose of the drill. When we got good at that (sitting without moving or falling asleep), we moved on to sitting across from each other with our eyes open. If one of us moved our big toe or looked down for a split second, the other had to say, "Flunk!" Then we'd both start all over again. The goal was to be able to sit and confront another person comfortably without feeling the need to speak or do anything else other than look at the human being in front of you.

Also part of the communication course is a Training Routine called TR-0 Bullbait, where the coach focuses on doing whatever it takes to get a reaction from your "twin," called "push the other person's buttons." The goal of the trainee is to not show any emotion or reaction at all, no matter what is thrown at him or her. If you speak, roll your eyes, cry, laugh, or even blush, you are met with a "Flunk!"

Like most girls, I was always self-conscious about my appearance—whether I had a pimple, if my nails were dirty, you name it. Nicole, being my older sister, knew all this, and there was no one better at getting under my skin.

"What is that on your face?" Nicole said during my Bullbait session. "Are you growing something there?"

I instinctively touched my forehead.

"Flunk!" Nicole said.

Nic did it again and again until it no longer bothered me. Well, until not a trace of emotion showed on my face. It bothered me, but I couldn't show it if I wanted to pass the drill and move on.

My sister had it a lot tougher when it was her turn. A male supervisor, who was probably in his twenties at the time but seemed about fifty to me, tested her.

"You have big tits for such a young girl," he said to Nicole to see if she could pass the drill and "get her TRs in."

"Fuck you," she said.

"Flunk."

"You have big tits for a young girl," he repeated.

"I'm telling my mother."

"Flunk," he said. "Learn to confront what's happening in front of you and be above it. You are not a body, Nicole, you are a spiritual being."

He didn't stop until Nicole, too, didn't react any longer.

Our being on course made Mom, who by this point was working full-time for the church, really happy. After school and on weekends Nic and I would do a course, which would take a minimum of two and a half hours a day and run on average for a week or two, but then we'd have to wait around for about seven hours until Mom was done working. So we spent a lot of time distributing church pamphlets (passersby would sometimes yell things like "You're too young to be in a fucking cult!") and running the streets, dodging in and out of random buildings, which sometimes got us in trouble.

We didn't meet too many kids at the New York Org, although I remember one girl named Sherry, who was my age but appeared a lot older (could have been the cup of coffee she was holding), whom my mom introduced me to in the lobby there. She was in the Sea Org and because of her specific location and duties, she was required to wear a uniform of a white shirt and blue pants. I was no doubt dressed in my tight jeans and a shirt that said "Leah," and of course I had perfectly feathered hair and gold chains.

I looked at her outfit and asked her, "What are you wearing?"

"I work here and this is my uniform," she said.

Wait, here was a girl my age who worked at the same place as *my mother*. Here I am, running around like a dopey kid, and here's this girl with a uniform and a coffee cup. I thought she was super cool.

So after we started taking introductory courses we were encouraged to also start participating in introductory auditing, a form of one-on-one counseling, usually using an E-Meter (an electronic device that claims to measure thought and emotion). A Scientology practitioner asks the person being counseled specific questions, and using readings on the E-Meter, directs them to talk about points of emotional discomfort or upset until they are relieved. Children as young as seven can participate in auditing. Both of those practices of being on course and auditing are the two required paths to move up the Bridge to Total Freedom, which represents various states of spirituality.

Scientology was our life, not just in the New York Org but also back home in Brooklyn, where our mom started adapting the Training Routines to everyday scenarios. If Nic and I got into a physical fight over, let's say, whether to watch *Solid Gold* or *Fantasy Island,* Mom would shout, "You guys do TR-0," which meant we had to sit and look at each other until we loved each other again. Sometimes it took a while.

The whole idea of not reacting to other people, no matter what they said, was such a foreign concept where I came from. In our neighborhood, everything was an opportunity to get in someone's face. Bensonhurst people didn't hold back. But the fact that Scientology offered a different way of living was exactly the point, according to Mom, who wanted more for us than what Bensonhurst offered.

I understood that Scientology was about following the precepts, laid down in the policy by the leader, L. Ron Hubbard. If you did that, your life would be good. But if you committed overts, or transgressions, and didn't talk about them, didn't take Scientology courses and auditing, then you would receive something bad back from the universe. And the only way to really do things right for yourself, and the universe, was to stay connected to the church.

I never met LRH, the popular sci-fi writer who founded the church in 1952 and died in 1986. Still, he made a huge impression on me. The first time I walked into the New York Org, I was struck by the big bronze bust of him. He looked like a god, or at least someone standing in judgment. There were pictures of him everywhere, and he was always standing behind a big desk or writing something that looked like it had to be important.

I felt pretty special—everyone was telling me that I wasn't a kid but a "spiritual being" with past lives, and that we were all on the same mission to clear the planet—to eradicate insanity, war, and crime across the whole world, and create a peaceful earth by helping all beings free themselves with Scientology. I was told that I was now a part of an elite and important group who were the only ones doing anything about the planet. I decided that this man was going to know me. There was a little locked wooden box with a pen and paper so that you could write messages and leave them directly for LRH.

"Hi, Ron, my name is Leah," I wrote, by way of introducing myself. "I am doing a communication course with my sister."

Shortly afterward I got a letter back! It was typed out on a clean white piece of paper, folded perfectly, and at the bottom it said, "Love Ron," not a stamp but his actual signature. This was proof; I was special.

In general, I was now starting to grow used to and liking how the adults at the New York Org treated me with respect, which was so different than back in Brooklyn, where I was nothing more than an annoying kid. Scientologists praised me and my sister for "finding our way back." I was a grown-up to them.

Scientology was so very powerful to me as a child, because finally, after feeling subpar for so long because I never had the right clothes, apartment, furniture, food, toys, you name it, I now had something on other people. Traveling to the city, taking responsibility for my actions, working on my communication skills all contributed to my sense of superiority. I could do things my friends couldn't (like steal leg warmers without getting in trouble) because now I had this "technology" and they didn't. I used words like "affinity," which as a kid was pretty awesome. Or "You don't have to yell, just communicate," I would say to my friends' mothers. They were impressed that I could use a multi-syllable word.

My dad, however, wasn't so impressed. After he moved out of our apartment, he moved into a big house with Donna, the woman who became my stepmom. My sister and I spent weekends there with him and Donna, and then their two daughters, Elizabeth and Stephanie, and Donna's daughter, Christina.

During visits to my dad's, more often than not he would complain about my mother.

"Does your mother ever brush your hair?" he said, looking at me. "What are you, homeless? Doesn't your mother take care of you? Or is she too busy with that cult?"

Now that I had been doing my communication course, I was going to get my "TRs in" to confront him. So over dinner with Nic and my stepfamily, all seated around a huge table covered with the best whipped potatoes, corn, salad, and warm Italian bread with butter, I summoned the courage to take on my dad.

"I don't think you should be talking about my mother," I said in a voice that was a little less assured than I had hoped for.

"*Wha?*"

"I don't want you talking about my mother."

"Or what?"

"Well, no 'or.' I just don't want you to . . . It's, like, not nice."

"You don't come into my fucking house and tell me what's nice—"

The heat in my body rose so quickly I wanted to crawl into my own face. Whenever my dad spoke in that tone, it always felt like being slapped.

Don't react. Don't react. Remember Bullbait, Leah.

"Dad, I really think it's better if you just communicate with us without putting us or our mother down."

"Oh. Is that what we should do? We should *communicate*? Is that what L. Ron told you to say?"

He was laughing now, and despite my best efforts to keep it together, I started to lose confidence in what I was saying and how I was saying it.

Why couldn't my dad treat me like an equal the way people at the church did? Why couldn't he value me as someone who had something to say?

These were the kinds of exchanges that proved what Scientology was teaching us—that people who don't get the ideals of Scientology are not as able, or not as healthy and mentally sound, as we are and will attack it. And now I believed that was right. It *was* us against them.

I⟶ WAS AROUND THIS TIME that the Sea Organization recruiters came
to talk to my mom and Dennis, and us girls. The Sea Organization
was founded by L. Ron Hubbard in 1967 to staff his three ships, on
which he'd taken up residence after the UK denied his visa exten-
sion. He wanted to live outside the jurisdiction of any governments
and away from the media, and he said he was continuing research—he
produced the "OT" levels on the ships. These levels—OT is short for
"Operating Thetan"—are the secret advanced levels of the Scientology Bridge that you move onto only after you achieve the State of
Clear. Originally the people with him were sailors, brought on to
keep the ships running. The crews then started taking on more functions within Hubbard's Sea Org, and the main ship *Apollo* grew into
a center for training Scientology staff from around the world. Subse-
quently those people who were with Hubbard and the Sea Organization were entrusted with the highest-level functions, secrets, and
control of Scientology internationally, tasked with clearing the planet
through multiple lives as they were reincarnated over and over for all
of eternity.

The Sea Org continues to be made up of the most devout and
dedicated Scientologists. A clergy of sorts, who work for the church
and are held to the highest standards within the organization. Although there are no official numbers, I have heard that there are
close to 4,000 Sea Organization members in the United States and
roughly 20,000 Scientology parishioners total. So roughly one in five
members tends to be in the Sea Org. (The church claims to have
roughly 10 million parishioners worldwide, but this number apparently includes anyone who has ever bought a book, taken a course,
or entered a church building. Estimates of the actual worldwide
members are closer to 35,000.)

The recruiters told Mom and Dennis, "This is the best thing for
you, for the planet—you have a responsibility. Look at your girls,
what are they doing? They're going down the wrong path. They're
hanging around bad people. A criminal element. What kind of a life
is that?"

By this time I was going through a combo package RunDMC/ Puerto Rican phase where I wore only Adidas, had a mullet, sang Menudo songs (even though I didn't speak Spanish), and hung out in Cropsey Park with a bunch of break-dancers. At least that's what I thought they were. As it turned out, they were also part-time drug dealers. But I didn't know about that. Back then everybody carried a fanny pack.

The recruiters preyed on my mom's concern for us to have a better life and her devotion to the religion. They said, "Your girls can do what they want to do in the Sea Org. Leah can act right away in the Scientology movies, and Nicole can train to be a lawyer for the church. The planet is going downhill, your help is needed, and in the end what will be your answer to this question: 'Did you help?'"

Mom and Dennis had already committed themselves to Scientology, bought it hook, line, and sinker, and now they were told they needed to do more.

So not only would we be saving the planet as Scientology dictates, but we would also be doing the things we loved. And Mom and Dennis could move up the Bridge for free (this was provided only to Sea Org members) and with no distractions from the outside world. Plus no more paying bills, as the Sea Org would provide us with housing, food, clothing . . . It was all just too good to be true. Who could blame Mom and Dennis for signing us all up for that?

Chapter Two

B Y THE TIME NICOLE, MOM, AND I GOT OFF THE PLANE IN
Tampa, it was two in the morning and I was exhausted but
excited. I was leaving home for something big. I had already
made huge sacrifices—like leaving behind my Smurf collection—
but that's what you do when you are on a mission to clear the planet.

We were headed to the Gulf Coast city of Clearwater, Florida—
the mecca of Scientology, otherwise known as Flag (a carryover from
the Sea Org term "Flagship," which itself was a carryover from Hubbard's ships when he moved back to land in 1975). We had come
there to get the whole planet up to Clear—the goal of Scientology.
Clear is the state on "the Bridge" that you achieve through Scientology auditing when you no longer have a reactive mind, which is defined as the "hidden source of irrational behavior, unreasonable
fears, upsets and insecurities." The Bridge is the route or guide to
each higher state. As the Scientology literature states, "One walks it
and one becomes free."

It would be a fresh start for all of us, including Mom and Dennis, who were now married and expecting a baby in three months.
Dennis had stayed back in Brooklyn to deal with getting rid of everything in our apartment and to accumulate more money knowing

that we wouldn't be making much after this point. He planned to join us in a few weeks.

While on the plane, I had imagined the welcome we would get when we landed. I pictured men in suits waiting for us at the gate. "Ron has been expecting you," one would say to me before handing me a freshly pressed military uniform. Then they'd lead us to a stretch limousine with tinted windows. I wasn't sure if Scientology had a flag, but if there was one it'd be flying from the hood.

Instead, the airport was pretty much deserted upon our arrival, aside from a guy working a floor buffer.

We made our way down to baggage claim, where I took my suitcase and Nicole took the other two, since my mother was pregnant.

Mom kept looking around as if someone she expected to be there was missing. Nicole and I followed her out of the terminal. Once we got outside, Mom looked left, then right, and her worried expression began to scare me.

"Ma, is anyone going to pick us up?" I asked, but she ignored me and walked back into the airport, where she found a pay phone. She fished out a quarter and made a call, but no one on the other end picked up. Nicole and I shot each other a look and stayed quiet. Mom tried calling again. This time she let it ring for a long, long time until someone finally picked up.

"Where are you?" she yelled.

". . . I don't have money for a cab . . . Okay, fine. I'll get one now, but somebody better be there to pay for it."

After a half-hour drive, we arrived at the Fort Harrison, a historic hotel that had fallen into disrepair before L. Ron Hubbard bought it in 1975 with the idea of turning Clearwater into the spiritual headquarters for all of Scientology. The large old-school lobby looked like the kind you see in movies—horror movies. There were marble staircases that descended to a large room with soaring columns, iron chandeliers, a black-and-white-checkered floor, and creepy chairs that looked like they belonged in Dracula's castle. It was dead quiet until Mom started hitting the bell on the front desk.

No one was there to receive us. When someone did finally show up, we were escorted to a cabana room near the pool. We were allowed to stay here, among paying parishioners, until space opened up for us at what was to become our regular berthing, or housing for members of the Sea Org. We were among Scientologists who had flown in from all over the country to do their services and/or upper OT levels (those above Clear on the Bridge).

Eventually we moved thirty minutes away from the Fort Harrison to what would be our new home. We pulled into what looked like a deserted motel. It was a Quality Inn.

The motel housed Sea Org members and some staff who worked at the Fort Harrison and surrounding orgs, or churches. This Quality Inn was running very low on quality. It was shabby, disgusting, and depressing. The pool we passed on the way to our room was literally a swamp.

The Sea Org member who was showing us around said to my mom, "Vicki, you come with us, and the girls are going to the girls' dorm." The only way you could get your own room was if you were married or had a baby. My mom's room was in the back of the motel, while we were in the front. Our room, one that would normally accommodate one double bed, was crammed with three bunk beds, which slept six girls. In our tight acid-washed jeans, cropped shirts, mullets, Nic wearing a puka shell necklace and me with a rope chain featuring a charm that read "Little Brat," we definitely didn't look like any Scientologists they knew. After we walked into our room and over to our beds, one of the girls said, "Ummm . . . you are not allowed to wear perfume. You might want to do something about that. I can't breathe."

Another girl on the far right top bunk blew the smoke away from her cigarette like it was bothering her even though she was the one smoking. It took a second, but then I remembered: the girl from the New York Org! She looked at me tentatively, but in another instant I could see she remembered me too. Sherry jumped off her bunk and gave me a hug.

From there we were shown the galley, which is where we were to report if we wanted meals. They served breakfast from six to seven-fifteen only. The floors were sticky with old food, and the plates so slick with grease that my eggs slid right off and onto the filthy parquet below. I held out my plate for more eggs, but the cook said, "Get out of my line and learn to get in present time," and just like that, I wasn't going to eat.

Later, we met my mom at the recruitment office. The head of recruitment put down on the desk a white piece of paper with two sea horses flanking the words "Sea Organization Contract of Employment."

"You have to sign a contract to be here," the officer said.

I looked at the contract and was baffled. I was asked to pledge myself for an eternal commitment to the Sea Org for a billion years in order to bring ethics to the whole universe. In accordance with Scientology beliefs, members are expected to return to the Sea Org when they are reborn over time in multiple lives.

"Mom, we've got to sign this?"

"Yes, you have to sign it."

"Nic, are you going to be here in a billion years?"

"Yeah," she said. "Are you?"

"Oh, definitely."

"What are you going to look like?"

"Really fucking old."

We both started laughing, but Mom shot us a look. Then we both signed.

Ironically, even though she was promised by the recruiters that she could become a member of the Sea Org, my mother, who at this time had been affiliated with the church, worked for it, and been on course for a few years, didn't qualify for the organization, because she had done LSD over a decade ago.

After we signed our billion-year contracts, Nicole and I were put on the EPF, or Estates Project Force, part of the basic Sea Org training for new recruits. It was a lot like boot camp. All EPFers spent twelve hours a day doing hard labor, like pulling up tree roots with our bare hands, working heavy machinery on the grounds of the Fort Harrison and the Sandcastle, or cleaning bathrooms and hotel rooms. Then for two and a half hours each day, we would do the basic courses for the EPF, in which you learned the Sea Org policies and rules and what it meant to be a member. We were all given detailed check sheets, which listed all the actions we needed to take in order to complete each course. The first course being how to study Scientology.

In studying the policies, we quickly learned that there is no middle ground or room for interpretation. Any question we asked was answered with "What does LRH say?" You couldn't ask your supervisor for help, other than "Where can I find the policy that says what I do here?" If you disagreed with something, the supervisor would answer that with "Okay, well, let's see what you don't understand here."

Once, as a requirement during my coursework, my supervisor gestured toward a Demo Kit, one of which was located on every student's study table. It was a little basket filled with everyday objects like paper clips and chess and checkers pieces.

My supervisor told me to physically act out the sexual policy for Sea Org members with the objects in the kit, in a room filled with other trainees—some reading, others doing drills.

"By using these things here, show me what the sexual policy is," the supervisor said. Policy stated it was forbidden for Sea Org members to have sex or physical contact of any kind before marriage. So I took a paper clip and a chess piece, to stand for the girl and boy, and rubbed them together, saying, "This is not allowed." Then I had the girl and boy touching each other side by side. "This is not allowed." I put the girl and boy on opposite sides of the Demo Kit basket and said, "This is allowed."

The supervisor took my check sheet and signed it, so that I could move on to the next assignment.

One day when I was working, Mike Curley, an older man who

was the head of the EPF, singled me out right away. He was tall and gaunt, reminding me of a cowboy from the movies.

"You're a little troublemaker, huh?" he said.

"I don't know. I've been told that," I replied, trying to be cute.

"I can tell you right now, you will address me as 'Yes, sir' or 'No, sir.' Or 'Mr. Curley.' Nothing else."

"Oh. Right. Okay."

"Not 'Oh. Right.' 'Right, sir.'"

Nicole chimed in to say, "We don't know the rules here."

"Well, you're gonna have to figure them out, because I'm putting you in charge of the Sandcastle Hotel crew," he said, looking at me.

Me? I was all of thirteen. Again, in Scientology children and adults are viewed equally. So it wasn't odd to them that I might be in charge of some adults on my watch as well. I now had responsibilities that no teenager back in Brooklyn could imagine. I was learning something here in this weird environment that combined lots of freedom and lots of structure. Yeah, they made us do hard labor all day, but I was no longer being treated like a child.

I rose to the occasion and did the job I was tasked with, and came up with a plan to reward my "crew."

If we got the Sandcastle cleaned in half the time, with good feedback from the guests via questionnaires they filled out, then the next day we could spend the other half of the day sitting on our asses at the pool. I was a boss running a crew and I was going to make some serious executive decisions. And I had read on my course that you reward good work. In my mind I was taking my orders directly from LRH.

With the incentive of possible time off, the crew was motivated to clean better and faster. We got positive feedback from the guests and headed to the Sandcastle's pool after we finished cleaning.

We were all lying by the pool when Mike Curley walked by. He did a double take when he saw us.

"What the hell are you doing?" he said, his face turning a deep shade of red.

The thought that I might need to clear my plan with anybody

hadn't even crossed my mind. I considered myself an executive of the Sea Org now.

"I've read the policy—"

"Get up, clean up all these deck chairs, and meet me at the dock," he said, then stormed off.

When we got down to the marina, Mike was waiting for us in a motorboat. After we crammed into the small boat, he started driving out of the marina and into the bay, into the real ocean. He was dead silent, his eyes in his weather-beaten face staring out at the horizon, until we were so far out that the marina was no longer visible. Then he cut the engine and started screaming at me.

"Never do you sit in a public place. You are Sea Org members. Don't you know that the pool at that hotel is for paying guests only, not for you to be enjoying?

"Do you understand me?" he yelled.

Actually, he was shouting so loud that I almost couldn't decipher what he was saying. Was he even speaking English? I wasn't sure.

"Mm-hmm," I said.

"It's 'Yes, sir!'"

I thought I was following LRH and rewarding my team. And I didn't know who these paying Scientology people were, but I was a Sea Org member, a bad motherfucker from Brooklyn clearing the planet. So, just like I'd practiced with Nicole back home, I pushed down my emotions, got my TRs in, and stayed silent. I mean, maybe Mike didn't know LRH had written me personally. That I had come back from another life?! Hello?

Mike kept trying to get me to say "Yes, sir." But I couldn't do it.

Then he picked me up and before I even realized what was happening, he threw me overboard.

The shock of the moment and the freezing water took my breath away, and for an instant I thought I was going to drown. But I sputtered and began frantically dog-paddling.

"Yes, sir!" Mike shouted.

I couldn't do it. The words just wouldn't come out. Once I gathered myself, I became calm. The waves were choppy but I was okay, I could swim. I began to tread water. This had become a battle as far as I was concerned. Although I wasn't sure if I would win.

Mike, who was following a policy practiced by LRH called over-boarding, which entails throwing a crew member overboard as a form of reprimand, picked me up by my shirt again, but this time it was to pull me back into the boat. We returned to the marina in silence. I was soaking wet and humiliated at what had happened, but there was a part of me that thought that deep down, Mike Curley might just respect me for not backing down.

A FEW WEEKS AFTER WE moved to Flag, we went back up to New York to see my father.

Shortly after we arrived, as we were sitting around the kitchen table, he asked, "What are you doing there in Florida?"

"I'm a housekeeper," I said.

"Your mother moved you to the cult to be a housekeeper?"

"Well, yeah. We clean hotel rooms that people pay money to stay in."

"You're learning to clean hotel rooms? That's what you're learning?"

"Well, yeah, but we just got there. It's part of basic training."

I started getting flushed. I felt the need to defend my position and what we were doing to help clear the planet, but I was not able to present it to him the right way and ended up ultimately doing the work a disservice.

"How much are you making?" he asked.

"Fifteen dollars a week."

"Donna," he yelled to my stepmom, "get me the Help Wanted section from the paper."

He found an ad and showed it to me. "You see this? A hundred twenty-five dollars a week for a housekeeper. And you're making a lousy fifteen bucks."

"Well, Dad, they're giving us room and board," I said, once again trying to defend it. But ultimately it was no use. He was convinced that he was right and he felt the need to belittle me and what I believed in to prove it. Little did he know that by attacking Scientology, he ended up simply pushing me back into its arms. *Them* against *us*. I thought, this guy has no idea that I am fighting for *his* eternity.

We returned to Florida, and I have to admit, Dad pointing out that I was making only fifteen dollars a week along with all of the hard labor was starting to bother me a little. I was here to do important work and be sent on vital missions. And more important, to wear heels, stockings, and a uniform with a cap, Navy style. I imagined myself clicking around the organization in my heels and yelling at people to clear the planet. But that just wasn't happening.

It was right about then that I noticed that one of the kids from my Sandcastle crew was wearing a uniform and was "on post," meaning that he had a real Sea Org job that definitely was not cleaning toilets.

"How the fuck did you get off the EPF?" I asked him.

"You have to complete the courses and show up to study time," he replied.

Nic and I had been taking the opportunity of study time to hide in the bathroom and take a nap in the tub or take the hotel shuttle buses back and forth from the Fort Harrison to the Sandcastle, enjoying a break and some air-conditioning. Up until this point I was under the impression that my bad attitude was what was holding me back from moving on from the EPF. That once I had a more positive mindset, I would be magically rewarded, promoted, and assigned a uniform and, of course, the all-important heels.

Nic and I quickly changed our ways and got on course. We wanted off of the EPF, and soon.

While I was making progress and heading in the right direction with my training, there was one thing I couldn't come to terms with. I thought a lot about my infant sister, Shannon, a sweet little blond, blue-eyed thing. Whenever I could, I went to visit her in the nursery, where she stayed during the day while my mom was working. "Nursery" was a charitable term for the motel room in the Quality Inn filled with cribs of crying, neglected babies, flies, and the smell of dirty diapers. The only ventilation came from a huge fan by the window.

This was where Sea Org members and staff dropped off their babies at seven in the morning and then picked them up at ten in the evening when their workday was over. We had an hour for lunch, but the shuttle took half an hour to go from Flag back to the Quality Inn, so even if parents wanted to visit their children, they would have to turn around practically as soon as they arrived.

I took advantage of any opportunity to sneak away and check in on Shannon. The first time I went to the nursery I was devastated by what I found. The person in charge was a kid like me, just some random teenage Sea Org member on post, who was hardly qualified to be taking care of children. Shannon was crying and soaked with urine in her crib. Before changing her and returning to my post, I vowed I wouldn't let her grow up this way. The neglect was overwhelming. I would immediately demand that the person on post clean up and change the babies. I would sometimes leave my post for a while to take Shannon out of there. I complained to my mother about it, and she complained to her seniors, who threatened that she would be taken off her job and demoted. She continued to voice her concerns about it and they told her to write it up in a report, but nothing was ever done. It really weighed on me. Though I was buying into the program, it raised a question inside me: While I didn't care so much about me, I wondered if we were doing right by this baby.

It was at this time that my mother revealed that we had no home to return to. Dennis wasn't coming to join us after all. At first he'd made excuses that he could accumulate more money by staying behind, but ultimately he had found someone else, gotten rid of the apartment, and moved on. He and Mom weren't together anymore. They were getting a divorce. Dennis, the man who claimed he would never do anything to harm us, who made us change our whole lives and live within the world of Scientology, who cheated on our mom while she was pregnant, had now left us. We were heartbroken. This hit us like a punch in the stomach.

I knew even then that moving in with my dad and stepmother was not an alternative. The Sea Org and its practices may have been hard on us, but at my dad's house my sisters and I would be called cunts, ingrates, and selfish assholes for crimes like pulling the laundry out before it was completely dry. Dad would tell Nicole and me over and over again throughout our childhood that he wasn't even sure if we were his real children because our mother was a slut. And on top of this, during the brief time we did spend with my dad, we lived in fear of his violent episodes. To us, the thought of living with him was worse than joining a "cult."

We realized now, more than ever, that we didn't have a choice but to stay in Florida. We had nowhere else to go. We couldn't leave our mom there to raise a baby on her own. Being in the Sea Org was what our mother wanted for us, and so though we worked long hours and lived in a filthy dorm, we were committed to staying by her side.

"I promise you girls," Mom said, "it will get better."

Chapter Three

NICOLE AND I WERE NOW PUT ON POSTS WITH THE REST OF the Sea Org. Like the adults, we worked fourteen-hour days and picked up the wonderful adult habits of drinking coffee and smoking cigarettes.

One habit we didn't pick up was going to school regularly. LRH had deep disdain for the conventional educational system. Scientology abided by the idea that as long as you were on course, getting an education in Scientology, going to traditional school was not all that important. Your education in Scientology—the main goal of which was to teach you how to learn Scientology—was the imperative. We were taught that getting a Scientology education was the equivalent of getting a doctorate in the real world. Who cares about calculus when you're clearing the planet? So because attending school wasn't enforced, the motel room at Flag that was designated "Schoolroom" was usually empty, and although I was still technically in eighth grade, I hardly ever went.

At Flag we did find moments to act like regular kids. Sherry and I played stupid pranks on the Sea Org boys, like putting shaving cream and Vaseline on the door handles in their dorm. We made them over and attempted to turn them into break-dancers in the lobby of the motel. We'd find little victories by using the hotel loud-speaker to page people at the Fort Harrison: "Mrs. Dickington, please come to Reception" and then doubling over with laughter. During "libs"—a few hours off or, if you were lucky, a whole day off once every two weeks—we would take the bus with some of the other kids to the mall to walk around, even though we had no money to buy anything.

During this time, Sherry and I would stay up late in our bunks and share our life stories. Sherry had grown up in the Founding Church of Scientology in Washington, D.C., where her mother and stepfather had been full-time staff members. Just a child herself, she was frequently left in charge of the babies and children in the day care, often going on walks where she pushed two strollers at a time.

Her brother, Stefan, had already joined the Sea Org, a year earlier, and was at Flag when recruiters from the New York Org came to D.C. to find new candidates for the Sea Org. With her parents' approval, the recruiters agreed to be Sherry's guardians. So at the age of eleven she was shipped to New York.

All alone in a big, strange city, she was left to fend for herself. The recruiters were her guardians legally, but they did nothing to care for her. "No one made sure I brushed my teeth or had a winter coat," she said. She had been there only a week when an executive screamed at her. Sherry called her mom to ask if she could go home, but her mother said she needed to stick it out.

This type of thinking becomes a parent's reality. Everything is about the church, the bigger picture. Parents refer back to policy for major and minor decisions, looking to the phrase "What does LRH say?" to advise them. All this is part of "doing something big here."

After that, Sherry barely had any contact with her family. Phone calls and letters were rare, and she visited her mother and stepfather for only one week every other year.

Her stepdad had taught her all these folk songs that she would sing for me at night. I fell asleep to "Where Have All the Flowers

Gone?" or "You Are My Sunshine" as I sucked on two fingers and held a blanket.

Even though we were treated the same as adults, we were really just little girls.

AFTER BEING AT FLAG FOR a number of months, we had really gotten into the Sea Org rhythm. We got on the bus at eight in the morning, were on post for the next fourteen hours, smoked and drank coffee throughout, and developed systems for pretty much everything. I even had a system for dealing with our roach-infested dorm room (turn on the lights and wait for them to scatter before you jump into your bed). Despite the long workdays and specific procedurals, I found openings and made the system work for me.

One of my tasks on post was to deduct bills from guest accounts—including their food tickets. We staffers were Sea Org members, but the guests were all regular parishioners who had come to participate in auditing and training. Sea Org members and regular parishioners—or the public, as we called them—ate different food in different places. We ate rice and beans night and day or liquid eggs; they ate steak, lobster, roasted chicken, anything you could get in a normal hotel. We weren't supposed to fraternize with the public in the first place, but with our salary of fifteen dollars a week, we didn't have the money to eat at the hotel's restaurants anyway.

My epiphany was that I was the person taking the tickets! That meant I could easily go into the Lemon Tree and the Hourglass, the public restaurants, or the canteen where they served snack food, and order a chicken sandwich or a piece of chocolate cake under a phony account name. Then in a couple of days, when my tickets came into the office, I could take them to my room, burn them, and flush the ashes down the toilet. And that's exactly what I started doing.

I didn't tell a soul what I was up to and I never got caught for my food scam. My attitude during this time was like "I gotta eat. I'm a Sea Org member, part of an elite group, and I'm clearing the planet, so get out of my way." I was being trained to make the impossible happen. Rising above my own mental and physical limitations. I was feeling fierce. Having said that, I still had to live and operate within the very strict constraints of the Sea Org.

Scientology is based on thousands of policies that leave no room for interpretation. Your actions are either "on policy" or "off policy." One of the challenges Nicole and I had was keeping track of these many policies. There were so many and they were so hard to keep straight that we didn't always know when we were breaking a rule. That's what happened one day when the two of us were walking through the building while on post. A girl around our age, walking in front of us, stopped when she got to a door, paused in front of it, and told us to open it for her.

"Are your arms broken?" Nicole said. "Open your own fucking door."

"I am a Messenger."

"What are you delivering?"

We had no idea that she was a member of the Commodore's Messenger Org (CMO), or even what that was. Well, we found out soon enough when we were routed to the Department of Inspections and Reports, otherwise known as Ethics, the department that deals with enforcing policy.

Waiting for us in his office was a Master-at-Arms (MAA), essentially the person you were sent to when you were in trouble. Sort of like the strict parent. There are Ethics Officers throughout Scientology, and their job is to apply ethics technology to Scientologists at all levels.

The MAA waiting for us walked around carrying a wooden stick, and his office was decorated with a picture of LRH and the Bridge, like pretty much every other room. There he showed us an organizational board with all twenty-one departments that made up Scientology. At the very top, of course, was "L. Ron Hubbard."

"So when you're talking to a Messenger, you are talking to LRH," the MAA said. "And when you're disrespectful to a Messenger, you're being disrespectful to LRH."

He showed us all these policies about Messengers and said that

from now on we were to address all CMOs as "Sir" or "Mr." no matter what their gender.

My takeaway from the MAA's speech was that being a CMO
was the shit. On our way back to our berthing, I told Nicole that I
was going to be a Messenger.

"You're an asshole."

"I might be an asshole, but you're still going to be calling me 'Sir'
in about a minute."

I made an appointment with the Messenger recruitment office.
The recruiter, reviewing my Ethics folder, which contained reports
on all my "crimes," had a different take. My record showed that I
had a "problem with authority" and flirted too much with boys. "If
you are pristine for six months, I will reevaluate you," he said. I accepted his review and vowed that he would see me again and that I
would get in.

A few days after the Messenger incident, Nicole, my mom, and I
were summoned to the Ethics office, in the CMO building. The
Ethics Officer told me that he had a Knowledge Report that a friend
of mine had written up about me. Knowledge Reports are a system
of Scientologists reporting on one another, basically setting up the
idea that *not* telling on your friends bars their freedom as well as
makes you an accessory to the crime. It's like systematic tattling. The
report he had on me stated that Danny Burns (my first boyfriend,
whom I claimed as soon as he arrived at Flag and kissed a lot) had
touched my boobs over my blouse. Sex before marriage was forbidden for members of the Sea Org, as was heavy petting—but kissing
was okay. In his office, the MAA told me what Danny and I had
done was "heavy petting and against policy."

"But he did it lightly," I said, confused.

That only seemed to make the Ethics Officer even angrier. He
told me to look at the reference in the policy and find the definition
of "heavy petting," which he made me recite back to him.

Unbeknownst to me, the same friend had written a Knowledge
Report about Nicole and her boyfriend that said they were having

sex, which was even more serious than Danny touching my boobs. It also wasn't true. Nicole was like a nun about that stuff, and we were both still virgins.

The MAA was sufficiently alarmed and called a code red. Two highly trained security officers of the church (a pair of fifteen-year-olds) launched an investigation into our so-called sexual perversions. They burst into our dorm room, riffled through our drawers, and found a pair of my underwear with a hint of lace, probably from Hanes Her Way, and a baby doll pajama top that belonged to Nicole. This was considered the evidence that my sister and I were sexually aberrated (a Scientology term that means "wrong behavior or a departure from what's rational and a straight line").

The Ethics Officer told my mother that he had no other choice but to send us both to the RPF. Nicole had been mouthing off to the MAA earlier and was being accused of upsetting him with her "hostile communication." I guess "Fuck you" could be interpreted that way.

The mention of the RPF, the Rehabilitation Project Force, sent a chill down my spine. I knew what that was from seeing the RPF members in their musters, which were the formations we all had to assemble in at any Sea Org gathering. Beginning of day, end of meals, group announcements—you name it, we got in our proper musters for it. The RPF mustered separately from the rest of us, so they were easy to identify. In 110-degree Florida heat and humidity, these men, women, and even children were forced to wear all black from head to toe as they did heavy MEST work (MEST is an acronym for matter, energy, space, and time) like cleaning grease traps in the kitchen or scrubbing dumpsters. And that wasn't all they had to do for their "spiritual rehabilitation." They also had to run everywhere they went—to the bathroom, to the galley, anywhere. They had virtually no liberties. As long as they were in the RPF they worked pretty much seven days a week, 365 days a year, and that's not including all the time spent doing security checks for their transgressions. No matter how high they had been in the organization

before, once they landed in the RPF, they had to call everyone—
even EPFers, the lowest form of Sea Org—"Sir," and they were not
allowed to speak unless spoken to. The RPF was the ultimate form
of punishment and your time there could last for months or even
years during which you basically weren't even considered a person.

"Absolutely not," Mom said. "My girls aren't going to the RPF."

The MAA stared at my mother, and she stared right back with
her green eyes that could be childlike or very, very hard. In that moment she reverted from her acquiescent Scientologist self back to the
Brooklyn survivor. My sister and I were frozen as we watched the
silent standoff between the two adults to see who was going to win.

My mother requested a fitness board, referring to a council that
could determine our fitness as members of the Sea Org. We had
heard this was a way to get out of the Sea Org without too many
repercussions. The council would eventually ask the question "Are
you here on your own determinism?" and you would respond "No,"
and be told to leave.

Shortly thereafter we began packing. Sherry, who had been asked
by an Ethics Officer to write up a report on anything she knew about
my physical relationship with Danny, was sad to see me go, and I
was sad to say goodbye to her. But she wasn't surprised. "You have a
strong personality and they don't want that in the Sea Org. You're
more trouble than you're worth," she said. "I'm surprised you lasted
as long as you did."

Chapter Four

WE WERE ON THE 405, THE VERY LAST BIT OF THE DRIVE that had taken several days from Clearwater to Los Angeles, when after heading up a mountain, we suddenly saw a sea of lights spread out below us. My first real vision of L.A.

With my sister and me facing the prospect of being thrown into the RPF, Mom knew we had to leave Clearwater. Despite everything that had happened, my mom still very much believed in Scientology and our family's place in it, and so did I. In moving to L.A. and joining up with other Scientologists we looked forward to the security of this larger group, a real community. Even though Nicole and I didn't make it in the Sea Org, that didn't mean we didn't have a place in clearing the planet. And like all Scientologists, we didn't want our eternity threatened. We learned pretty early on that we come back again and again, over the course of millions and millions of years, as the body is just the vessel for the thetan-spirit.

We didn't have much money, but thankfully a friend of my mother's from Brooklyn who now lived in Los Angeles offered to take us in. A Scientologist herself, she said the church was really strong out there; L.A. has the greatest concentration of Scientologists in the world.

California was nothing like what Nic and I thought it was going to be. We had pictured L.A. as a beach town filled with blond people in bikinis. But Hollywood, where we were staying, felt like just another big city. "Where's the damn water?" Nicole asked. I was just as disappointed as Nic that L.A. wasn't straight out of a scene from *Baywatch,* but I was still excited to be there. I could hardly wait to start fulfilling my dreams of being an actress.

My mom's friend and her husband let us sleep on the floor of their apartment. "We" now included baby Shannon, Mom's new boyfriend, George, whom she had met in Clearwater, and his two teenage sons.

The tiny apartment was a block from the Blue Buildings, a gigantic complex of ten buildings that made up the Church of Scientology's West Coast headquarters. The imposing concrete Art Deco building was the former Cedars of Sinai hospital, erected on Fountain Avenue in the 1920s. It is known as "Big Blue" because of the color it was painted after being acquired by the church in 1977.

By the time we arrived in California, I should have technically been in the ninth grade, but because I missed an entire year of school while in Florida I was enrolled at King Junior High School. Not very inspired to return to school, Nicole and I persuaded our mother to let us quit. She felt, as do most Scientologists, that studying Scientology is more important than getting a traditional education. So as long as we were on course, my mom was okay with it. (Plus, I would say things like, "Ma, I'm going to be an actress. I will hire an accountant who went to school, I promise.")

Now that we were no longer enrolled in school, we immediately set out to get jobs. Everyone in our family was hustling to find work, since we all needed to chip in to eat, pay the electricity bill, make car payments—and stay on course. Our religion didn't come free. The courses Nic and I were taking were still introductory, so they weren't expensive compared to what it cost to do more advanced courses. Still, the range of $45 to $300 per course was a fortune for us.

Plus, I was starting with a deficit. After I left the Sea Org, I was saddled with what's called "a freeloader's debt." Sea Org members take courses for free in exchange for being on post, but if you leave of your own volition, or are thrown out or found unfit, you owe the church money for those "free" courses you took while in the Sea Org. I owed thousands for the courses I took in Clearwater. I wasn't allowed to be on course again until I paid my debt, so I went on a payment plan.

Practicing Scientology imposed a lot of financial pressure on everybody, but it also opened opportunities to make money. In businesses run by Scientologists, lack of experience, age, or education didn't seem to matter. The kind of training provided by being on course was good enough. So after my mom found a job at a solar-heating company, American Sun, which was run by Scientologists, I begged her to find me work there as well, and unbelievably, she did.

It was a telemarketing position, where the barrier of entry was pretty low, but still, since I was just a teenager, the job was nothing short of a miracle.

My job was to call people who were listed in a huge binder, and to stick to a script that went something like this:

ME: Hello, [sir/ma'am]. I am calling to congratulate you on winning an all-expense-paid trip to Laughlin, Nevada! All you have to do is have a representative from American Sun come out for you to retrieve your certificate.
CUSTOMER: What's the catch?
ME: There is no catch, [sir/ma'am]. You simply need to set an appointment for someone to come out and enlighten you on how solar heating could drastically cut your cooling and heating bills down. After you listen to a ninety-minute presentation on solar heating for your home, you will receive this trip at no cost to you. We have a rep in your area tomorrow afternoon on another appointment. Does that work for you?

Even I thought this was a racket. But my boss assured me it was the real thing. The free trip was from Tuesday to Thursday, and it was to Laughlin, which apparently was the fucked-up part of Nevada where they have $2.99 buffets and penny slots. But it was real, and it was free.

So I took my seat in the large room of rows and rows of telemarketers and looked up at a big board on the wall. On it was every telemarketer's name—including mine—with little suns that represented how many confirmed appointments each caller had made. Well, I was going to get suns all the way across the board! Yeah, I was definitely going to rock this. I dialed my first number with total confidence that came to me both from my inherent personality and from what I had learned in Scientology. There simply is no "no" in Scientology.

"Hello, ma'am," I began.

When it came time for the woman to say, "What's the catch?" she actually said it! Even though my supervisor had told me they always said it, I couldn't believe it actually worked. But when I got to the part about setting up an appointment, the lady on the other end of the line didn't go for it. No problem—there were more names where hers came from.

By the end of the day, however, I realized that booking appointments wasn't as easy as I'd thought it would be. In fact, I hadn't booked a single appointment all day. When the next day didn't go any better, I decided to take matters into my own hands and go off script. Mostly, the people I called cut the conversation short by hanging up on me. So when one man did just that, I called him back to give him the real talk.

"Hey, it's me again," I said. "Listen, you do have to sit through this boring thing on solar heating, but you don't need to buy it. Just, like, do the presentation and you literally get a trip. It's Tuesday through Thursday, okay? But it seems like you aren't that busy."

He hung up on me again. And I called him again. This time I didn't care about making a friggin' appointment; I wanted to give him a piece of my mind.

"What is this? What are you, some kind of animal?" I shouted (sounding like my dad). "You don't hang up on people!"

The man hung up again and then called the company to file a complaint about me. Not only did I never get a single sun by my name—I soon got fired.

I wasn't so upset when American Sun let me go, because by that point I realized there was a whole network of Scientology businesses in the vicinity of the Blue Buildings (which was important, since I didn't have a car). My sister got a job down the street at a place called George's General Store, which sold accessories needed for Scientology sessions and recommended vitamins.

Canvassing the area around Fountain Avenue, I went into the restaurant right across from the Blue Buildings, New York George's (no connection to the general store). My strategy was to use the fact that I was from New York to get my foot in the door. The owner, Randy, a Scientologist, interviewed me and agreed to try me out as a cashier, because I wasn't trusted to be a waitress with the attitude I had on me, as he could attest to from my days as a customer there. "Just sit here on this stool, take the money, make change, and try not to lose us any business with your mouth," Randy said.

"Can I at least—"

"No," Randy said. "Take the money, make change, and that is it."

To pass the time, rather than just sit there I took it upon myself to clean the doors every five minutes with Windex, clean the cash register with a Q-tip, and put all the bills facing in one direction. You could say I had an obsession with things looking neat and clean—and I still do. Eventually Randy promoted me to waitress, a job that I know most people complain about, but I absolutely loved it.

I mimicked my grandmother, who used to clean the whole table after we finished dinner and before coffee and cake. "You don't want to sit in macaroni," she'd say. "Let me make it nice." So before I served the coffee (with the napkin in between the saucer and the cup, naturally), I'd say, "Let me make it nice," and then I'd clean the table, which customers found charming.

I even loved being a waitress when customers were busting my balls, an occupational hazard. One of my regular customers was a guy named John Futris, who owned a Scientology graphic design company called JFI a few doors down. They printed all of the church's literature. John was always smiling, but he was a pain in the ass with his muffin ordering. "I would like a blueberry muffin, with the top cut off, but not in half, the top should be smaller, and then I want two pats of butter, one on the top and one on the second half. But make sure the butter is not frozen, so warm it a little in your hand first, and then a coffee with half-and-half and one sugar." Every day.

This went on for a couple of months until one day when John asked me what I really wanted to do, I told him eventually I wanted to be an actress but my immediate goal was to make more money. "I believe you'll be a great actress one day," he said, before asking me if I typed and wanted a job that'd pay more.

"Yes and yes," I said.

I quit New York George's that day. I was moving up in the world, going corporate. I only prayed my eyes would go bad so I could wear glasses, which would go perfectly with the pencil skirts I planned to wear.

John called me into his office on my first morning and said, "I need you to take this down in shorthand because I need you to type up a letter."

"Yup."

I wrote down what he said (sort of) and went back to my desk to type it up. I sat and stared down at the typewriter. I didn't know how to type; I didn't really even know how to load in the paper. I could have sworn I took a class in school once. Or was that in a movie I saw? Whatever. How hard could this be?

An hour later, John called me on the intercom and said, "Is that letter ready to be signed?"

Looking at the catastrophe that was the letter (I had used about half a bottle of Wite-Out), I knew I couldn't show it to him. So, as I walked into his office and looked at him sitting behind his big wooden desk, I said, "John, I lied to you. I can't type," and I started to tear up.

"Honey, you lied about typing? Why?"

"Because you are from Chicago and I just really wanted to work for you and I . . ."

"Leah, you are too cute."

John fired me.

As his secretary.

He did offer me another job as his personal assistant. My first task was to go up to his house on Mulholland Drive and bring his shirts to the cleaners. Easy enough. But I was bewitched by his Greek wife, Valerie, with her blond hair and her long, pretty nails. Valerie was also from New York, and she laughed at everything I said. She was always pinching my cheeks and saying, "You are so cute." Who wouldn't be smitten? It was hard to believe hours had gone by.

John fired me.

As his assistant.

And hired me as his accounts receivable person, where I was given a crash course in getting people to pay their bills. While I may have failed him as a secretary and an assistant, I quickly learned the art of manipulating people into paying their bills on time, all the while using church tactics to find their weaknesses and prey on them.

When I wasn't working I would hang out with a bunch of kids around Nic's and my age whose parents were Sea Org members, but who themselves no longer wanted anything to do with the Sea Org and Scientology. As mentioned, in Scientology, minors are considered spiritual beings and not children in need of protection and guidance. You are the only one responsible for the condition of your life, regardless of your age. The Sea Org members believed that their kids could make up their own minds. As a result, these kids could no longer live with their parents, most of whom had berthing in the Blue Buildings. Even if that meant they ended up practically squatting, or sleeping in a stranger's apartment, their parents felt that it was the child's decision to make. They weren't running away from a home where a mother and father worried about them.

Nicole and I were compassionate and we hung out with these kids. They got us—meaning they knew the ways of Scientology even if they chose to leave it—and we, like them, had basically said "Fuck you" to Sea Org, if not to Scientology. Shouldn't we be friends with these people and set a good example for others?

So with everyone basically left to their own devices, some kids lived with other regular Scientology parishioners in the neighborhood. Others buddied up and moved into their own apartments with one Scientology kid or kids old enough to sign a lease. Or kids lived with complete strangers if need be.

We spent our days working, our evenings going on course, and our nights together smoking, playing gin rummy, and scrounging for jobs, even food. Hanging out in front of Hannon's (which was a local mini-mart) at the corner of Edgemont and Fountain, we formed a tight-knit community.

We were children trying to be adults. Whenever we met someone who was struggling in his or her life—be it with drugs or alcohol or other addictions—we were convinced we could save them with Scientology. It didn't matter if they were twice our age or battling demons we couldn't begin to understand; we thought we had the knowledge and skills to help!

During this time I wavered between acting like a typical teenager and like someone who thought she was a spiritual being. I carried on with my friends and partied and drank thinking, *I have all the answers in the world, nothing's going to harm me.* I would walk in at three in the morning after a night out and hear my mother say, "What the fuck? Why is it okay to come in at three a.m.?"

"Who cares?" I would say.

"I care. You still live under my roof."

One morning my mother found me at home instead of on course. She asked why I wasn't at church. I told her that I had been drinking and so I couldn't go on course (Scientology policy states that you are not allowed to be on course within twenty-four hours of drinking). She started yelling at me and I laid into her about how I work, I go on course, am I a spiritual being or not? According to Scientology we are all equals. "What, are you going to wait for my body to turn twenty-one?" I tried to use Scientology against her and she responded less as a Scientologist and more as a mom: "Don't use that shit against me, Leah. I'm still your mother."

Later that day, she filed a Knowledge Report on me. When I showed up on course the day after that, my supervisor summoned me almost immediately, took out an Ethics routing form, and wrote my name on it. It was a printed form that directed me to proceed to the Ethics office.

I had fucked up. I was off to see an MAA, who was just one of a whole network of Ethics Officers in Hollywood, working in concert to investigate and make sure everyone was in-ethics. In other words, they were on our shit. The only thing required of us was that we stay on course, and the only people we had to answer to were Scientology officials.

"What's happening?" asked the MAA, a heavyset woman with curly black hair. "Why didn't you make it to course yesterday?"

"Oh, I was tired."

But the MAA didn't buy it, and she employed an investigative technique called "pull a string." The piece of string sticking out represents something that doesn't make sense—like the idea that I wouldn't come to course because I was tired. Further questioning is pulling on the string—finding out why I was tired. And this MAA was going to keep pulling until she got to the bottom of it.

"Why were you tired?"

"I'm not sure."

"Were you out late?"

"What's late to you?"

"What's late to *you*?"

"Um, like, two a.m."

"What do you do until two a.m.?"

"Hang out."

"Does hanging out mean doing drugs?"

"No."

"Is anyone who you are hanging out with doing drugs?"

"I don't know." I was starting to grow more anxious.

"Well, because you can't be connected to that, right? So if you're connected to that, see how that has a domino effect in your life? You didn't make it to course, right? Things don't just happen. Everything has a cause and effect."

"I didn't do drugs. I wouldn't do that."

"Good, because they are the single most destructive element to a person's spiritual and mental well-being."

"I drank!"

The MAA sat back and looked me straight in the eye. It wasn't accusatory but instead kind of calming.

"Good, so who else was involved?" she asked.

I quickly reverted from peaceful back to worried; I didn't want to get my friends in trouble.

As if she could read my mind, the MAA said, "It's not about tattling, Leah. You know what the policy says. You're not narcing on them; you're helping them. Is it great that they're staying out and getting drunk till two in the morning?"

"No, I guess not."

"So what's the greatest good here? It's to tell the truth. And if we all did that, we'd all be helping each other to live a better life. It's about not being a wog" (a term for non-Scientologist, short for "Well and Orderly Gentleman"). Wogs are considered to be ignorant and unenlightened and to be avoided for their lack of priorities.

The MAA scribbled as quickly as the names rolled off my tongue. She was connecting the dots for a Knowledge Report. Every person I mentioned would be routed to Ethics. But I didn't feel guilty. Not only had I given up what I had done, but I was helping my friends. I made a vow to myself to be a better person.

I'm going to be good.

I'm going to be on course.

I didn't want to be average. I didn't want to be acting like a wog. *I am more than this. I am a Scientologist and I am here to help clear the planet.*

Chapter Five

❧

IT DIDN'T TAKE LIVING IN L.A. FOR LONG BEFORE I REALIZED THAT you didn't need actually to be *in* anything to say you were an actor. I would meet people all the time who said, "I'm an actor."

"What are you in?"

"Well, right now I'm in the fry station at McDonald's."

I got it: You didn't have to do shit to be an actor. You didn't even have to necessarily believe in yourself. You just had to have the confidence to say it out loud.

An acting job represented a way out of poverty for my family and me. It's a dream a lot of people have when they come to L.A., but I felt particularly responsible to change our living conditions for the better. After we slept on my mom's friend's floor in Hollywood for a while, we moved into a house on Los Feliz and Edgemont that looked like a mansion from the outside but inside was a dump. Nicole and I had to sleep in the dining room. We had no money for furniture. My sister had two jobs—everyone was working so hard to contribute toward our food, housing, and Scientology. It was an exhausting life, and all I could think about was moving us up and out. I also felt I had to be something bigger than a Sea Org member to ever regain respect after being a deserter, so I thought the only way to do so was to become a celebrity, or what Scientology calls an Opinion Leader (one who is persuasive and whose opinion matters).

If I wanted to do more than just *call* myself an actor, I needed an agent. Even I knew that. So I talked to Sherry, who was now dating actress Juliette Lewis's brother Lightfield, about getting me an agent.

Sherry had left Flag and the Sea Org about a year after I did, returning home to D.C., where she got a part-time job at a copy shop and did some door-to-door sales. She wasn't in school, and she and her mother weren't getting along. We kept in touch and I knew how unhappy she was, so I told her to come meet me in New York when I went back to visit my dad, and once there, I convinced her to come live with us in L.A.

George, whom my mom had now married, partitioned off a room within our living room for her, and I got her a job waitressing at New York George's and then at John's printing company.

Sherry was eager to help me, and as promised, Lightfield introduced me to an agent, albeit a children's agent.

Natalie Rosson was everything I expected her to be. An older lady with coiffed blond hair, a lot of bracelets, and an office in the valley.

"So, do you have any experience?"

"Nah. Zero, but I was *taw-king* to my friend who . . ."

"Well, you need to lose that accent."

"Totally."

"I'm not going to sign you just yet because you're a little . . . right-off-the-boat. I'll send you out on a few auditions to see how you do. But don't run around saying I'm your agent."

"No problem, Nat!"

"And don't call me Nat."

"Yep."

My first audition was for a soap opera. Lightfield talked to me about what to expect. He knew a lot about the business from his family. His sister would later go on to success with films such as *Kalifornia* and *Natural Born Killers*. Their dad, Geoffrey Lewis, was a veteran TV and film character actor and a big Scientologist. Lightfield explained that I needed to get the "sides"—the portion of the script I would be expected to perform at the audition—so that I could familiarize myself with the material.

In the soap opera audition, one of my lines was, "Do you think I'm a whore?" In my Brooklyn accent "whore" sounded like *"hoo-wha."*

Pointing to the line, the casting director asked, "What is this word you are saying?"

"Hoo-wha?" I asked.

"What's that?" she asked.

"It's a girl who has sex with guys for money."

"No, I'm asking in what language are you attempting to speak?"

I laughed. She did not.

My non-agent Natalie called and had these words to say: "It is not going any further."

I said, "I don't know what that means. Are we breaking up?"

"No, I am telling you you didn't get the part."

Next I was sent to see Bob Corff, one of the top voice coaches in the business. After we had worked together for one session, Bob said, "You know, I'm going to go against what your agent is saying. I think you should keep your accent. Your personality is going to get you where you want to go, and your accent is part of that."

"Bob," I said, "I couldn't agree with you more."

Natalie next set up a meeting with a casting director named John Levey. He would go on to cast a number of popular shows like *China Beach* and *ER*. But most importantly for me, at the time he was casting *Head of the Class,* the ABC sitcom about a class of kids in an honors program at a public high school in Manhattan. My plan was this: Get on the show, meet Brian Robbins, who played the character Eric, have him fall in love with me. He was from Marine Park, Brooklyn, which was just a couple of miles along Kings Highway from Bensonhurst. So it was destiny; we'd get married and be a power celebrity couple who never forgot our roots.

During this time I had been working at Survival Insurance, a Scientologist-owned company, where I assisted insurance brokers. I headed out at lunch and spent money that was supposed to be for my car payment on a cute mini and a white tee at the five-dollar store and a brand-new pair of skippies from the Payless next door. I figured that once I got the part on *Head of the Class,* I would make all the payments that I had missed on my new car. So it would all work out. I drove over to the Warner Bros. lot to meet John Levey. Not knowing how it worked, I assumed that once he approved me, I would be sent to the set to marry Brian—I mean, to work on the show.

This was my second audition and my agent had not given me any sides. Instead I planned to charm John with my whole tough-girl shtick, turning into a full-on *cuginette* as soon as I got in front of him. With my Brooklyn accent thicker than usual, my hands waving all around, and a lot of "fucks" sprinkled in, I started talking about how "this one's a jerk-off and that one's a jerk-off in Hollywood."

I had this big casting director laughing at my act, and in my mind the deal was done. Get the director's chair ready with my name written on the back. I was in!

"You're adorable," John said. "Go outside for a minute to look at the sides, and then come back in to read."

"Oh, there's more to this?"

"Yeah, honey. You've got to audition."

I was confused. I thought that I *had* been auditioning. But I didn't say anything. I walked out into the lobby only to return to the room a few minutes later.

As I started reading the sides with John, I became a different girl. My smile wobbled, my hands shook so badly that the script made a rustling noise, and my voice cracked. I went from sassy to loser in two seconds flat. It was like having an out-of-body experience. I could see it happening to me, but there was nothing I could do to stop it.

The audition did not last long.

"You are so damned cute. You're just a little new at auditioning, so I am not having you come back tomorrow for producers because you are very green. Don't worry, though. I know you now, and I'm going to keep you in my pocket. I'm going to call you. I promise."

But I did worry. I walked out of the studio defeated. I had blown it. My big chance to be an actress, marry Brian/Eric, and be a big star in my family's eyes and to the church, to get out of poverty and live happily ever after was squashed. As well as be on TV. Oh. And make that car payment. Or payments.

BUT BY THE TIME I got to my car, parked across the street in the Taco Bell parking lot, I was back to being a fighter.

Fuck that.

I called Information from the Taco Bell pay phone and asked for the Warner Bros. casting department. "Hi," I said when I got the secretary for John Levey's office on the line. "I was just there. I've got to tell John something. Can I just talk to him real fast?" Miraculously, she put me through.

"What's up?" he asked, and I began crying.

"I'm sorry I was so nervous. I didn't know. Like, I thought I already had the job. I can do better. Please, give me another chance, I was nervous, not prepared . . ."

I don't know if it was because I was crying so hard and he felt sorry for me or what, but John said, "Okay, come back tomorrow at four. There's a producers' session. Maybe you'll do better."

Oh, I'd definitely do better. I thanked John for the second chance, told him I wouldn't let him down, and then called my agent's office, where I left word with her assistant about what had happened.

I was pretty pleased with myself until later that day when I got a call from my agent screaming at me.

"If you ever harass a casting director again—," she yelled.

"Wait a minute. He told you I harassed him?"

"You listen to me. You don't call them directly. That's not the way it's done here in Hollywood. Got it? If you pull a stunt like this again, I am going to drop you so fast."

John Levey was the biggest jerk-off in the history of Hollywood. For him to call my agent and say I was harassing him after he told me how fucking cute I was? When I made it big, I was going to thank John Levey for being such an asshole. Publicly, while accepting an Emmy. I had it all planned out: "And lastly, I would like to thank John Levey, jerk-off of all jerk-offs, for being a two-faced . . ."

I was at work the next day when the phone rang around five in the afternoon.

"Survival Insurance. This is Leah. Can I help you?"

"Leah, it's John Levey. Why didn't you show up to your appointment?"

I didn't even let him finish his sentence before I started in.

"You asshole! I thought you were going to be my buddy. And instead you complain to my agent that I'm harassing you? What kind of dick fuck . . ."

John told me to shut up and went on to say that he never said anything like that to my agent. He explained that he had called Natalie's office the day before to confirm the appointment and let her know there would be more people in the room so that I'd be prepared. He had told her assistant what I had done to get back in the room with him.

"Look," he said, "your agent said that because you had the balls to call me. And I'm telling you now, I don't want you to change, Leah. Don't listen to her or people like her. You did what your heart told you to do. And I hope you always do."

"Thank you, John," I said.

"No problem."

"Sorry about calling you an asshole."

"No worries."

"And a dick."

"Okay, honey, I got to go."

"And a fu—Hello?"

Okay, I guess he had to go.

But *Head of the Class* wasn't going any further.

Still, he made good on his promise—that he would keep me in mind for any part he thought I'd be right for. He was my champion, calling me once a week for auditions, where invariably I got nervous as soon as I got in front of the producers.

"Don't turn into an asshole when you get into the room," John would say while walking me down a hallway in the studio for my audition.

"You're the asshole."

"You get crazy when you get in there. You get weird. And you start rambling. I want you to shut the fuck up," he said, right before opening the door to the room where the producers were waiting. As soon as we stepped inside, his entire demeanor shifted. Beaming a huge smile at the suits, he said, "Hello. This is Leah Remini. You are going to love her."

Well, they didn't love me. Instead, what I got from that audition and dozens if not hundreds more was "It's not going any further," and an all-new rejection: "They went another way."

Apparently my car wasn't going to go "any further" either. Side note: When the Ford Motor credit guy tells you that you are behind in payments ninety days and that they are going to repossess your car, they mean it. Despite the fact that you went out of your way to make them laugh. My car was repossessed shortly thereafter making getting to auditions, where I would lose roles, all that much harder.

Each time I went to an audition my mom would say, "I know you're gonna get this part," and each time I had to come home and tell her that I didn't. That we were going to eat Taco Bell again for dinner. That we couldn't buy furniture. While my mother never discouraged me, it broke my heart having to face up to this failure in her eyes. It killed me that I couldn't help my family, and that we were living this way.

I understood this failure of not landing any of the roles I auditioned for to be 100 percent my fault. According to Scientology, I either wasn't applying the technology I was learning well enough or

I wasn't applying it correctly. Clearly I wasn't dedicated enough, because if I were I would have the job. I equated my struggles as an actress with punishment for my behavior. So I was always trying to be a better Scientologist, believing that the technology would provide the assurance for success. The more I worked in the church, the more success I would have in my career. This was the mantra we were taught.

I heard over and over how the more successful a person was, the more impact he or she could have for the church. I thought I could also make more change happen in the world if I were famous. I pictured myself one day on the cover of *Celebrity*, Scientology's answer to *People* magazine. In this way my two goals of advancing as a Scientologist and as an actress became intertwined.

My mom's attitude was that if I wanted to be an actress badly enough, "You'll make it go right." That's a widely used phrase that hints at a major concept running throughout Scientology. Either you are an able being, meaning someone who can overcome any obstacle to achieve a goal, or you are simply an average person who can't make it happen. I couldn't be average.

I didn't give up—either in the church or as an actress—and finally I was rewarded with something good. John Levey wore the producers down until they agreed to give me a small walk-on part and my first line on none other than *Head of the Class*!

It was 1988 when I arrived on the set of my favorite show. It was the first time I'd been on a comedy set. Instantly I knew I was home. The smell of the stage, the heat from the lights, the energy from the audience when they cheered each cast member. And then when an actor got that first laugh—the sound was a drug. *I want this. I want to make people feel this.*

I knew I had to make an impression even though I had a pretty nondescript part. I was in a scene where three girls walk by Eric (my future hubby). The first says, "Hi, Eric, three o'clock. Don't forget," and walks offstage. The next girl: "Hi, Eric, three-thirty. Don't forget." And finally me: "Hi, Eric, three-forty. Don't forget."

How was I going to separate myself from the other girls with that one line?

I decided to add a dramatic pause *and* a wink.

When it was my turn I took a deep breath and went for it. "Hi, Eric. [*Pause*] Three-forty. [*Wink*] Don't forget."

"Cut!" the director said. "That's great. Now can you cut all that other stuff you're doing and just say your line and walk off like everybody else? Okay, doll?"

"Doll, that's cute." Maybe he wasn't really seeing the magic before him. I'd do it one more time—after all, he called me "doll."

I cut the wink, but I kept the dramatic pause.

"What did I tell you about all that other shit you're adding in there? Just say your line and get out."

"Okay. Will do."

So I cut the wink *and* the pause, and added only a little look back at the end, like one of those you do to see if a guy is checking you out.

"Let's take a camera break here," he said.

Cool, I thought. *They see the magic before them here. I think they will have a meeting now and discuss how to add me into the show.*

The director called John Levey to the set.

"Are you deaf or just annoying?" John said to me when he arrived. "They want to recast you, because you're so annoying. You're not taking direction. You've got to listen. This is not your moment. Steven Spielberg's not going to see this episode of *Head of the Class.*"

He was right. And it wasn't going any further.

Chapter Six

I T WAS THE FALL OF 1988 WHEN I LEARNED ABOUT THE PART OF A "sassy girl from Brooklyn with a heart of gold" for a potential new sitcom. Sitting at my desk at Survival Insurance, where unfortunately I was still working, I took down information for my audition from my agent on the phone, writing the description for the character Charlie Briscoe and the name of the show, *Living Dolls*, on the front of the weekly memo for the Monday-night meeting I always tried to get out of.

ABC and Columbia Pictures Television wanted a spin-off of *Who's the Boss?*, the popular show starring Tony Danza as a retired baseball player turned housekeeper. The way the *Living Dolls* spin-off was set up was that Charlie is the best friend of Samantha (Alyssa Milano) from her old neighborhood. Charlie runs away from home, naturally, and goes to Samantha's house, where she is discovered by a modeling agent, played by Michael Learned (the mom from *The Waltons*), who, wowed by Charlie's beauty, decides not only to make her a model but also to have her come live with her and a few other models.

The breakdown for the character of Charlie Briscoe was a teen with a smart mouth, a sense of humor, a New York accent, and a heart of gold. When I heard that, I told my mom, "This part is perfect for me! If I don't get this part, Mom, I don't think I'm going to act anymore."

"What's the show about?" she asked.

"Models."

"Who are you going to play?"

WHILE I KNEW THAT I was right for the part and I could do the job, I was still nervous. I was really counting on this role and this series to change my life.

Creator Ross Brown and executive producer Phyllis Glick had me work on a scene a few times. Whatever they saw, they liked it enough for me to get a call back. But right before I left, the casting director gave me a piece of advice for when I returned: "Look like a model."

Thanks, genius. Let me do that real quick. Should I also wish for eight more inches of height and higher cheekbones?

"I can't be taller and prettier than I am," I said.

"Listen, sweetheart, when you come back, wear some makeup."

"Good note."

I could put on makeup, no problem, but the bigger issue was my nerves. As my time with John Levey showed, I was always great one-on-one or schmoozing a room. However, the minute I was standing in front of all those producers with those sides in my hands, I became a wreck. In a few days I was going to have my network session for *Living Dolls*. I could already picture all those suits and the shaking script in my hand.

After pretending to work at Survival, just killing time, I walked into the apartment I shared with my family and found my mom and a group of strangers waiting for me. They were all Scientologists.

My mother introduced me to Bob, a friend of hers from the church who was a self-proclaimed acting manager. She had approached him about my problem and asked if he could help me prepare for my big audition for ABC. "You need to get comfortable reading in front of a crowd," he said.

Bob had me do some exercises straight out of the Scientology course Success Through Communication. It was intended to teach participants how to speak with intention and purpose. I worked from my sides. "Flunk," he said whenever he couldn't hear me.

Next, Bob had me do the sides in different tones along the Tone Scale. That's a Scientology concept of the "successive emotional tones a person can experience," with a tone being "the momentary or continuing emotional state of a person."

The scale runs from 40.0 at the top, which is known as Serenity of Beingness, through Body Death at 0.0, and all the way down to 40.0, Total Failure. Church policy states that if you are below 2.0 (Antagonism), you are a detriment to yourself and others.

Scientologists do drills so they can learn to tell where people are on the Tone Scale and can stay clear of people who go below a certain point on the scale.

Bob felt that actors needed to learn their lines in all tones of the scale so they could find the tone the character was in.

"Do it in Hostility," Bob ordered me.

I tried.

"I didn't get that," he said.

I tried again.

"Now do it Numb."

"Not enough intention," was Bob's response to my effort.

We went on like this for another two hours.

AT THE PRODUCERS' SESSION FOR *Living Dolls* the next day, I was bolstered by not only the rigorous drills that Bob had put me through but also the support of a whole Scientology community that had come out to encourage me while I did the work. No one could take that away—not even the casting agent, who introduced me to the producers this way: "Okay, the next actress is *not* a Brooke Shields, but she gets the material. She's fresh from New York, and very funny."

I worked the room the minute I got inside.

Don't blow it, Remini.

And just like in every good made-for-TV movie, I nailed it! My audition was good enough that I convinced the suits I could play a model. If that's not acting, I don't know what is. I was so grateful to the Scientology technology that made it happen and the members of my church who rallied around me.

After five excruciating days, my non-agent Natalie called and as I went to pick up the phone, I was thinking, *Please don't say "It's not going any further" or "They went another way." Please change my life, please change my life. I don't want to have a picnic table as a dining table, I don't want to scrounge for car payments anymore, please I've been good, I've been on course, okay I am cheating on my boyfriend but I will give that up tomorrow in session, please give us a better life. Please work, Scientology!* . . . All that in the seconds it took for Natalie to say, "You got your first series." I was hysterical—screaming, crying, cursing. And further she said, "I am going to need you to come to my office and sign contracts." Not for the series, but because she had finally decided to officially take me on as a client and be my agent.

At eighteen years old, I felt this was going to be the ticket out for my entire family. Mom, George, Nicole, Shannon, and I had lived in seven apartments since moving to Los Angeles, and each was just as disgusting as the last. But now I could finally say, "I am an actress, a real one." I would make my family proud and the church proud.

I gave notice at Survival Insurance by sending out a company-wide memo announcing: "My fellow co-workers of Survival Insurance, I bid you all adieu, even those who didn't believe me—I'm off to be a big star. Please feel free to take my clients."

A few wrote back via interoffice mail.

—Break a leg!
—When do you leave?

—You owe me money.

—I thought you were fired a long time ago.

—I didn't even know you worked here.

—Leah, you never had any clients.

I had a new set of co-workers—my cast mates, and I loved all the girls: Alison Elliott, Vivica Fox (right after the pilot she was replaced with Halle Berry—oh, shit, we were replaceable!), and Deborah Tucker. The producers wanted us to have fun and bond as well as look great, so they treated us to personal training sessions and haircuts at a fancy Beverly Hills salon.

Getting the star treatment was more glamorous and exciting than anything I could have ever imagined. I also felt strangely comfortable with it. Like, *yes, this is where I belong.* But my real training for *Dolls* was on the set of *Who's the Boss?*

Before I was transformed into a fashion model with my own series, I had two weeks on the set of *Who's the Boss?* working with seasoned actors like Judith Light and Katherine Helmond. But no one was more influential for me during that crash course in how to be a sitcom star than Tony Danza.

Tony taught me the importance of turning the page *before* the next line so you don't ruin the rhythm of a joke. Because there's nothing worse than if someone else has a joke, and you're like, "Hold a second . . . hold, hold, hold," while you fumble with the pages.

And always say hello to your crew. Always know their names. And make eye contact. Tony was big-time all about the crew and any people who became part of the set. He told me that it was important to introduce yourself to the guest cast. Make them feel at home. Don't ignore people.

Tony was very warm *and* efficient. He was strict in the way his set ran, which I learned when I broke one of his cardinal rules: Never keep an audience waiting.

Throughout a TV show taping before a live audience, actors often have quick changes when you have to change outfits for another scene. Because the dressing rooms aren't usually located on the stage, there are quick-change rooms backstage, which are basically structures made of felt held together by a clamp with an actor's name in tape on it. On my first day, as I was walking to the quick-change room for a wardrobe change, Tony stopped me.

"You can't be walking," he said. "There are two hundred and fifty people waiting out there, and once the audience is tired, that's it. There's no people laughing at your joke. This isn't about you. You have to think about the audience. You've got to *run*."

After the show, he took me aside.

"You know why I'm hard on you, right?" he said. "Because you have it and you can be great. I've got to teach you these things now so you don't get yourself into bad habits."

Tony was very loving and giving in a fatherly way. He was the one who taught me right from wrong on a sitcom set—and after my time on *Who's the Boss?* I wanted to be just like him. I wanted to talk to my cameraman, be gracious to my guest stars, and run my ass off for my quick changes. I wanted to follow his beautiful example. Why not be nice and courteous?

Working on a sitcom is the best job you could ever have. It's very similar to a play, where you rehearse, rehearse, rehearse, and then perform in front of a live audience. From the cameramen to props to wardrobe, everybody's excited when it's showtime. You rehearse all week on an empty stage, with no audience, running through the show for the director, then for the writers, then writers and producers, then writers, producers, studio, and the network, just for cameras. But on show night, the audience loads in, the deejay plays the music, the comic starts to warm up the audience—you can hear them laughing (or not) while you are backstage in makeup or your dressing room—your camera guys and girls are dressed up a little more, and there's just an extra something in the air. The audience is there to see you. *YOU.* Magic.

Being on TV also meant I could make more of an impact as a Scientologist. Even though I didn't get any special pass from my supervisor, who on the news of learning about my new gig asked me what my course schedule was going to be.

"Well, I can't be here at all on Friday because I'm filming," I said.

"So you'll have to make up the time on Saturday then," he said.

If being a practicing Scientologist was hard before I became a regular on TV, after I started on *Living Dolls* it was crazy. After a twelve-hour day on set when everyone else was headed home to flop into bed or on their way out to dinner, I had to go to the church to spend two and a half hours on course. Still, there wasn't any part of me that was unhappy.

When I got the part, I immediately moved Mom, George, Shannon, and myself into a three-bedroom apartment in Burbank. My mom, like a lot of Scientologists who put most of their resources toward Scientology rather than themselves, was the kind of person to get a secondhand couch or keep a dress forever. Meanwhile, I was working very hard *not* to be that kind of Scientologist. The conditions we had been living in embarrassed me, just like they had when I was a kid. And just like when I was in Brooklyn, I knew that if I was going to get what I wanted—matching furniture, normal snacks, coffee cups with saucers—I had to make it happen.

I believed that I would be the one to move us up and out. My family was now going to live a better life and I was going to be the one to lead the way. I convinced my mom that we needed to move out of Hollywood and into Burbank. She obsessed about the money it would cost and so did my stepfather, George. Like most Scientologists, he cared more about working toward his eternity. Everything else was just materialistic and a waste of time. But I got to Mom one day when I said, "LRH had very nice things, Mom. We need to live better." I knew this would appeal to her.

So we moved into Parc Pointe, an apartment complex. Mario Lopez and Jennifer Love Hewitt were a couple of our neighbors. Standing on our balcony, overlooking the pool downstairs in the center of the courtyard, I thought, *We made it, people! We're living in Burbank, California!*

Shortly before our move, Nicole had decided to move out on her own, and she got an apartment nearby. Ever since we'd left Clearwater, my sister's interest in Scientology had waned. As the years passed, she left the church and moved toward Christianity. I didn't have a problem with it, but my mother did. She attributed anything that was wrong in my sister's life—everyday problems like money issues or boyfriend trouble—to the fact that Nicole was no longer a Scientologist. Looking back, I should have pointed out, *Wait, we have the exact same problems and we are still* in *Scientology.* At the time however, I was under the impression that our achievements in the church outweighed anything else that might be going wrong in our real lives or any other non-Scientologists' lives, for that matter. Still, I never gave Nicole a hard time about no longer being in the church.

In September of 1989, when the first episode of *Living Dolls* aired, it seemed like everything was going my way. Life was exciting, from the telex I received from then-ABC president Bob Iger telling me to "have a good show" to coming to the attention of the New Kids on the Block. Well, I wasn't exactly the one who got noticed by the hottest boy band at the time. It was Halle Berry. Thanks to her we were invited by the guys to their show and backstage afterward.

Even my dad, who I hadn't heard from in a while, called to say he had seen me on TV and that he was very proud of his little girl. It was a surprise, because my dad didn't reach out often. If we spoke on the phone, it was because I called. And if I saw him and his family in New York, it was because I was the one who visited him. He asked what Tony Danza was like and could I get pictures. Then he said, "Why don't you make a movie with Marty Scorsese? He's from the old neighborhood."

"I'd love to, Dad," I said. "But I don't have his phone number."

He said, "Well, get it somehow. Don't you have an agent?"

I said, "Hey, Dad, you know it's not easy to get on a series, right?"

MY MOTHER WAS GENUINELY PROUD of me. She always thought I was funny—she used to say, "Oh, my God, Leah, you make me *laugh*" all the time—but now I was on television making other people laugh. I was on top of the world, my family was proud, my church was proud. I was on my way.

In television, however, there is a thing called ratings. And we didn't do well in them. And we were told that we were being canceled. We were all completely devastated. None of us was ready to move on. We had just gotten started.

After shooting the twelfth episode of *Living Dolls* in December 1989, we had a wrap party, which was the worst thing I could imagine.

On top of the sadness I felt to be leaving this group of people I had become so close to so quickly, I had no idea what I was moving on to. I worried about making the payments on my brand-new car and paying the rent on the apartment filled with all the new matching furniture that I had convinced my family I could afford. To my mom and George I pretended that everything was going to be all right, but on the inside I was dying from the pressure. I didn't understand why I was being punished. What had I done?

Chapter Seven

Y OU'RE NOT GOING TO DO THIS SHOW," MY AGENT SAID.
Not going to do this show? It's Saved by the Bell.

I was now with a big power agency, ICM, which I had
been encouraged to move to after I got *Living Dolls*. Still, I didn't
care how big and powerful these guys were; I was grateful that a
popular sitcom was offering me six episodes, and I was going to
take it.

My agent's rationale for turning down the role of Stacey Carosi—
who has a romance with Zack (played by Mark-Paul Gosselaar)—
was that since I was coming off of a series, it was beneath me to take
a recurring role on a show. I thought, *Not having money to pay my
rent is beneath me.*

The series that I had just come off of in the fall of 1991, *The Man
in the Family,* lasted for only seven episodes. It left me back where I
was before *Dolls,* auditioning for guest appearances on popular sitcoms. I just wanted to belong somewhere again, on a show I could
call my own. I was exhausted already. I did a pilot, it didn't go any
further; I got another series, it got canceled before it aired. Each
time I swore I was going to give up, but then I'd just get back up
and keep going. (All told, I've been on more than twenty-five even-

tually canceled television shows in my career, and have appeared in even more pilots that never made it to air. While I would never complain, I certainly did feel anxiety. This is not an easy business to be in.)

It seemed like all the actresses in L.A. were going out for the same roles—after a few rounds of endless auditions at the studios, I was able to identify the girls who were my competition for these coveted spots. So when I walked into an audition for the part of Rhea Perlman's daughter on *Cheers* and saw one of my regular contenders, I was like, "Ugh, there's Aniston."

Jennifer Aniston and I had become friendly from seeing each other so much at various auditions. She was normal, unlike most other actresses, who, if you tried to make small talk, like asking where they were from, would accuse you of trying to "psych them out." One girl I tried to shoot the shit with got up and walked out. So when you find someone, like Jennifer, who isn't douche-y, you develop a natural camaraderie.

When I saw her in the last round of callbacks for the *Cheers* audition, I said, "Fuck, I hope you don't get this one. I need to pay my rent."

Jennifer just smiled and said, "I hope you get it, then."

The part of Carla's daughter was kind of a no-brainer for me, but you never know. So when the casting agent came out and said, "Jennifer . . ." I was thinking, *You have got to be fucking kidding me.* But the agent finished the sentence with "Thank you so much, but we're going with Leah this time."

Jennifer couldn't have been sweeter. "Congratulations, honey!" she said, and I could tell she really meant it.

My first day on the set of *Cheers* I was totally awestruck because it was such a huge show and it featured major, Emmy-winning actors. While I was watching rehearsal, Ted Danson came and sat next to me. I tried to play it cool, not wanting to bother him. So when he said, "Would you run lines with me?" I assumed he was speaking to someone else and completely ignored him.

"Is that too much?" he said.

"I'm sorry. Were you talking to . . . ? I actually didn't know," I stammered. "I heard you. I just didn't know if you were talking to me."

"Yes, darlin', I'm talking to you. Would you mind? I'm so bad on my lines."

"Of course!" I said. We went through his lines and when he did the scene for real I felt completely responsible for his success, like I was Ted Danson's acting coach or something.

So, I had landed the role of Carla's daughter on *Cheers,* but of course, as TV history would tell, Jennifer Aniston got hers with *Friends.* When the show was still being developed and was called *Friends Like Us,* I tried out for the part of Monica. As soon as my agent and I read the script we knew it was going to be a hit. And it was filming over at Warner Bros., right across the hall from John Levey's office. If this wasn't meant to be, I didn't know what was.

The way it worked back then was you'd go to the studio first to audition, and then if you made the cut you went to the network. If you didn't make it, you would get the "It's not going any further" line, but if you did go on, it was a long day. It came down to me and this other girl at network. We became friendly during what seemed like an eternity of them asking us, individually, to go in and read, then sit outside, then calling one of us back in, then out, and so on. Eventually the casting director came out and said, "Thank you so much." Here was the embarrassing part, where one of us would exit a failure. It's hard to walk out with your head held high when you've been rejected.

"You can both leave," the casting director said.

We were surprised but relieved. The girl and I assumed they were going to tell us at home who got the part, which was probably for the best. We walked out of the building and into the completely empty parking lot. It was a Saturday, so no one was at the studio. We chatted on the way to our cars, wishing each other the best, and then we saw Courteney Cox walking toward us, then past us and right into the building. *Motherfucker!* We both knew it right away: *She* had the part of Monica.

I knew *Friends* was going to be a hit. This killed me. I cried for days. I swore I would never ever audition for another show. Ever. Because this had been the one that was going to be my ticket. This one was so tough to get over.

In addition to hustling for parts, I had all my Scientology work to deal with. I was a dedicated parishioner, going through auditing and courses, but still there were always things required as a parishioner that I felt uncomfortable with, like the drills we had to do on certain courses. One was to spot different levels on the Tone Scale. You had to stop complete strangers on Hollywood Boulevard, get them to answer questions, and then assess their tone: 2.5 for Boredom, .07 for Hopeless. As part of a course on the Tone Scale, we were sent out with clipboards and required to pretend that we needed people to answer questions for a survey being conducted by the Hubbard Such-and-Such Research Center, but it was all just a ruse for us to practice assessing different tone levels. The surveys weren't real. Most people were like, "Fuck you. I know who you are and what you're doing."

I took a shortcut to try to get out of doing the drill. "I'm an actress. I can't be out here. Someone might recognize me from my not-so-popular and canceled series," I protested. "John Travolta did it," the supervisor said. "*You're* going to do it."

I was pretty much always on course a minimum of two and a half hours a day at the Celebrity Centre on Franklin Avenue, which was the building reserved for people in the arts or their associates to get services. After I became a working actress, I always went in through the main entrance, but there was a special one that led to the President's Office—a private area reserved exclusively for celebrities, like John Travolta, Tom Cruise, and Kirstie Alley, and other VIPs. I didn't get that role on *Friends,* so I wasn't "there" yet.

In the theory room of the course room, which is just for reading, I would sit as still as a statue, because a supervisor was always walking around, looking for manifestations of study problems. If someone scratched his head, the supervisor would come over and ask, "What word don't you understand here?" I always tried my best not to blink or breathe. If you yawned, you were pretty much dead in the water.

"Get your course pack and come into the practical room for a checkout on your materials," the supervisor would command.

Being checked out sent me directly back to elementary school, where teachers seemed to take sadistic pleasure in pointing out a kid's gap in understanding in front of everyone in class. In quizzing me, the supervisor asked for definitions of words in the course packet, then examples of how to use those words in a sentence. Sometimes starting at the top of the page, which read "Sussex, England," and if you didn't know where that was, you would have to re-read the whole thing again (Sussex was where L. Ron Hubbard once had a home and is now the highly coveted Church of Scientology called St. Hill Manor). They went back as much as ten pages in the course to find something I had forgotten. It could be the third point in the ten points of "Keeping Scientology Working" or reciting verbatim all twelve "antisocial personality attributes." Then I would have to go all the way back in my course to that point. It was frustrating, but the objective was to get the correct data and technology per HCOB (Hubbard Communications Office Bulletin). That meant doing it exactly right. I mean *exactly*.

Being on course was time-consuming, but when a parishioner was getting audited, there was no time limit. An auditing session could be twenty minutes or twenty hours. As determined by L. Ron Hubbard policy, you were expected to do twelve and a half hours a week of auditing or study. If you were not a good student before Scientology, you certainly would become one.

Auditing is all about rooting out hidden pain, stress, or anxiety with the use of an E-Meter and then getting rid of it. The E-Meter, short for "electropsychometer," is an "electronic instrument that measures mental state and change of state in individuals," according to the church. During the process, the preclear, or PC (person getting the auditing), is asked a set of questions or given directions as he holds on to two empty "cans" hooked up to the meter. It is believed that the thoughts in a person's mind affect the flow of energy between the cans and cause the needle on the dial to move.

When you are being interviewed by the auditor, there is a "mental image picture." This is a Scientology term for something you can "see" in your mind, most often demonstrated by asking someone to close their eyes and think of a cat and then describe what it "looks like." These mental image pictures include emotion, pain, or stress, which changes the flow of the current and moves the needle.

The auditor's job is to keep the session focused by using the meter and observing the reactions on the needle. There are twenty-eight "needle characteristics" that auditors have to know verbatim. A little shaky movement on the dial means you are having a bad thought about the thing you are talking about, or about something you are not telling the auditor. If the needle falls to the right, it tells the auditor to pursue what the PC is thinking about or talking about.

That is one of the hardest parts about being in session—there might be something you really want to get off your chest or to understand better (a fight with a boyfriend, problems with your mother, an issue with a colleague at work), but if the needle doesn't move when you talk about a particular subject, you have to move on. In Scientology you further discuss only what's reading on the meter.

Auditing can also become a form of self-editing, when it comes to criticizing others. The theory in Scientology is that if you are critical of someone, you have "similar transgressions of your own."

For example, if you were to say, "My boyfriend beats me," that would be seen as saying something critical to the auditor. He would then turn it around and say, "I got that, but have you done something similar to him or others?" The word "critical" in Scientology is very different.

Hubbard defined critical thought as "a symptom of an overt act having been committed" or "a withhold from an auditor." What Hubbard meant is that critical thought is a bad thing; it indicates a criminal act. "Overt acts" and "withholds" are the equivalent of crimes against life and freedom in Scientology. The new definition thus makes it a crime for members to think critically, particularly about Scientology. Any "critical thought" by the Scientologist is immediately suspect. This redefinition makes criticizing anything about Scientology extremely difficult for members, as it is reflected back on them as something they did wrong. Hubbard's message is clear: Critical thought is not the sort of thing any good Scientologist should be engaged in.

As a result you start to edit what's happened to you in your mind, and thus you can fail to address what is bothering you because you know it would end up all coming back to what you did to provoke that situation.

There are also other problems that can get in the way of covering those items that might be bothering you in your life. Scientology auditing follows a precise series of steps. Each addresses one or more conditions that everyone supposedly needs to overcome. Thus, your auditor directs your problems as required for you to move up the Bridge.

For example, the steps on the Bridge predetermine what will be addressed next. The auditor would then say: "In looking at earlier interviews and auditing, I have found that in your life you have a problem with communication."

Your auditor then proceeds to ask: "From where could you talk to your mother?"

You give various answers, but the auditor continues to come back again and again, looking for more answers. You grow frustrated and exhausted as the auditor comes back to you with the same question dozens of times, trying to unblock you. Then you surrender. You have a realization that gets the required reaction on the E-Meter that signifies this step is complete with a "floating needle."

You finally say: "I can communicate with my mother from any-where."

In the end, the "ability gained" is that you can communicate with anyone on any subject. Through auditing it has been proven, unequivocally, that you did indeed have this problem but just were not aware of it. And now that it's been proven to you that you did have a problem with communication and that problem has now been eliminated.

At the end of every session, once the needle has floated, the auditor says: "Thank you very much. Your needle is floating, we're going to end session now."

You now leave, feeling that you've accomplished something. *Didn't know that was there, but now I'm clear of it.* But the mind fuck lies in the fact that *they* assigned *you* the problem and not the other way around. And afterward, if you realize that you still have a problem with communicating with your mother, you are taught that that person is a wog, or "down tone." (Being down tone means existing at the lower level of the Scientology Tone Scale, which is a listing of the various emotional states you can be in. The higher you are on the Tone Scale, the happier and healthier you are. So, if you're down tone, it means you're unhappy and unhealthy—and potentially dragging higher tone people down with you.)

The process could produce a great sense of cathartic relief. Here was a problem I wasn't even aware of, that I may have created for myself, and after much back-and-forth, I was able to overcome that problem.

So while in session I would feel the euphoria of self-discovery and growth, back in the real world I was still angry, depressed, and judgmental. Looking at my diaries from that period (journaling was frowned upon by the church, but I did it anyway), I would note that I still wanted more for my life and my family's life. My Scientology realizations were great in the church building, but I would start cursing when I couldn't find my car in a parking lot or when I had no money left in my bank account. It just wasn't there for me in real-life situations, this sense of accomplishment of having solved problems. It really existed only when I was in the presence of other Scientologists, who completely bought into it.

What I didn't realize at the time was that all the understanding I gained through auditing only related back to my life in the church and helped me be a Scientologist. My "gains" in Scientology were not relating to the real world. I was so entrenched in the church that it had become my everything. I couldn't question that.

Chapter Eight

WHEN IT CAME TO MEN, I NEVER REALLY DATED SCIEN-
tologists, even though it was encouraged. I was embarrassed by a lot of people in the church who didn't pay
attention to practical things like how they looked and who talked in
a language that was strange to the outside world. Just like I wanted
a normal mom as a kid, now I wanted a normal boyfriend.

Dating outside the church also probably meant there was a part
of me that was subconsciously trying to keep something for myself
that wasn't connected to Scientology. Most of my family was in the
church, as were most of my friends, and I spent much of my free time
on course or being audited. My romantic life gave me that tiny bit
of freedom away from the weight of saving the planet. My fantasy
was that I'd meet a regular, cool, normal guy who *wasn't* a Scientologist but was open to it. Hopefully fucked-up enough to desperately
need it.

Looking back now, I am sure that the way my father acted and
the way I perceived him ultimately informed the way I looked at
men both when I was growing up and as an adult. I interpreted his
yelling and his dominance as strength, and I ultimately adopted the

same behavior and took it on as part of my own persona. I believed that this was the way a man was supposed to be and this was how a woman felt, being charmed by him. He yells, she cowers. To me this all made sense—except that in my relationships, I was usually the one doing the yelling.

I treated men badly and didn't have much respect for them. I had a list of very specific things that could get a man written off my list pretty fast (including, for example, men who wear sandals—shallow, I know). Always a keen observer since childhood, I also kept a mental list of what I thought a man was:

> Men say horrific and hurtful things to their wives and daughters (and are forgiven).
> Men are strong, women weaker (or men appear strong, but they are weak).
> Men are charming.
> Men wear cologne.
> Men get manicures.
> Men have clean cars.
> Men cheat.
> Men don't care about their families.
> Men go and start new families.
> Men hurt women.
> Men do not value anything.
> Men break their word and women forgive them.
> Men appear to be the dominant species.
> Men win.

FROM THE AGE OF EIGHTEEN through twenty-five, I went through a very promiscuous period, going out with all kinds of guys, from gorgeous soap actors to athletic beach bums. But I was never really attached to anyone in particular. It was mainly sex without any emotional connection.

Now, look, I don't want to give you the idea that I would sleep with anyone. I wasn't picking up random men and bringing them home. I just wasn't faithful. And sex was a substitute for really being there in a relationship.

I would do things that men would normally do to women to "get back at them." But I was only hurting myself. If I had sex with a guy, afterward I would say things like "Listen, ummmm, I have a very early morning, so you have to go. You can't sleep here," or "I have to go now. I haven't been home all day and my dog has to be let out" (I didn't have a dog). I would do this to a guy before he could do it to me. If I spent the night or committed to them, I would be made vulnerable. I was convinced that they would eventually either cheat or leave me anyway. Why open myself up to another man breaking my heart?

My mom always wanted me to be with someone in the church, because she thought it would help me with my problems with men and intimacy in general.

"I don't know, Ma. I just don't respect men," I confessed to her. "I have bad intentions toward them. Obviously it comes from Dad and Dennis. I want to break their hearts, like my heart's been broken," having been let down by many of the men in my life.

"I never want them to get the upper hand. Even if I feel something for them, I tell them to get the hell out."

But like any good Scientologist, my mom offered answers that led directly back to the church.

"You'll handle that in session," she said, and that was it.

She didn't judge me (and for that, she is always the person I go to, then and now)—she subscribed to the idea that anything bad I was doing wasn't really the doing of her daughter; instead it was my reactive mind, which I was on the road to dealing with and getting rid of. The main thing was that I stay on course and move up the Bridge. If I did that, everything would sort itself out.

All of my non-Scientology boyfriends would tell me I was fucked-up and that clearly Scientology was not working for me because I kept cheating or leaving. This made me go in search of someone even more fucked-up than I was. Someone I could fix, to avoid fixing myself.

In 1996 the universe provided me with Angelo Pagán. A man with a history of cheating, and three kids. Perfect. Now, I'll preface this by saying this is not a love story. I mean, it's a story about love— just not the kind that you hope to tell your kids one day.

It all began with a WB sitcom I was on—*First Time Out*— which, naturally, was soon canceled. The show's star, Jackie Guerra, who became a good friend, invited me out to a Cuban nightclub to "celebrate" getting canceled. I wasn't exactly feeling celebratory about being on the unemployment line yet again, but when I heard that Scott Baio, who had directed the last episode of our show, was going to be there, I quickly said yes.

Maybe I'd marry Scott. He might make this better. There was no doubt about it; I wanted "Charles in Charge" of me, and "Chachi loves Leah" sounded kinda nice. Now that he was no longer my director in a professional relationship, maybe there was something there.

As soon as I walked into the Cuban club El Floridita, I fell in love with the place. It was the tiniest nightclub I'd ever been to in my life. A small parquet dance floor surrounded by tables, a drop ceiling, red walls, and strung-up Christmas lights were the sum total of El Floridita's décor.

After Jackie, Scott, and I had dinner, the band started playing salsa music, and soon after that this guy walks in. He's got thick black hair, caramel skin, and huge dimples. He went right up to the microphone and just started singing without doing any kind of warm-up.

I was intrigued by this Cuban Frank Sinatra, but by now the club had become really crowded and the dance floor was packed with people dancing salsa, so we decided to leave as I'm not good with inhaling other people's sweat (that's why I don't do things like yoga). My fascination with Scott Baio had waned in the hours we were there because he was wearing high-top Reeboks. I told you, I'm very judgmental.

The next day I was still thinking about the singer. I called the club and found out that he performed every Wednesday night, then told Jackie that we were going back to El Floridita. The following Wednesday we got a table on the floor, right by the band, and had just sat down when Jackie spotted someone at the bar: "Isn't that Carlos? He was on our show. He had a few lines."

"I don't want him over here, Jackie." I didn't want to be sitting with some asshole guy when Cuban Frank Sinatra walks in.

"Why are you such a bitch?"

"What kind of guy comes to a club by himself?"

Jackie just rolled her eyes and got up to talk to Carlos. Meanwhile, Cuban Frank Sinatra walked in and started to sing. So I put my purse in the empty chair next to me, because I didn't want "Carlos, Mr. Few Lines" sitting with us. Jackie had brought him over anyway. I turned my back to him completely, as if I were totally absorbed by the band. That is, until I heard him tell Jackie, "My friend Angelo's the lead singer here. I came to meet him." And with that, I turned around and said, "Jesus, Carlos! How rude of me to turn my back to you! Eat something with us!" as I removed my purse from the empty seat.

"Jackie, how rude are you? Carlos! Have some *platanos*."

Sure enough, when the band took a break, Angelo came right over to say hello to Carlos, who introduced him to Jackie and me.

"Do you dance?" he asked me.

"With you? Yes. But I don't know how to dance salsa," I said.

"I'll teach you."

On the dance floor, as Angelo's going one-two-three, I'm doing the check:

Smells good, check.

Dimples, check.

Good teeth, check (although the bottom row are a little fucked-up, but I found that sexy as hell).

Strong arms, check.

Then the last item on the checklist: shoes and socks. I was petrified as I looked down, because if you have white socks on, you're dead to me. *Dead to me.* There's no fixing you. You're beyond help. As a person, there are certain things you should know, and one of them is black pants, black socks, black shoes.

Please, God, please.

And he had black socks and good black shoes. Check!

With Angelo it was instant magic. Like what movies are made of, songs are written about. But to be sure this magic was real, I needed to test it out.

With my checklist complete, I decided to break the number one rule of dating, and I asked him, "So, when are we getting married?"

"Ha, ha, ha," he laughed.

"Ha, ha, ha," I mimicked him. "It's going to happen, Angelo. I know you're uncomfortable in this moment, because you probably just think you're going to get laid. And that is going to happen. Right away. But here's what I'm saying to you: We're going to get married at some point."

"That's funny. I mean, I'm already kind of married."

Suddenly, the rom-com movie I was in came to a complete halt.

"What do you mean, you're 'kind of married'?" I asked.

What it meant, according to Angelo and which I believed, was that he and his wife were legally married but separated.

I said, "Why are you married already?"

He said, "Well, where have you been? I've been waiting for you."

Magic. I am a sucker for cologne and a good line. "What time do you get off?" I asked.

I was head over heels for Angelo with the dimples in a way that I had never felt. I wanted to be with him as much as possible, but it seemed that he could never sleep over. There was always a reason. An early work shift or he needed to take his young son to school. If I had used an ounce of the life smarts I prided myself on, I would have known why Angelo could never stay the night and why we rarely met until late at night. When I look back on it, it's clear I didn't want to know.

After I had given Angelo a lecture about going after his dreams, (he was selling electronics during the day and singing at night, which left no time for him to pursue his dreams of being an actor), he came to me and confessed the truth.

"I have to tell you something," he said to me one night. "I'm really starting to like you, and I'm starting to feel bad about the person that I'm being. I'm not separated. I'm a cheater—and not just with you. I have been a cheater my whole life."

This guy is so fucked-up, he's perfect for me!

I admired Angelo's honesty and candor, and I think it made me fall even more in love with him. I didn't want to give him up. So, even though Scientology hadn't helped me with my infidelities, I decided the church was going to fix his: "I need you to go to this place and make a change in your life."

Angelo did a small intro course called Personal Values and Integrity, which was about exactly what the title said. It discussed morality in a very simple way, stressing the importance of the participants' confessing to any and all transgressions with exercises such as writing an essay on the topic "When have you been dishonest?"

God bless him, Angelo threw himself into the course and began to tell me about every woman he had been with in the recent past— and there were a lot. Girls in the club, a dancer he knew from back in San Francisco, an entire bridal party! The more truths he told me, the more he wanted to tell. While most people might hear about these transgressions and be devastated, I had learned from Scientology that this behavior was not representative of the real person Angelo was. He just hadn't been "cleared" yet. All of this was still his reactive mind. A person could admit to the most heinous things and feel no remorse. But learning to admit to feeling guilt and to take responsibility was a whole other thing, which Angelo was now doing. We're taught to respect the person who has the balls to do that and admire him for it. Admitting you've done something wrong is the first step toward salvation, as defined by Scientology. According to LRH, each of us has something like 800 million overts—meaning transgressions—and you are never going to get them all out in one lifetime, but it's being aware that you have them and need to work on them that makes all the difference.

Angelo's history with women was what the church calls an ethical blind spot. Every man he knew growing up, including his father, cheated. It was accepted. What wasn't okay was to leave your wife for your girlfriend. So for Angelo to finally admit to himself that he was in fact a cheater was a huge first step for him. And the fact that he was willing to do something about it was even more impressive to me as a Scientologist. This was someone who could confront things and make real change. Angelo felt like that perfect mix I was waiting for, a "normal guy"—not a Scientologist—but someone who could quickly get with the program and get with Scientology.

My mom had a completely different take on the situation. "This guy isn't actually divorced," she said. "He isn't even separated." Maybe it was the echo of her own situation with my dad and Dennis, who had both left her for other women, or that she wanted more for her daughter than being the other woman, but she showed a hardness with me that I had never seen before. For the first time, my mother, who had supported me through many things other mothers wouldn't have, expressed utter disgust toward me. "I don't even know you," she said. "I did not raise this person."

My mother's reaction brought me back to my senses. Angelo was married with three kids. I was so focused on his ethical blind spot that I had completely ignored my own. Suddenly I asked myself, "What are you doing?" And the answer was horrible: I was destroying a marriage. Which opened up a new blind spot. I had no real respect for marriage. What did it mean? Clearly, it meant nothing when it came to my dad or my stepdad Dennis.

And just as clearly, I had no respect for the family unit either.

I went to the only place I had to work out my crisis of conscience—the church. I eventually and begrudgingly told them that I was having an affair with a married man, who had a son with his current wife. I was told I needed to make up the damage. It was determined that the way for me to do that was to pay for Angelo and his wife to go to marriage counseling offered by the church.

Scientology couples counseling is vastly different from typical relationship counseling. The church teaches that a marriage can't survive if one partner has any unknown transgressions against the other person. You need to reveal in excruciatingly specific detail what it is you've done wrong. Scientology doesn't factor in how much this kind of truth can break a husband's or wife's heart. Unlike other religions, where one can relieve guilt by talking to a member of the clergy, Scientology forces its parishioners to confront their partners face-to-face and admit their transgressions, no matter the consequences.

So I did it. I told Angelo that he needed to give his marriage a chance, and the only way he was going to do it was through counseling, which I would pay for because of what I had done by sleeping with him. Although he was as sad about leaving me as I was about leaving him, he had realized the impact the values course had on him and knew that for the good of his family he should give counseling a try.

I felt no relief for making up the damage. Instead, I got to watch Angelo and his wife walk by me at the Celebrity Centre, where they were going to counseling, holding hands like newlyweds. My church was telling me, "Do not contact Angelo." And again I was back in auditing and ethics to deal with my hidden evil intentions toward men, which clearly had not changed.

The church took little pity on me. On top of paying roughly five thousand dollars for the counseling Angelo and his wife did in the church, I now needed to meet with his wife in person and apologize for what I had done. I was beyond humiliated, but I also felt like I deserved everything I was getting.

I met Angelo's wife at a coffee shop and stumbled with my words.

"I don't have the answers. I can't justify what I've done," I said, unable to apologize not because I wasn't sorry but because an apology felt weird. "I'm sorry" weren't the right words. An apology didn't do it.

His wife, however, had no problems expressing herself. I sat there and took my punches.

I WAS DYING OF A broken heart, but Angelo never felt better in his life. After I met with his wife, he called me on the phone to thank me for all I had done for him.

"This is a whole new way of life for me," he said. "I never thought I could be honest like this. I mean, to look at my wife, tell her I've cheated, and have her still hold my hand. Oh, my God, Leah. Thank you."

Fuck you. Fuck you. Fuck you. Fuck her. Fucking hell.

"You're welcome," I said, barely able to get the words out and pulling the receiver away from my mouth so he couldn't hear me crying. "I hope you have a happy life now with your wife and your son, and I am sorry for what I have done to you all. I hope you can repair it."

From that call on, I plunged into a well of despair, confusion, and self-doubt. Did I do the wrong thing by doing the right thing? Is that the way this love story was supposed to end? I guess it wasn't a love story after all. In the end, though, I understood what had happened through the lens of Scientology. The purpose of my meeting Angelo was to do penance for my years as a cheater. The pain I was feeling was my punishment, and I deserved it. I was told by the church that I must no longer talk to Angelo, so I didn't, and he didn't call me.

I was still feeling pretty low several months later when Angelo called out of the blue. I was shocked that he reached out to me. I didn't want to hear that he was happy. I was steeling myself for it, though. He told me he had some things he wanted to talk to me about. We agreed to meet at a restaurant.

After we sat down, Angelo told me about what he had been going through since we had last seen each other. The couples counseling had been really therapeutic for him because, as he said before, it was the first time in his life that he was truly honest with a woman. But an unintended consequence of no longer being burdened by his own guilt was that he began to realize that his wife had her own set of issues and her own skewed set of values, telling Angelo that he could still have a girlfriend but he didn't need to leave her and his family to do that. He just needed to come home. But Angelo didn't want to be that guy, he wanted to be better. He was realizing that his own core values were changing as a result of his time spent in the church, but his wife's were not. Previously he overlooked anything she did because of his own bad behavior. He had been trying to make it work, but it felt like he was back to living a lie. He had already told his wife he was leaving.

"So it's either with you or somebody else," he said, "but I want to be happy."

I wanted it to be with me.

Chapter Nine

⚓

THIS WAS IT. I WAS SURE OF IT. *THIS* WAS GOING TO BE MY BIG
break. A sitcom in the time slot right after *Seinfeld*? It didn't
get any better.

When I got a lead role in the new series *Fired Up,* a mid-season
replacement on NBC's Must-See TV comedy block, I wasn't just
thrilled. I was relieved. Finally, my chance. Finally I will arrive home.

Fired Up, which first aired in the spring of 1997, was exactly
what I had been working for all these years. This was a sitcom with
some serious pedigree. Kelsey Grammer, of *Cheers* and its spin-off
Frasier, was producing the half-hour comedy starring *NYPD Blue*'s
Sharon Lawrence as a self-centered promotions executive and me as
her mouthy assistant. Our characters quickly got fired from their
jobs, and were forced to move in together and team up to create a
business as equal partners. Mark Feuerstein, who in real life is one of
those really good guys, played my brother in the show. Since I've
known him, Mark's proven himself to be a good friend and one of
maybe five "real men" I've met in this business.

Although we were getting an audience of about 15 million (which
would be a monster hit these days), we were still losing about half the

audience of about 30 million viewers who tuned in to *Seinfeld* every week. The network changed our time slot for the second season. With that, *Fired Up* lost its audience. Our last episode aired in February 1998.

The death of that show represented yet another failure as an actress and as a Scientologist. At twenty-seven years old, I was having to go back to the drawing board once again.

There were so many starts and stops in my career, ups and downs, moments of triumph and then heartbreak. It always felt like "This is it" and then it wasn't. Although that's the nature of the business in Hollywood, when it is happening to you it seems like the end of the world. My failures in my professional life ended up driving me toward the church, which taught me that because I wasn't successful on a regular basis, I was doing something wrong in life. Being a Scientologist means you are responsible for all the bad things that happen to you (and anything *good* that was happening was due to the church), so it was only natural to assume that the cancellation of *Fired Up* was somehow caused by my transgressions or some technology that I was misapplying in my life.

So when my agent Harry Gold called me about a new series for CBS, *The King of Queens,* about a blue-collar couple in Queens, I instantly came up with a reason that this wasn't going to work. I loved the idea of this show, but I felt America had left it behind and networks were looking more toward making sitcoms about young, sophisticated dot-commers.

What's the point? I thought. *I am only going to do the pilot and it won't get picked up or it will go to series and get canceled.* My heart couldn't take it. So I passed on it.

Harry swore up and down that this was my part, my show. "Will you just meet with Kevin James?" he asked, referring to the Long Island comedian set to play the part of Doug.

It was Les Moonves, the president of CBS, who ultimately got me out of my funk. When he heard the news that I didn't want to meet on *The King of Queens,* he called my agent to say, "Who the fuck does Leah think she is, passing on a show when she just came off some shitty show for NBC?"

Oddly enough, that kind of honesty always cheers me up. I got up and showered and took the meeting with Kevin. Les Moonves was a "real man" I needed to work for.

As soon as I walked into the room, Kevin took one look at me and said, "I'm sorry. Were you too busy not counting the money you weren't making on your canceled shows to make it to this meeting?"

I was in love.

Kevin had me crying from laughter in the first five minutes of our meeting.

Some changes were made from the pilot to the series. The important change to the original pilot was the addition of the legendary Jerry Stiller as my wacky father, who moves in with Carrie and Doug after his third wife dies and he burns down his house with his lucky hot plate. Originally, Jerry, who perfected the art of the crazy dad as Frank Costanza on *Seinfeld,* didn't want to do the pilot, but it was awful without him. When the show got picked up, he agreed to the part, we reshot the pilot, and it was like night and day. The concept for the show was simple. *King of Queens* was unpretentious and, most important, funny.

Still, as I stood next to Kevin backstage on that late September day in 1998, waiting to be introduced to the live audience, I knew better than to take a single second for granted. The emcee (the guy who warms up the audience before the taping) introduced everyone in the cast individually. Because Kevin and I were last, we had a moment to take it all in. I looked around—at the back of the sets, which were just plywood over sturdier wood frames with jacks to hold them upright, and at the cheap staircase that led to the back of the kitchen set. There I saw a name in a heart engraved into the wood—a leftover from another set, another show, another time.

"Look, Kevin," I said, "we should always remember that we're lucky to be here. There were shows before us and there will be shows after us, so let's never take it for granted."

Kevin got it completely, and we looked up at that rafter before greeting the audience at every single show. We were always aware of how fleeting this opportunity could be. And at the last show, nine years later, Kevin pointed to that same piece of wood, but I couldn't look at it.

Even if we had wanted to forget that we could be canceled at any minute, no one let us. Despite the fact that we averaged about 12.7 million viewers our first season (thereby keeping 95 percent of the viewers from our lead-in, *Cosby*) and we hands down beat *Conrad Bloom,* which we were up against on NBC (sorry, Mark, but you did okay), our success was called "modest." We certainly weren't a critical success, that's for sure. The press either ignored us entirely or wrote pretty bad reviews.

"The performers are pleasant enough, and Ms. Remini almost gives Carrie some zing," some guy wrote in *The New York Times* when the show debuted. "But they can't overcome the stale setup. As for the title, there is no obvious connection to Queens, for which residents of the borough can be thankful."

So, yeah, we never really got too comfortable. At first it was "Let's see if we can make it past the first thirteen episodes." Then we prayed to get the last nine ordered to complete a full first season. Even then, most of us said, "Eh, we'll see if we make it to Season Two." The threat of cancellation always hanging over us actually had a positive side, though. Even if any of the cast had fights with the writers or complained about atrocities against humanity, like not having a sesame bagel, there was still an underlying appreciation for everything.

Although I did more than my share of complaining, I loved *King of Queens*. (I hate when people say, "Enjoy it," when you're complaining about something. I am enjoying it. But I also enjoy complaining about it. It's one of my favorite pastimes.) I loved the audiences and the crew, but above all I enjoyed the everyday-ness of the job. I never got bored of saying hi to the guard at the gate of the lot, or seeing my name on my parking spot, or listening to the latest from makeup and hair. The same thing, the same people, week in and week out—the routine was the part I loved. I had a home. Finally.

And I had Kevin, who has ruined me for life. He was my first leading man; and despite doing other shows with other leading men, I've never found anyone who could compare favorably to him. When I was acting with him, I felt safe. I knew that no matter what the joke or the script was, Kevin would find a way to make it better. He was gracious, the kind of actor who would often say, "Give Leah the joke instead of me"—unheard of in a town full of ego-driven males.

Yes, we fought, like many married couples who were together every day for years. And yes, I treated Kevin just like I treated my husband, meaning I drove him crazy like any good wife would. And there were days when we didn't even speak until the cameras were rolling, but we always made up.

If Kevin and I were like a true married couple, Jerry Stiller was definitely the crazy and wonderful father of the show. Kevin and I would constantly tell him, "There'd be no show without you, Jerry." And it was true. He was so funny, but he had no idea how funny he actually was. We would be in rehearsal and Jerry would say his line and do his Jerry thing, and then Kevin and I would laugh and break character, and Jerry would just look at us like "What's happened?"

His wife, actress Anne Meara, was the same way, so talented and loving, and she would say, "You two are fantastic together." Or she'd pop her head into my room and say, "You got the goods, sista."

I miss her.

When he was done with his scenes but still had to stay for curtain call, Jerry would take off his TV clothes and put on his street clothes, which were usually a tank top and pants pulled up way too high. Out he'd saunter from his dressing room in his backstage grandpa attire, drinking a martini. Anne would come by and say, "Jerry, look at ya, what the fuck are you doing? Put a shirt on!" When he made us laugh, he always looked around like he wanted to know what we were laughing about. "It's you, Jer!" we'd say. He'd just lift his martini and shake his head. "It's you kids. You kids are the show."

It's a cliché, but there was a lot of love on *The King of Queens*. The only time I felt a distance from other people on the show was when the topic of Scientology came up. I kept my religion very much to myself. Even though I had to go directly from the set to the church nearly every day, I didn't let anyone know where I was headed. If Kevin or any of the other cast members or crew invited me for a drink or dinner, I declined with one excuse or another. I didn't want people on the set to think I was weird based on the amount of time I had to spend at the church.

As much as I tried to keep the different aspects of my life separate, everyone knew I was a Scientologist, and because of that I still sometimes felt judged for it. If I looked at someone directly in the eyes or for a beat too long, they might say, "What, are you going to sign me up for a course now?" It hurt when people pointed out my quirks and acted as though everything about me was a manifestation of my oddball faith. I thought, *Couldn't I just be considered a diva or a bitch like everyone else? Why does it always come back to Scientology?*

On the flip side, I felt an added burden on set because of my Scientology outlook. If I had a bad day and snapped at someone or acted like a brat because I was given the wrong call time, I was guilt-ridden. The church would have frowned upon my actions, always pressuring me to set a good example, and that if I didn't, it might prevent someone from becoming interested in joining Scientology. I was never at a loss for reasons to beat myself up, and I worried about what bad effects my actions might have.

As we went into the second season of *The King of Queens*, and the network decided to shoot the opening credits in Queens, things were looking pretty positive for our show. To take the whole cast to shoot the opener in New York was a real vote of confidence. I got to spend time in Bensonhurst and went to the San Gennaro Feast, an annual celebration in Little Italy that I used to go to when I was a little girl.

It was a real hometown-girl-makes-good moment. My dad, two half sisters, and Angelo had appearances in the opening sequence, and on the street fans shouted things like "We love you, Carrie!" or "Where's Arthur?"

It was loyal fans like those that got us a third and then a fourth season, a huge milestone that meant the network had a hundred episodes, enough to sell to syndication. Going into our fifth season in 2002, *King of Queens* continued to dominate our Monday night eight o'clock time slot, as we had done every season before, thanks in part to our comedy block that included *Yes, Dear* and *Everybody Loves Raymond.* Even the critics admitted that our show wasn't as unfunny as they first said it was. *Variety,* which in its original review wrote, "If only Doug and his show were funnier," now said that Kevin had "the finest timing on television, and his couch potato humor is pitch perfect." *Entertainment Weekly,* known for its snarky editorial tone, called us TV's best comedy in its 2002 year-end issue.

There was one hurdle *King of Queens* couldn't seem to clear— and that was winning an award. Any kind of award. Emmy had no love for us. No one, not even the sound-mixing guys, got so much as a nomination for our show. We had a hit show, but it was a blue-collar show. But I thought we could at least get nominated for a People's Choice, whose ceremony aired on our own network. Can't you even buy these things? Was it really people voting? I mean, shows like *Bette,* which didn't even make it through a full season, won one. I'm a big fan of Bette Midler, but come on. I knew we were the people's choice, because I had people coming up to me every day, saying we were their choice!

Kevin told me not to worry about it. "If you ever feel bad about yourself, Leah, I need you to go to Germany," he said. "Swear to God. We're like the Beatles over there."

As we went into our sixth season it was announced that we were moving to Wednesday at nine o'clock. In what *EW* called "sitcom suicide," we were going up against *The West Wing, The Bachelor,* and *The O.C.* But the best of all was our lead-in—*60 Minutes!* What genius came up with that scheduling? When Kevin was asked about his reaction when he heard the news from Les Moonves, he said, "I threw up and wet myself immediately." He turned it into a joke, but as we faced our sixth season with such a dismal time slot, no one was laughing. The nagging voice in my head that predicted bad things so many times, the one I worked hard to quell for hours each and every day at the church either on course or in session, seemed to get only louder.

Chapter Ten

INSIDE THE SCIENTOLOGY ETHICS OFFICE AT THE ADVANCED OR-
ganization of Los Angeles, the MAA looked through all my folders, which held every Knowledge Report written about me since
day one of my life as a Scientologist.

The system of Knowledge Reports is one of the major ways the
church gathers intelligence on members. It is policy that you have to
report on anything that is considered unbecoming to a Scientologist;
otherwise you are considered complicit. As LRH described it, "Anyone who knew of a loafing or destructive or off-policy or out-ethics
action and WHO DID NOT FILE A KNOWLEDGE REPORT
becomes an ACCESSORY in any justice action taken thereafter."

The Ethics review of all my folders was part of the standard pre-
check to be invited to do OT I, the first of Scientology's eight Operating Thetan upper levels. But before you can start in on this long
and costly process, you have to undergo extreme scrutiny when an
Ethics Officer reviews all your church files that hold every one of
your transgressions.

My Ethics Officer, Julian Swartz, didn't seem like the type to
overlook anything. I sat on the other side of his desk while he
thumbed through my files in silence. Most of the reports in my

folder were of a similar nature: "Leah threatened to have my legs broken," "Leah told a student to 'go fuck yourself' when that student complained about her wearing perfume" (off-limits with the church as scent can provide distraction to other people in the room who are studying).

Finally he asked, "So why aren't you married?"

It was 2002, and Angelo and I had been together for six years, during which we supported each other in everything we did—including Scientology. Not only was he on course, but he also understood when I went to the church straight after work and was there until nine or ten o'clock most nights.

"I don't know," I answered. "It's not important."

"You don't think it's important to set a good example to the public? Does Angelo not want to marry you?"

"Of course he would marry me if I wanted."

"Then get married," he said.

I didn't know if I wanted to get married, but I was like *Eh, if it's awful, there's always divorce.* Scientology doesn't exactly put a premium on the sanctity of marriage. Or on relationships between parents and children, for that matter. The church demands that rather than placing value in your own future or your future as a married couple, or a family, you place value and focus only back to Scientology. Divorce is rampant among church and Sea Org members, as is the dissolution of families.

That night at home, I told Angelo what had happened during my pre-check and how it was suggested that we weren't married because he didn't want to marry me.

After all the complications that attended the start of our relationship, sealing the deal was as simple as saying, "Make it happen, man."

On Christmas Eve of 2002, Angelo and I went to dinner at a restaurant down the street from our house, and after we were seated at a booth, he announced, "Baby, get anything you want on the menu."

"Oh, okay, Angelo. Thanks."

When the waiter came, I ordered the calamari as an appetizer and the steak. Angelo went into his pants and took out a wad of money.

"Let me just check," he said, peeling the bills off, "because the steak is pretty expensive."

"Let's stop with the attempted comedy bit. Put your money away; you look crazy. You're the looks of the operation, OK? And I'm the funny. Let's know our lanes. Because when you step into mine, things go awry."

"All right. I'm going to the bathroom," he responded, but when he came back he said, "You're right about staying in my lane, because I think I lost a hundred dollars doing my little bit."

"Oh, Angelo."

He knelt down on the floor and stuck his head underneath the table where I was sitting to look for the money.

"Anglo, get up. You look like you're going down on me. We'll get it later."

"No, no, no, no, no."

"We'll just get it later. Stop."

"Oh, here it is."

"Grab it, babe. God."

When Angelo came back up from under the table he wasn't holding a hundred-dollar bill. He was holding a small black velvet box.

"Will you mar—"

"Who ordered the calamari?" the waiter interrupted.

"Bro, bro. Do me a favor? Can you give us a second?"

"Sir, are you okay?"

"Yes. Man, I'm good. I'm good," he said in Spanish. Some "Mano, Mano" shit and "por favor."

"Oh, my God. Oh, my God." I was crying, while the waiter tried to step over Angelo's feet to get to the table with the calamari. I took the ring box.

"I didn't ask you yet," Angelo said.

"I know."

"What's your answer?"

"I don't know. Nobody's ever asked me that."

"Nobody ever asked you that! What?"

"I don't know what I'm saying! What? You asking me to marry you?"

"Yes, baby!"

"Oh, my God."

"Did you order the calamari?" the waiter asked.

"Yes, we ordered it," Angelo said. "Just put it down."

On the night of July 19, 2003, we got married outside at the Four Seasons Hotel in Las Vegas. It was, I kid you not, 110 degrees easy.

VH-1 was shooting our wedding for a special, so when they asked us to come up with a location for the event I thought Vegas would be convenient for a lot of the guests coming from L.A. as well as make for a fun weekend. I pictured all my guests, tan and relaxed from a day around the pool, looking and feeling sexy and elegant.

What I did *not* picture was everyone—including me—melting under the brutal rays of a desert summer sun. I mean, had somebody told me, "Hey, dumb-ass, you know Vegas is boiling hot in July," I wouldn't have planned a poolside ceremony and reception. Instead I put 125 guests through sheer misery. As Kevin told *People,* "The best part was toweling off."

Right before I walked down the aisle, I surveyed the landscape and the different buildings, and saw what I thought to be a paparazzo on the roof of the building. Still looking to be accepted by the Hollywood "in-crowd," I was both delighted and disgusted. Paparazzi were a true sign of making it in this business, but what kind of fucking pig crashes a wedding? To get a picture? On my wedding day? Man, *Star* magazine must really want to get this exclusive. Emmy, here we come, People's Choice . . . I can feel it in my hands! Kevin and I had arrived. Even so, this was not the place and time, really!

I called my security guy over and said, "There is a paparazzi piece of shit on the roof trying to grab a picture of me and I want him removed."

"Where?" he said.

"Really? You have to get a better eye for these things. *Right there!*"

"That guy?" he said as he pointed directly at the stalker pig.

"Yes," I said. "Obviously. "

"That's your wedding photographer," he flatly replied.

"Oh. Motherfuck . . ."

DURING THE CEREMONY, WHICH I pared down to the most nondenominational seven minutes of the Scientology wedding vows and which was officiated by Susan Watson, the former president of the Celebrity Centre, I looked over at Kevin, who gave me the wrap-it-up sign, which almost made me pee in my white lace G-string.

Even though it was so hot that later I'd have to soak my feet in the pool, I was so happy to be marrying Angelo and to have all these people I loved around me to witness it. Most especially, my mom, my sisters, and my friends, including Sherry, who had left the church when she was twenty-one.

Just like with my sister Nicole, Sherry's departure was a slow one. When she moved to L.A., all of her friends were Scientologists and she worked at Scientology companies just like I did. But the big difference was that she wasn't active in taking courses or getting auditing, while I was.

Even after she left the church, she remained friendly with our Scientologist community and was still invited to get-togethers. You are allowed to be friends with non- or ex-Scientologists, as long as they aren't antagonistic toward Scientology. If they are, you are expected to disconnect or break off all ties with that member, who is considered a Suppressive Person. A person is declared by the church to be an SP for a variety of reasons, which may include going to the authorities about the church or making any kind of negative comment about it publicly or in the press. Both are considered suppressive acts that can have devastating consequences for relationships. And furthermore, if the church were to find out that you remained in contact with an SP, you would then be declared an SP as well.

Before Angelo and I were married, his ex-wife sold a story to *Star* magazine about her version of everything that had happened—including their Scientology marriage counseling. When the magazine hit the stands, I was called into the Ethics office at Flag, where I was doing auditing. Some random Scientologist had written a Knowledge Report on me after seeing the article.

"Leah, either you disconnect from Angelo or he disconnects from his ex."

"Are you kidding me? You're telling me Angelo can't see the mother of his son? How is he going to see his six-year-old boy?"

The Ethics Officer shrugged and said, "I am not telling you that. What does LRH say? The policy says what it says. Read it out loud. You can make your own decisions."

I loved Angelo's three sons: his oldest two boys who lived with their mom in San Jose, and his youngest, in L.A., whom we had every weekend and certain days each week. Sometimes I got to pick him up from school when his mom was busy, and he was always a real source of joy in my life and had given me a wonderful taste of motherhood.

Whenever the question of Sherry came up in one of my checks, however, I would always say that Sherry wasn't anti-Scientology, even though she was. Unlike many Scientologists, I didn't feel I had to give up every piece of information in my head to the church. I rationalized it to myself by saying that Sherry wasn't pulling me out of Scientology, which is the important thing.

Since Sherry left the church, her life hadn't become a disaster, as we are made to believe by the church. Far from it. She put herself through night school, earning a hard-won degree from UCLA at the age of thirty, then started her own tech business. She also married a nice, successful guy and had two sons.

I never dwelled too long on that contradiction. The church's response to my question "Well, how come that one left the church and they seem to be doing okay?" was always the same:

"But are they happy, Leah, truly? What about their eternity, Leah?"

Yeah, I thought, her eternity might get fucked up, but they seemed happy and much less fucked-up than me.

Instead I chose to focus on my own happiness. No sooner were Angelo and I married than I was telling him I wanted a baby. But sex was not exactly fun for Angelo during this period. A typical "lovemaking" session between us went like this:

"Babe, it's on," I said.

"I'm in the middle of *SportsCenter*," Angelo yelled from the other room.

"No. It's got to happen now."

In that moment, I predicted he had given me a girl. Angelo, who already had three boys, didn't believe it. But I was adamant. "You've been so horrible to women your whole life that God is going to give you one girl that you can't mess with, who's going to wrap you around her finger," I said. "I'm telling you, you're having a girl."

After I got pregnant, I couldn't wait to find out that I was right about my prediction. During an early ultrasound, I pestered the doctor, who said he couldn't really "tell if it was a girl."

Oh, my God. Either he has the smallest penis ever or she has the biggest vagina. Either way, this is not good. If my kid has a little dick, I've got to tell him how to use it. And if it's a girl with a very big vagina, we've got to talk about that too. I want to be prepared.

"We need to know, Doc. We need to know."

He ordered an amnio (which was encouraged as I was close to thirty-five), which confirmed it: We were having a girl! Angelo was in trouble.

I gave the experience of being pregnant everything I had, particularly the eating part. At my four-month doctor's visit, the OB suggested I talk to a nutritionist.

"Why, Doc?"

"Because you've already gained all your weight for the whole pregnancy and then some."

I was floored. I knew things were bad, but I didn't know they were this bad.

"*I'm* not asking for Big Macs. It's this kid! I can't control what she wants me to have!"

"You're going to have a hard time if you keep up like this," he said.

"You're telling me *I* gained all this weight? You're telling me all this weight is just me? She has a head, right? How many pounds does a human baby's head weigh? That's gotta be something! Did you take that into consideration?"

"The entire fetus is probably around five ounces."

"Really? Jesus. A liver doesn't mean anything, I guess."

All told, I gained—wait for it—eighty pounds over the course of my pregnancy. And it was no mystery why—I went three-Egg-McMuffins-and-four-hash-browns crazy. I kept Stephanie, the poor craft services person on *The King of Queens,* busy making me food. "We just feel like mac 'n' cheese," I said to her. "The baby needs it."

When Stephanie returned with a bowl of mac 'n' cheese, I told her I would need more than just the sample portion.

"That was the whole box," she said.

"From Kraft?"

"Yeah. Kraft Macaroni and Cheese."

"This is the WHOLE box? I just want to make sure," I said.

"The whole box," she said.

"Did the FDA start regulating portion sizes? I don't understand."

She smiled in sympathy and walked out of my room.

While a lot of actresses in Hollywood can hide their pregnancy on-screen with a strategically placed pillow or a bigger purse, on *The King of Queens* I had to use a couch. I was so huge that I literally had to stand behind furniture to hide my belly. Kevin relished the fact that I was so fat. "This is so great," he said. "I look like the skinnier one here for the first time!"

At first I was really into the whole pregnancy thing. I rented a heart monitor, and I would sit there for hours listening to her heartbeat. Or I went into her little room. I loved going in there, because it already smelled like a baby. I sat in the rocking chair or folded and refolded her baby clothes about a thousand times. I would imagine her in my arms.

By the eighth month, however, I was over it. At my OB appointment, I told the doctor, "I think she needs to come out." He replied that my request was not only crazy but also illegal.

"My feet are so swollen I can't even wear flip-flops, man. Seriously?" I made noises during this time that I didn't even realize were coming from me. I would wake up in a panic, looking for the wild boar that had entered my room, only to realize it was me.

The doctor had been right about gaining so much weight making things hard. Getting up from the couch left me out of breath. One guy asked me if I was having twins. Don't ask anybody that *ever*. I started telling people who asked when I was due, "I already had my baby," just to be a bitch. "Yeah. I had her nine months ago."

When I went into labor and headed to the hospital, they put me in a room with a view of Jerry's Deli. All I could think about was why I hadn't gotten my tuna fish on a kaiser with fries before I went into the hospital. I was miserable.

My plan was to be a good Scientologist, and not use an epidural, but when I felt the real thing go down, I yelled, "Get that anesthesiologist in here before I kill somebody!" The doctor was on it and told me he didn't know why I had waited so long. I didn't even try to explain to him that the church teaches you that drugs will make the baby susceptible to what is said during labor so that it gets recorded in your child's reactive mind, the place where pain is stored. So if I said to a nurse, "You are a horrible person," my daughter might go through life acting out the role of a horrible person, thinking I was talking to her.

Similarly, that's the reason Scientologists espouse the concept of "silent birth," which LRH described in *Dianetics* as providing an environment where no one—not even the doctors or nurses in the room—talks during the delivery. Again, it's because in times of pain, loss, or unconsciousness, "words, in particular, spoken during these moments, can have an adverse effect on one later in life." Women can make sounds during birth; they just aren't supposed to say any words.

Once the doctor gave me the epidural, I was myself again—and talking. "I'll deliver three babies with this shit," I boasted. "Somebody do my hair. I don't want to be ugly when the baby comes." Shannon started heating up the flatiron.

It took forever for me to be dilated enough to start pushing, and even then I didn't think the baby was coming. It felt like nothing was happening. I regretted that I hadn't planned a C-section—the celebrity thing to do. And while someone's already down there, they get a quick nip and tuck. I hadn't thought this out in a celebrity way.

Then, all of a sudden, the epidural went away. It was like it erased any memory of itself, and I experienced a kind of pain that if there had been a large rock around, I would have bludgeoned myself with it. That's how bad it was. Nobody tells you this shit. When they say it's like your period, they're lying. Having a head and a full body emerge from your vagina is nothing like getting your period.

"Ma!" I screamed. "Help me! Help me!"

"Lee, there's nothing I can do." She shrugged helplessly.

Oh, and did I mention that this entire thing was being taped for a VH-1 special about my pregnancy and childbirth? Yup. Of course they edited out this whole part where I was cursing. In the final show, I looked so serene the whole time, but in truth it was as far from a silent birth as you could get.

"Reach down, now," my doctor said.

As soon as I could touch her, I turned primal and started to pull her out.

"Give her to me. Give her to me. Give her to me."

I had had visions of this moment long beforehand and made it clear in no uncertain terms that when I had my baby I wanted her cleaned up before she was handed to me, preferably with Johnson and Johnson's baby shampoo (because I like the smell), and then wrapped up in a nice white blanket. You know, like what you might find in a forties movie, with me in a white head wrap and great eyebrows.

Instead, when she actually arrived, I was sweating and fat. I reached down to grab her and pulled her right up onto my chest, and couldn't stop kissing her. I was crying, Angelo was crying. My mom, Nicole, and Shannon—everyone.

"She's beautiful," my mom said.

On June 16, the day after my thirty-fourth birthday, my daughter, Sofia Bella, was born.

A couple of days later when the nurse told me I was ready to go home I looked at her like she had three heads.

"I can't stay here a week?"

"No."

"So when Courteney Cox had her baby here just a week ago, you kicked her out? I bet not, because she was on *Friends*."

"She left in the same amount of time as you."

"And I bet she had a better room." (Better show, better room.)

"Nope, same room."

"Really? Hmmm. Okay. BUT, I'm not ready to leave. You are just going to trust us with this baby? Isn't there any psychological test I'm supposed to take?"

"You'll be fine. If she has a fever of a hundred and four, come back."

"Whoa. Why would she have a fever? What are you talking about? What if she has a hundred-degree fever?"

The hospital staff practically had to push me out the door. And the minute I stepped outside, everything felt like a threat. We were in the middle of Beverly Hills, which was filled with exhaust. "My baby's lungs are going to be ruined!" I yelled. Driving home, I was sure that everybody on the road was trying to kill my baby. They knew I had a newborn and were responding by saying, "Let's get into an accident. She wasn't on *Friends*, fuck her baby."

In the hospital, Sofia was the perfect baby, lying there in her little plastic bin sleeping her ass off no matter how loud people were talking. What I didn't realize was that she was resting up for home life when suddenly she became allergic to sleeping.

Every night, as soon as the sun went down, Sofia started crying. I started to develop a phobia of the dark. "I don't want night to come," I said to Angelo. "I'm scared." It almost felt vindictive on Sofia's part. Like, as soon as she knew there was no one to relieve us, that's when she started up. At five o'clock, our house became a ghost town because visitors don't come to see your newborn at that hour. I was begging the sun, "No, no, no! Don't fall! Don't go, sun!" And then . . . "Whaaaaah!"

When friends asked what time would be good to come over and meet the baby, I answered, "Five o'clock. We're seeing people at five o'clock. At ten p.m., and midnight." Angelo and I began reconnecting with folks we hadn't talked to since the second grade.

"Hey, what are you doing? You want to come over and visit? We just had a baby. Come at 2 a.m. You can hold her for five hours if you like."

We tried everything to get her to stop crying and sleep. Gas was the big theory, so I did that thing where you push the legs into the baby to let the gas out. Not only did it not work, but I worried I was breaking her little legs. Then I discovered that her diaper was cutting into her thighs and leaving little red marks. Maybe that's what she was crying about! I yelled at Angelo that he had to make sure to leave a finger of room in her diaper when he closed it up. As I laid her down on her changing table to diaper her, she started crying again.

"She doesn't like to be on her back! Maybe she has a thing with falling!" I said while putting a pillow to prop her head up.

"She doesn't *not like* anything, Leah," Angelo said.

"Of course she does *not like* something, Angelo. She's crying."

"I have three kids."

"That you didn't raise."

Low blow, but all is fair when you're sleep deprived.

Angelo and I had the nastiest "deaf fights" where instead of speaking, we mouthed the words—"Fuck you" or "I want a divorce"—because we didn't want the baby to be any more upset than she already was.

Things were so insane that I called the doctor and said, "There's something seriously wrong with my baby. You need to come right away. I can't put her in a car. Things are very bad. Come quick!"

He dutifully came over right away and examined her.

"She doesn't sleep. She's crying all the time. All she's doing is eating and peeing and crapping, and crying."

"That's what newborns do."

"So you're saying nothing's wrong with her? I want to be clear about this conversation for the lawsuit. You're saying there's nothing wrong with her."

"There's nothing wrong with her. Welcome to parenthood."

"So you're telling me that normal babies never sleep and always cry?"

"As I said, 'Welcome to parenthood.'"

"Are you even a real doctor?"

And with that he closed the door behind him, leaving Angelo and me standing in the entryway of our house. With our crying baby.

Sofia continued to cry her head off for the next few months. Everyone thought they could cure her. Everyone, including every Scientologist I knew, offered advice. As new parents we felt as if we were doing everything wrong. They told us that it must be something about her environment or that technology wasn't being applied correctly. Friends would take the baby and do a Scientology assist (a hands-on form of auditing that you can do anywhere, without any equipment). They would take her outside and have her touch a tree, a leaf, the grass. All she would do was continue to cry and scream.

So when I woke up one morning and didn't see Angelo and the

baby in my bedroom, I ran downstairs in a panic. I almost ran past him in the den, where he was—*gasp*—sitting on the couch, drinking coffee.

"What's happening?" I panted, looking over to see Sofia drooling in front of the TV. "What is that? What are those ugly things? Why are they making that sound? Why is she being quiet?"

"Shhh," Angelo said. "They're Teletubbies, and they are magic."

I looked at our daughter, who was mesmerized, as if this show had suspended her brain. It was genius. She was like a vegetable. Could we just sit here and have a cup of coffee? Could this be real?

"How much time do you think we have?" I asked.

"Don't ruin it," Angelo said. "Just enjoy."

Chapter Eleven

W HEN SOFIA WAS FIRST BORN, I HAD A SUPPORT SYSTEM
most women can only dream of. And yet, there were still
times when I would run to the grocery store for no reason
at all, just to get out of the house. I would walk up and down every
aisle—even aisles no one ever goes down, like the one with auto
supplies—feeling like the worst mom ever. There I was, hiding out
in Albertsons, because I needed to be away from the bottles, the diapers, the crying. Just for a moment I wanted to feel like my old self.

In addition to figuring out how to be a mom, I had to also continue to be the breadwinner for my family, which meant losing all
the weight I had gained during my pregnancy. I had only four weeks
after Sofia's birth to return to the *King of Queens* set, and the pounds
were not coming off quickly.

I had never really had body issues, even though I was in an in-
dustry where women are constantly scrutinized for their weight, but
after Sofia was born I got a complex. I kept thinking of all those
actresses who seemed to be back to their old selves by the time they
left the hospital with their newborns. I worked out three or four
times a week, did the fat flush, tried the cayenne drink cleanse, suf-

fered through the cabbage soup diet. Some people in the business suggested diet pills, but because I was a Scientologist that was off limits.

So I returned to work still forty pounds overweight. Everyone on *King of Queens* was encouraging after I had Sofia. The producers accommodated me in any way possible so that I could bring her with me to the set. Still, I needed a full-time nanny. Even though I interviewed a bunch of candidates, Trish stood out immediately. Taking Sofia from my arms, she said, "Bless," in her English accent, and then started noticing things that I adored too, like the rolls on my daughter's legs. I was so impressed by how loving Trish was, because for me, that was what it was all about. I just wanted to know that when I couldn't be with Sofia, somebody who loved her was with her. The clincher, however, came when Trish put my daughter on her big, huge bajunga tits, and Sofia fell right to sleep. "Those are magical tits, which I'm sure your husband has told you," I said, and the deal was sealed.

Trish was a traditional nanny and not a Scientologist, and I preferred it that way (even though all of my church friends urged me to use a Scientologist nanny). I didn't use Scientology tools in dealing with my daughter, because I didn't want her to be ridiculed for anything that seemed strange to the general public. For example, I was told that if she got hurt, I was not to react but perform a Contact Assist, which "consists of putting an injured body part exactly on and in the place it was injured." So if she hit her leg on the corner of the coffee table, I was supposed to remain quiet and gently touch the hurt part of her leg to the exact spot on the table where she hit it—and continue to repeat that action until she said it was better. Instead, the second I heard Sofia crying from a fall or bang, I was shouting, "Are you okay? Mommy will kiss it better." I refused to raise Sofia in a way that would make her incompatible with the rest of the world as I felt I was, and as were many second-generation Scientologists.

Even though Sofia is now eleven, I still have Trish. What can you do? I'm a family person. Whether it be the cast and crew of a television show, a friend, or a nanny, I quickly grow attached. It's hard for me to let go of people.

Going to the playground with Trish and Sofia when she was a toddler was certainly an education. After we had been watching Sofia sit in that disgusting sandbox for a while, I asked Trish how much longer we were going to stay.

"Love, we've only been here two minutes," she said.

"I'm just asking, because in the baby world time is totally irrelevant. Like, if we just started to randomly pack up, she wouldn't know if we'd been here for an hour or five minutes."

"Darling, usually parents stay until the kid's nap time."

"That's two hours from now! Is an ice cream truck going to come by? Is anything going to happen? Is there a crime in progress we could stop? I mean, this is just not enough."

"Let's take her on the swings."

"God."

Most moms used to look at me with a confused expression and say, "You don't love playing with your daughter?"

Then I would start lying about it: "Aw, of course I love it. I mean, God, every moment's a joy."

"I just cherish the time, which is going by so fast that I'm thinking about having another one."

Out of your own vagina? Why would someone do that to themselves?

I thought there was something wrong with me, because I never understood the joy in playing with my kid. When Sofia got older and she insisted we play Barbies while she was in the tub, I usually lasted about four minutes before I tried to weasel out of the game.

"My Barbie is tired," I would say. "My Barbie wants to go sleepy."

"No, she doesn't want to go sleepy. She just got up," Sofia would insist.

"No, she needs to go sleepy, because she stayed up all night. She stayed up all night because she wanted her ba-bas and she's so tired right now. So mine's going to go to bed."

I really admired other parents I saw running around with their kids. I thought, *How nice is that for their children?* But they also left me racked with guilt—until one mother, out of the dozens I met, told me I shouldn't feel bad. "You're not your daughter's playmate," she said, and I nearly burst out in tears, because I needed to hear that so badly.

I loved my child and liked to watch her be happy. While I wasn't so much a "player," I did love spending time with her. I also loved taking care of her, protecting her, and setting up her future. But playing, eh.

And while I may not have been the best mother in the world, I was the one paying the bills, providing for my family, and trying to clear the planet. Between Sofia, work, and the church, I had a tall order to fill. When I returned to *The King of Queens,* the time spent at the studio and the hours spent every day at the church left me lucky to have any time at all with my daughter. And I felt the weight of it, often thinking that I wasn't giving adequate attention to one or another part of my life.

Now that I was on my OT levels and diligently participating in auditing and my studies, my commitment to Scientology was more consuming than ever. I was typically at the church all day if I wasn't at work. On top of that, I was a celebrity, which meant that I had more responsibility than ever to be a positive—and active—member of my church.

My special celebrity status that came around the time I was on *Fired Up* also had its benefits. When I went back to Flag to work on my OT levels twenty years after leaving the Sea Org, I fully expected other Sea Org members to look down on me, because it's pretty much policy to view ex–Sea Org members as deserters. But because I was on TV and had appeared on the cover of Scientology's *Celebrity* magazine, I was treated within the church like, well, like a star.

It was so strange to be staying at the Fort Harrison like any other parishioner. Occasionally, I would have flashbacks to that nightmare period of my life when as a teenager I was ripped from everything I knew in Brooklyn only to end up cleaning hotel rooms at Flag. After

I returned, every time I ate dinner in one of the hotel restaurants I remembered how I used to steal food because I was so hungry.

During one of my sessions at Flag, I gave this up as a transgression and my auditor asked how much I thought I owed to make up the damage for the food I stole twenty years earlier.

"I don't know," I said. "How much was custard and hamburgers for three months in the eighties?"

"Well, let's just round it up to forty thousand dollars. Okay?"

Forty thousand dollars?

I was dumbfounded, but I was also trying to get onto my OT levels so I paid the church forty thousand dollars for this transgression.

The real surprise of the trip, though, wasn't my huge bill for snacks I stole back then. It was seeing Mike Curley, the head of the EPF when I was in Clearwater and the guy who threw me overboard into the ocean. I spotted him while I was walking out to the Fort Harrison's pool; he was still doing the same job, leading a group of shell-shocked young Sea Org members.

I stopped him and asked, "Do you remember me, Mike?"

"Yeah," he said. "You're the little ballbuster Leah. You're a big celebrity now. I saw you on all our magazines. You do so many great things for the church. I always knew you'd make it. I always knew you had something."

"Even when you threw me off that fucking boat?"

He laughed and said, "You were okay."

I had imagined this moment more than a few times in my mind, that I would confront him for the way he treated me. Instead, he met me with admiration. "You know, I'm actually kind of glad it didn't work out in the Sea Org," he said, justifying his reason for being so happy to see me. "Because you do so much more for our church being a star." And with that, all of my resentment washed away in an instant.

All Scientologists are expected to present an image to the outside world that is so perfect and happy that people can't help but want to join. If you are a celebrity, your reach is that much greater. And celebrities are expected to use the full extent of their power to bring new parishioners into the fold.

However, I was never really comfortable with recruiting new members. Instead of getting new people into Scientology, my instinct was to do the opposite because I knew what an extremist religion it was. All in or all out. I knew how onerous the commitment to this religion was and how—despite what certain church representatives said—you had to leave any other belief behind, and I didn't want to be responsible for others making such a big decision. What I decided to focus on instead was assisting other participating Scientologists. So I started doing events to help people move up the Bridge faster, which I enjoyed. I gave speeches and seminars for those stalled on the Bridge, meaning people who after becoming Clear—achieving a state of total clarity and control over your thoughts and emotions—stay there and don't move on to their OT levels (like I did). I pushed by reminding them, "If you signed up for this, then you need to get on with it."

So while I wasn't overly keen on being a missionary, and dodged constant pressure from the church to bring new members in, I found that I couldn't keep my mouth shut when I saw injustice or someone having trouble speaking for himself or herself. Being so confrontational made me an unofficial advocate for Scientologists who were having problems within the church, because I would say anything to anybody, no matter how high their supposed rank. One of these people was Stacy Francis.

I had met Stacy through a friend and had instantly fallen in love with her. She was very funny, very New York, and very loud, just like me. But more than anything else, I felt drawn to Stacy because she reminded me of where I used to be, struggling and without family support. So I welcomed her into ours, becoming not just a friend but a kind of mother as well. I counseled Stacy through her first marriage, her pregnancy, her divorce. I was her daughter's godmother, and when they had nowhere to go for a month, I took them in.

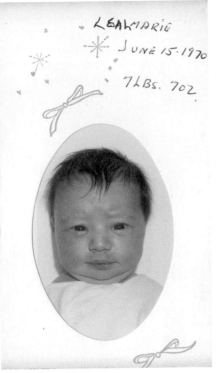

My mother's first words to my dad were "George, I love her, but wow, is she ugly." Really can't argue.

Clearly things were not getting any better a few months later, so the photographer placed this doll next to my head as a distraction.

Please note that my head is almost as big as my sister's whole body. I was less than a year old.

Okay, luckily we're starting to see a little hope for me here, alongside my sister Nicole.

I have no idea why we are dressed like this, although my sister could have doubled for Little Orphan Annie or Donnie Osmond, featured in the posters on the wall behind us.

Me in the arms of my mother, alongside her pimp (aka my father). It was the seventies, after all.

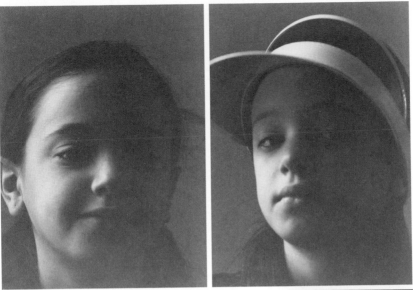

These photos were taken by my stepfather Dennis. Though he was not a professional photographer, I loved them and thought I looked amazing. Clearly I could play anything from innocent to complex. I was a thinker even back then. I put on a sun visor to show my range. Then I pulled out all the stops and put on my *Little House on the Prairie* shirt.

In Brooklyn's Cropsey Park. I thought the coat showed character. But what it really showed was a bad fashion choice.

Nicole, Dennis, and me at Christmas in Brooklyn. I don't know what's on my feet, but I love them and want a pair of them in my size right now.

Hanging out on Eighty-sixth Street in Bensonhurst with my posse.

Nicole and me in our Sea Org uniforms at Flag in Clearwater, Florida, holding baby Shannon.

Me in matching acid-washed jeans and jacket taking Shannon for a stroll on Fountain Avenue in L.A., where much of our lives took place.

The theme in these early headshots was Big Hair: The first one with hair off to the side. The second, with a pirate earring. The third, showing a little shoulder.

Alain St. Clair

I thought if the mullet didn't grab 'em, then certainly the popped collar would get me the job.

Working with Tony Danza and the cast of *Who's the Boss?* was an invaluable education and a great start to my acting career.

Leah:
   I can't even begin to explain what a pleasure it has been working with you.
   Stay pure! What I mean by pure is—don't let the fact that you're brilliant and you will make it in this business, affect what a special person you are.

   Please keep in touch.

   Love forever!

   Alyssa

Alyssa Milano couldn't have been nicer on the set of the show. I kept her sweet note to me.

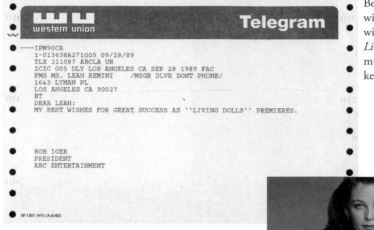

```
 ┌──────────────────────────────────────────────┐
 │  WU                              Telegram      │
 │  western union                                 │
 └──────────────────────────────────────────────┘

  ──IPM90CA
  1-013638A271005 09/28/89
  TLX 211087 ABCLA UR
  ZCZC 005 DLY LOS ANGELES CA SEP 28 1989 FAC
  PMS MS. LEAH REMINI    /MSGR DLVR DONT PHONE/
  1643 LYMAN PL
  LOS ANGELES CA 90027
  BT
  DEAR LEAH:
  MY BEST WISHES FOR GREAT SUCCESS AS ''LIVING DOLLS'' PREMIERES.


      BOB IGER
      PRESIDENT
      ABC ENTERTAINMENT

  SF-1201 (NY) (A-6/82)
```

Bob Iger's telegram wishing me luck with my first series, *Living Dolls,* meant so much to me that I've kept it ever since.

Here are the network publicity shots for *Living Dolls*. A very exciting time. In the first one I'm all smiles. In the second one I'm trying to pull off a *Dynasty* expression. But instead everyone just asked me if I was pissed off.

At the wrap party for *Living Dolls*. Crying, thinking I would never work again.

Even at the age of eighteen, I wanted to claim my star. I'm still waiting. . . .

My first new car, a Toyota Tercel that soon got repossessed.

My sisters Stephanie (who passed) and Elizabeth, Kevin James, me, and my dad shooting the opening credits of *The King of Queens* in Queens.

Angelo Pagan

With my *Saved by the Bell* co-star Mark-Paul Gosselaar in the early nineties in a makeout scene and twenty years later.

I was so excited to be working with Dick Van Dyke, one of my favorites, on an episode of *Diagnosis Murder*. A guest spot that led to another pilot that didn't go anywhere. But I did meet a legend.

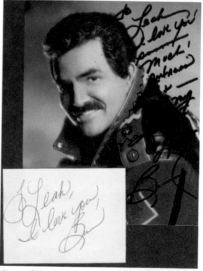

I had a recurring role on CBS's *Evening Shade*, which led to a spinoff pilot that aired as a TV movie.

One of the things I loved about Burt Reynolds was how every time he saw me, he gave me another headshot of himself. I now have a collection, which I cherish.

My guest star appearance on *Cheers,* playing Carla's (Rhea Perlman, pictured below) daughter. The scary thing is that I *didn't* hate this dress!

The night Angelo and I got engaged. I was crying so much I couldn't even eat my dinner. We went home immediately afterward and invited my mom and family over to celebrate with us.

Yes, very happy here, but then . . . the 110-degree weather in Las Vegas, not my smartest move.

I did finally get on *Friends,* but for only one episode, as Joey's girlfriend.

Me and two of the funniest guys I know.

Kevin James, my favorite leading man.

Kevin James

I kept blowing my lines here because my makeup artist had given me champagne before the show. Kevin blew my cover to the audience.

One time at a taping of the show, Kevin kept messing up his lines. He swore it would happen to me next and, sure enough, it did, as he raised his hands in know-it-all victory.

Here I am with the cast (Jerry Stiller, Kevin, Patton Oswalt, and Gary Valentine) celebrating our hundredth episode. Someone toasted to a hundred more. Kevin and I looked at each other like, yeah, right.

We surpassed this two-hundredth-episode cake with two hundred and seven episodes total.

I had a great time making *Old School*. Vince Vaughn and Will Ferrell made me laugh out loud every day both in between takes and while we were filming.

I was thrilled to have my mom and sister with me at the *Old School* premiere. As always, they were there to support me.

Getting a hug from Tom Cruise at the premiere of his movie *Collateral* in 2004.

One day when we were sitting outside, she gestured to the house and pool and asked, "How do I get all this?"

"Hard work," I answered. "It doesn't happen overnight."

"No, come on. It's gotta be that Scientology stuff that you're involved in. It must have given you a leg up in the business."

Stacy touched on a myth that the church has very successfully used to its advantage. Many people were under the same impression that there are tons of Scientologists in the film and television business and that we all help each other out. The real truth is that while the church would like you to believe it wields a tremendous amount of influence in Hollywood, that is simply not the case. Throughout my career I knew of one minor casting director who was a Scientologist, but other than that, no real movers and shakers. As a matter of fact, I think identifying myself publicly as a Scientologist probably hurt my career more than it helped it as far as perception was concerned. And while some of the courses the church offered provided me with better communication skills to help land roles, the time, money, and effort I invested certainly didn't outweigh the benefit for me.

"You gotta bring me in," Stacy continued, almost insisting.

I explained the basic tenets and courses and she said, "I want that Tom Cruise shit."

Having grown up as a preacher's daughter, she was questioning her faith, especially how it was not necessarily helping her to obtain her goal of being a professional singer.

I reluctantly brought her into the church, introducing her to some of the initial course work. I felt responsible for her well-being. I told her not to give out her address or phone numbers. The church is notorious for putting you on a mailing list—for the rest of your life—and piles of mail come to your house indefinitely. I had heard over and over again about people who signed up for only one single course and nothing more but who had to shut down their mailbox because they were inundated with so much mail and propaganda. If you failed to show up for a course and they had your phone number, they would call and harass you. I didn't want Stacy to have to go through that experience if she chose not to move forward with Scientology.

Stacy ended up joining the church, and from what I witnessed throughout our time there together, she was looking for validation and not getting it. While she was a bigmouth and a troublemaker, which I loved, she didn't have the celebrity status yet and all that went with it.

One time Stacy had brought her friend Brandy Norwood, the singer, to the church in hopes of recruiting her. After a few months Brandy started to pull away, and in an attempt to keep her engaged, she was asked by a church official, while she was standing next to Stacy, if she'd like to go to a barbecue at Tom Cruise's house.

Stacy immediately chimed in with "Where's my invite? What the fuck do I look like?"

She got sent for a sec-check for that one. (A sec-check—short for "security check"—is a hardcore form of interrogation using the E-Meter in which an auditor asks a long list of questions to make sure a person hasn't engaged in any hostile activities or thoughts toward the church.)

While I would often stick up for Stacy and others throughout my Scientology career, there were some people I would not stick my neck out for.

One Sunday in early 2005, Sherry and I had finished playing tennis, like we did almost every week, and we got in our cars to head for breakfast per our usual routine. Except on this Sunday, Sherry phoned me from her car to say her brother was going to meet us at the restaurant.

Although Sherry had left the church decades ago, we had an understanding that we'd leave Scientology out of our relationship. It was the only way I could justify maintaining our friendship. But now, by ambushing me with her brother, she had broken our code.

In the fall of 2004, Sherry's brother, Stefan, had left the church very publicly in a rift over his wife. Stefan and Tanja, who met in the Sea Org, had both been "up lines," meaning they were high-ranking executives working for the church's top leader, Chairman of the Board (COB) David Miscavige.

In 1999, however, as punishment for financial and ethical transgressions against the church, Stefan was sent to the Rehabilitation Project Force, or RPF, at Gold Base, the sprawling and remote five-hundred-acre compound near Hemet, California, also known as International Base. Stefan contended that it was because he had gotten on David Miscavige's bad side that he had been assigned to the reconditioning program for Sea Org members, the RPF. As mentioned earlier, these are the people who wear black, are required to run everywhere, are not allowed to speak unless spoken to, and perform the most demeaning and arduous manual labor with no days off.

I had met David Miscavige a number of times at various events, after which a few of us would go meet in the President's Office, the special area of the Celebrity Centre reserved for celebrities and VIPs. David, short, trim, and well built with blue eyes and light brown hair, had always treated me with respect, and I liked his wife, Shelly, a lot. She was tough and something of a rule breaker like me, but I also found her kind. COB's wife (also referred to as COB's assistant) for nearly two decades, Shelly could always be found at his side at any public meetings or events. She was also cc'd on all of his correspondence. She was devoted to COB, as she had been to LRH (to whom she reported as one of his original Messengers), and assisted him in many capacities.

I first met Shelly when we both attended a Tom Cruise movie premiere. She invited me to sit with her, and we quickly hit it off, afterward regularly exchanging cards and gifts at holidays. I remember she was so grateful when I had my makeup person get her ready for a CC (Celebrity Centre) gala. Meanwhile, she stuck her neck out for me when I brought a friend who was not a Scientologist to the Celebrity Centre to try and get some help with some issues he was going through. This was probably one of five friends I had ever brought into the church in my thirty-plus years with Scientology.

My friend was struggling in his marriage, and I thought that perhaps he might benefit from some of the courses or auditing that the church offered. I was not trying to recruit him into the church, just trying to have him apply some of the technology I had learned in hopes of helping him in his marriage. I handpicked who I requested to be in charge of his service, but I was met with resistance and told that I didn't have the right to decide who would work with him. I immediately went to Shelly, and she made sure that not only did I get the supervisor I wanted but no one pushed me out of being involved. I also didn't want anyone I brought in to be dragged into regular church procedure. I wanted to protect them from that.

The David Miscavige that my friend Sherry described that morning was very different from the affable COB David that I knew. According to Sherry, he threw Stefan in the RPF after Stefan objected to the amount of time COB demanded from Tanja, who was one of his secretaries. Stefan remained in the RPF for almost four years, during which time Tanja was encouraged to end their marriage. While they were apart, the couple ignored orders and remained in contact by cell phone. When David found out that his orders had been disobeyed, Tanja was removed from her position and demoted to a much lesser position. And that's when Stefan "blew"—a term reserved for Scientologists who leave without approval and without letting anyone know. In theory it is possible to leave the church on good terms, but it involves a lengthy process that involves endless sec-checks and usually winds up with the Scientologist deciding to stay rather than pay a costly freeloader's debt. Stefan had escaped, and for that he was labeled an SP.

"Sherry, come on," I said to her in my car. "You know that I can't talk to him."

She wanted me to talk to her brother who had now been officially declared a Suppressive Person. The church forcibly stated that all parishioners had to disconnect from any SPs and cut off all contact with them.

"Just listen to what he has to say."

"This is uncomfortable. Actually it's worse than that. You're putting me in a position that will have consequences."

"Please, for me."

Ugh. I was deeply conflicted. Despite our ups and downs, Sherry was one of my oldest and closest friends. We had known each other—and helped each other—when we had nothing *but* each other. Still, Scientology was now the framework for my entire life, and what she was asking me to do could get me in serious trouble, and my family as well. So I split the difference. On the way to the restaurant I called my MAA, Julian Swartz, to ask what we knew about Stefan.

"Why?"

"It's my friend Sherry's brother, and we're meeting for breakfast."

I knew the minute I said this, Sherry was going to come up in every sec-check for every OT level I'd get for the rest of my life. "Don't go," he said.

"I have to."

"Leah, I'm asking you not to go."

"I'm going, Julian."

"Well, then, we're going to have to talk."

"Okay. Then we're going to be talking."

I was so angry by the time I sat down at the table with Sherry and Stefan that I could hardly look at the legal documents he wanted to show me. He wanted to get Tanja out of International Base, but when he left Scientology the church offered him $25,000 in return for a contract that would keep him from ever contacting another Scientologist again—including his wife. He signed the contract so he could make copies and show an attorney, and soon after that gave the check back and voided the contract.

"I'm not taking the money, because I am going to get my wife out," he said to me.

"But I don't know why you felt the need to come to me," I said.

I didn't like Stefan when he was still in the church. I thought he was a terrible brother to Sherry and put her through the wringer when she left Scientology—so I certainly wasn't going to help him now.

"Stefan, look. What do you want me to do—pick up the phone and call David Miscavige? Honestly, it just shows how stupid you actually are. I don't have any power to break your girl out! All that's going to come from this stupid presentation is that I'm going to be thrown in a sec-check."

"Why won't you just read the documents?" Sherry asked.

"For what? You're not hearing me. There's nothing I can do—and Sherry, now I'm going to have to deal with why we've been friends all these years, and why I was lying about you not being against Scientology. So thank you for ending our friendship over this asshole."

With that, I got up and left. On the drive home, I called Julian, just as he had asked me to do and told him everything that had happened, which was nothing. When I got home, however, there waiting for me was a representative of the Office of Special Affairs, the legal branch of the church. For an hour or so, the OSA person grilled me on exactly what had been said and by whom, all the while taking notes that he slipped into a black briefcase before leaving.

When I closed the door behind him, I was devastated because, as per the church, that would be the end of my friendship with Sherry. I felt I had no choice.

Chapter Twelve

AS A CELEBRITY SCIENTOLOGIST, YOU ARE EXPECTED TO BE an example not only to the outside world but also to other Scientologists. Moving up the Bridge is important in setting an example for the group. And so is donating money. A lot of money. I donated millions of dollars over my life to my church to help set an example.

The church is relentless when it comes to fundraising and soliciting. The plea is always a variation on the same refrain: "You're a celebrity. You've got to step up, because if you do it, people who are not contributing will start to. So you need to do this to save the planet."

I felt a combination of coercion and responsibility. When I heard from the church the causes my money was being put toward, I believed them. They ranged from protecting religious freedom to helping workers who were at Ground Zero after 9/11 through the New York Rescue Workers Detoxification Project. In 2002, the NY Detox, as it's known, began offering free treatments to firefighters, first responders, and police officers. Based on LRH's writings, the detoxification regimen flushed poisons out of the body by employing an intense combination of multiple hours in and out of the sauna, high doses of niacin, jogging, and other elements. I donated over $100,000 to sponsor these first responders and fundraised on the cause's behalf for additional donations.

As my donations grew, however, so did my questions about where my money was actually going. In the wake of Hurricane Katrina in August 2005, I gave $50,000 for a special mission of Scientology Volunteer Ministers to take food, water, and supplies to the hurricane victims in New Orleans, an effort spearheaded by Kirstie Alley. When I asked to see some kind of evidence that actual supplies were handed out, however, I was given the runaround. Even though I knew church officials thought I was a pain in the ass because I complained all the time, I said, "Give me a picture of somebody from Scientology Volunteer Ministers handing out a fucking bottle of water in New Orleans, not a booklet about our beliefs."

"Why are you always questioning your church's intention?" asked my "handler," Shane Woodruff. (Shane had become my unofficial liaison with the church once I reached celebrity status.)

"Because I see Volunteer Ministers, with their yellow shirts on, handing out *Way to Happiness* booklets, as opposed to the water that you told me you were going to give them," I said to Shane.

I wondered if we were helping anyone other than fellow Scientologists or just giving off an appearance of this for all the world to see. Were we actually helping the world at large in the way I had been told? Those questions gnawed at me all the time, but particularly when I agreed to help open the Inglewood Org in the neighborhood southwest of downtown L.A. I agreed to donate $100,000 to get the basic books needed for the org to be considered a church, but I had my own set of stipulations that I made very clear. In a meeting I held with all the organizers, I said that they had to reach out to the community to find out what they needed in their neighborhood. I also demanded that we create a children's center, because mothers can't go on course for two and a half hours and stick their kids in some bullshit nursery. "Let's open up a center that's wonderful for the kids, so Mom can feel like she did something great for her child," I said. "You want my help? That's what I'm willing to put my name on."

At a follow-up meeting to discuss the Inglewood Org's opening, slated for Thanksgiving, the team presented me with its plan to meet the community's needs.

"We came up with this," one self-satisfied Scientologist told me. "We're handing out turkeys with a *Way to Happiness* book."

"First of all, the idea that you think anyone needs your fucking turkey is condescending. But on top of that, you have the balls to stuff it with *The Way to Happiness*?"

The entire room went quiet. I knew they were shocked not only by how I was talking to them but also because I thought their idea was terrible. In turn, I was angry not only because their idea was shitty but also because they didn't know it was a shitty idea. As I had felt many times before, I wished these Scientologists had better human technology.

"I'm out," I said.

In the aftermath of that meeting, the group working on the new org begged me to go to the opening. David Miscavige personally requested that I be there, and there would be hell to pay for everyone if I didn't show up. But they wouldn't back down on their turkey-and-booklet plan, so I compromised. I agreed to attend the opening but said I would only sit there. "I'm not speaking, because I don't want to be part of this org." (They picked me up at my house, probably just to make sure I actually went.)

There was always something the church needed money for. Nearly every single day when I came out of session at the Celebrity Centre, there was a member of the International Association of Scientologists (IAS) waiting for me in the parking lot. According to the official literature, the purpose of the group, formed in 1984, is "to unite, advance, support and protect the Scientology religion and Scientologists in all parts of the world, so as to achieve the aims of Scientology as originated by L. Ron Hubbard."

But the IAS is also the powerful fundraising arm of the church.

The IAS rep waiting for me in the parking lot would say, "Can we talk for a second?" and my heart would sink.

Did I care about mankind?

Did I care about the state of the planet?

Did I care about other Scientologists who were being persecuted as we spoke?

It was just money, and as LRH says, you can always make more money.

As I said, it was relentless.

I had given here and there to specific projects, but it was when the IAS came into my own house to make the case for why I needed to give even more that I made my first *major* donation.

I'll never forget how the IAS representative banged on my kitchen table, saying, "Do you see this?"

She had brought some anti-Semitic propaganda, used in Nazi Germany, that depicted Jews with large hooked noses and a caption that read, "The Jew is identified by their greedy long noses." According to the IAS rep, they were using the very same propaganda against Scientologists. "Do you see this? This is what's going on in Germany right now! They're making Scientologists wear armbands. You're Jewish. How can you let this happen?"

I couldn't let that happen—or any of the other crises the IAS brought to my attention. So I kept giving and giving and giving.

It was after I made a single donation of $1 million to the IAS that I first saw Tom Cruise in the President's Office. The mere fact that I was fit to be in Tom's presence was a huge compliment. The actor wasn't just an A-list movie star but a pillar of the church. Because of his good work on behalf of Scientology, he was called Mr. Cruise, which was a big deal, since in the church the honorific "Mr." was reserved for only the highest executives, including women in the Sea Org.

Usually when Tom came into CC, the building was locked down and the other celebrities who used the President's Office had to come and go by the other entrance. When this happened, I would sit in the courtyard or the waiting room, but on this particular day, my handler, Shane, met me at my car before I entered the office to say, "I just want you to know that Mr. Cruise is here, but it's fine for you to walk through." I had met Tom before at public events, but here I wasn't quite sure how to proceed. I asked if I should pretend I didn't see him; I honestly didn't know how to act.

Tom, who was already in the room, was on the phone. He gestured for me to sit down.

When he trained his gaze on me, I felt very important. He was the perfect example of what Scientologists call "in PR" in the world—someone who's highly regarded and brings goodwill and respect to themselves and to Scientology. We had a brief but pleasant conversation. He had that magical quality that makes the person he's talking to, in this case me, feel like the only one in the world. You feel that he is super interested in what you have to say. He brings an intensity to the interaction. That's very "Tom."

I figured that all I was doing for my church by way of time and money had resulted in Tom's approval. We were on the same team. Tom and me, super twin powers activate! I was never more ready to do this clear-the-planet thing.

Not long after that day when I first met Tom in the President's Office, I began to be invited to events and get-togethers involving Tom by his church liaison, Tommy Davis, who wasn't just any Sea Org member but from a prominent family within the church. His mother was the Scientologist and actress Anne Archer. With his pedigree and good looks, it was no wonder that he was Tom's liaison with the church and later became a spokesperson for the church.

Because of my record, I was approved for Tom's entourage, a small group of heavily contributing, with-the-program Scientologists that included EarthLink founder Sky Dayton, Marisol Nichols, Ethan Suplee, and Jenna and Bodhi Elfman. (Noticeably absent from the chosen few were Kirstie Alley and John Travolta. I had heard that Tom didn't like them.) The honor came with its own set of obligations.

You just didn't say no to "Mr. Cruise," even when it came to little things. Like when he invited me and Angelo over when I was pregnant with Sofia because he wanted to learn to dance salsa. Angelo had offered to teach him, but when we were called to come over it was a last-minute invitation, so I tried to get out of it or reschedule, but Tommy Davis, who had made the call to us, said, "Make it go right."

We drove onto the massive gated rental estate, which included formal gardens, a sunken tennis court, and a main house. As soon as we walked into the house, we were met by a Sea Org member who said that Tom had only an hour because he had to listen to his congresses, a newly issued set of tapes that we were all mandated to buy and listen to. "I wasn't the one who called us to come over and do Tom a favor, Tommy," I replied as we walked into the living room.

I was surprised by what I saw: in addition to Tommy Davis, there was Jessica Feshbach, another Sea Org member from an extremely powerful Scientology family. In the eighties, her father, Joe Feshbach, built a $1 billion hedge fund business with his brothers by aggressively shorting stocks. The Feshbach brothers credited their success to LRH tech and ran their firm with strict adherence to Scientology's principles.

But the most unexpected guest in the living room that night was the actress Katie Holmes. I didn't know Katie and Tom were dating, but I quickly got the picture since he couldn't keep his hands off her. What I didn't understand was Tommy's and Jessica's presence. Did they want to learn to salsa too? I felt uncomfortable as Angelo started to go through a few moves with Tom, as if these high-ranking Sea Org members were sitting there to supervise. They certainly weren't reining Tom in, as he was manhandling Katie, dipping her in a forceful way and then making out with her. "You guys might want to get a room because we haven't even started yet," I joked. In response I received a sharp look from Tommy and Jessica.

From that point on, we were invited to Tom's compound for dinner regularly. And almost every time we went over there, Tommy and Jessica were also there in the mix. In my view it crossed a line for any Sea Org member to be at Tom's home, since my and most Scientologists' understanding was that Sea Org members are here to clear the planet and deliver services, they aren't supposed to fraternize socially with the public or parishioners. If this had been a church event, and they were there in service to Tom and Katie or protecting them as their church liaisons, that would have been completely different. But this was just dinner with another Scientology couple at home.

When I got Jessica alone, I asked her what she was doing there.

"I'm on post," she said.

"We're having dinner. What job are you doing? I don't get your purpose here."

"I work for CC," she said, which was hard for me to believe given that I was at the Celebrity Centre almost every day and had hardly ever seen her there. It also didn't answer my question. I knew she and Tommy worked for COB.

Tommy's and Jessica's off-putting presence added to the weird feeling we got at Tom's house. It was hard to place, but there was an energy in the air, like we were being watched. It was as if at any moment you could be ejected from his Beverly Hills mansion and sent to Flag in Florida to scrub toilets.

As the dinners continued and we spent more time with Tom, I came to think of him as a big kid with his loud laugh, high energy, and goofy ideas of fun. Like when he invited some Scientologists and a few other celebrities like Will Smith's wife, Jada Pinkett Smith, to his house and announced he wanted to play hide-and-seek. At first I thought he was joking, but no, he literally wanted to play hide-and-seek with a bunch of grown-ups in what was probably close to a 7,000-square-foot house on almost three full acres of secluded land.

"I can't play—I'm wearing Jimmy Choos," I said.

"Well, good," Tom said with his signature grin. "So you're It, then." And with that he tagged me and ran to hide.

"Huh?"

I pulled my husband aside and in a quiet voice whispered, "Uh,

Angelo, you're going to go ahead and do this, because I'm not doing it. I'm not trying to play a fucking game of hide-and-seek in five-inch stilettos. Okay?"

People were terrified of offending Tom, and not without reason. Once when Angelo and I were over, Tom decided he wanted to make cookies. He walked into the kitchen, where a batch of prepackaged cookie dough had been prepared and was sitting on the counter, a perfect loaf ready for cutting and baking. Tom was looking for flour and other ingredients and must not have seen the cookie dough, and he instantly got angry.

"Guys, where's the cookie stuff?" he said, furrowing his brow.

His assistants came running in wanting to explain that it was right there, on a nearby counter, but all one of them could say was, "Uh, Tom." They both grew more flustered, and Tom got angry. "Goddamn it!"

Looking at the dough sitting on a cutting board, obvious to all of us except Tom, I wished his assistant would say, "Hey, the stuff is right under your nose, dumb-ass." But she didn't. She couldn't. Instead, Katie whispered something to Tom, who repeated, "Can I just get the stuff for the cookies, guys?" Although his voice was lower, there was still a seething quality to his request that made his assistant even more flustered.

Tom seemed like a child who had never been told no. People say that celebrities stop developing emotionally at the age of their success—which for Tom had been with *Risky Business* at twenty-one.

"Get in the fucking present time, is what you need to do," he then screamed at his assistant. As he lit into her, I thought about the time a friend had mentioned to me that she witnessed him taking his assistant to task for giving him a chipped coffee mug.

"You served me tea in a chipped mug? Do you know who gets served with a mug that's chipped? Fucking DBs," he said, using the initials for "Degraded Being," a term in Scientology that means degraded spiritual being.

Still not noticing the log of pre-made dough on the counter, Tom raised his hand above his head. "LRH is here," he said, then lowered his hand to his chin and said, "And Dave and I are here." Then, with his hand down at his waist, he said, "And you are here."

An uncomfortable heat rose in my body, just like it used to when I was a little kid being yelled at by my dad. It was horrible to watch someone I admired come undone and even worse to witness the fear in the assistant's eyes. Tom comes across with an almost presidential charm to the public, but seeing him treat people this way was utterly shocking. I've seen celebrities (myself included) treat people or staff poorly, but this was on another level. The whole scene was so painful to watch that I had to step in. "Oh, wait," I said, as if I had just discovered something. "Tom, is this it?"

He looked at the dough, the assistant looked at him, and I was looking at the both of them, all of us incredulous.

"Oh," he said. "Thanks." And that was it.

It was one thing to act like an overgrown child in his own home, but when Tom had his infamous *Oprah* incident, I picked up the phone and called Shane. I wanted to know what they were going to do about Tom, who proclaimed his love for Katie Holmes by jumping on the daytime host's couch in a move that creeped out most of America. His behavior reflected badly on Scientology and me.

"Leah, he's just very up-tone," Shane said, the term used for high on Scientology's emotional tone scale. Tom and the church had become a laughingstock, and we were calling it *up-tone*? "The guy's really happy, and you should be happy for him." Again, I felt like maybe I am just an asshole and maybe there is something really and truly wrong with me. Is that just a foreign concept to me? Happiness? Real love? I wondered if Angelo would jump on a couch for me.

Meanwhile, ever since my first time at Tom's house, I had been questioning why there were Sea Org members constantly hovering around. Well, I had my own theory; it was to make sure nothing upset Tom, and if it did, to immediately report it to the church, specifically to COB David Miscavige.

Once when we were at the compound for dinner, Angelo made a joke about some celebrity we were friends with. Jessica, who was acting as Katie's Scientology chaperone to keep the actress on track and doing Scientology, pulled me aside and asked me details about the joke. When I asked her why, she said, "I am just collecting the data." The next day Jessica wrote a Knowledge Report stating that Mr. Cruise had observed Angelo joking about another celebrity and Leah did nothing about it. We were both pulled into session immediately. I was furious. Tom was a big boy; if he had a problem with me or my husband, he could write it up himself, which was proper policy. And really, all for a joke about one of our friends?

In the church, though, Tom's status only grew, despite his public behavior. He followed his *Oprah* appearance with his even more infamous one on the *Today* show, where in an interview with Matt Lauer he chastised Brooke Shields for taking psychopharmaceuticals to deal with postpartum depression. The church's response was to hold a huge event for him at the Shrine Auditorium to present how prescriptions for Ritalin and other psychotropic drugs were down something like 500 percent, thanks to Tom and his recent comments. According to the church, Tom had single-handedly taken down the psychiatric profession. As I watched Tom get a standing ovation from all the Scientologists who filled the massive auditorium, I started to question my judgment. *Look at this guy*, I thought. *He's doing great things for the world, and you're criticizing his couch jumping?* I felt more than down-tone. *Maybe I am degraded and an S.P.?*

I certainly didn't think he and Katie deserved the scrutiny they underwent from the press after their daughter was born in the spring of 2006. Because the first pictures of Suri didn't appear until she was almost five months old, there was wild speculation about whether she existed and what this mystery baby was like.

I experienced a small taste of the media frenzy around this infant when I attended my first Emmy Awards show, a little more than a week before the Annie Leibovitz portraits of baby Suri appeared in *Vanity Fair*.

Tom's kid was the last thing on my mind that day. Kevin had been nominated for lead actor in a comedy series, which was exciting for everyone on *The King of Queens* because in our nine seasons on the air no one had been nominated for a single Emmy. While walking the red carpet on a day that was so brutally hot I was sweating everywhere, I stopped to do an interview with Ryan Seacrest.

"So, Leah. This is an exciting time," he said.

"Yes, it is, Ryan."

"We heard you saw Suri."

I didn't see that coming.

"Yeah. You know what's also big news, too? Kevin James was nominated for an Emmy for the first time in the history of the show."

He gave me a kind of look like I had an attitude, which of course I did. But this was only the start of it. Every single fucking interview on that broiling red carpet was about that baby.

"You've seen Suri. What's she look like?"

"You know what Tom and Katie look like? That's what the baby looks like."

"What is she like?"

"Well, I don't know. What are babies like?"

"Is she a real baby?"

"Last I checked."

(To add insult to injury, after all that bullshit, Tony Shalhoub stole Kevin's Emmy. It was not my night, despite the fact that I had Kevin's Emmy speech written out for him, beginning with "I want to thank Remini for . . .").

Of course I didn't bring any of that up the next time I saw Tom and Katie. At the end of the night when they walked us out to our car, Tom said, "Hey, we have some news. You have to keep this hush-hush."

It wasn't hard to guess what the news was.

"We're getting married," he said, "and we want you guys to come."

I was excited for them, but I wanted to prove I was theta, not a DB or low-tone—that I could be really happy and up-tone—so I started jumping up and down. (In the car, later, Angelo said, "The jumping up and down was a little much.") Tom, who seemed pleased with my reaction, then asked if we wanted to invite our friends Jennifer Lopez and Marc Anthony to the wedding.

"Don't you think you guys should?" I asked, confused.

"Well, we don't really know them that well," Katie said. *Right,* I thought, *exactly my point. And you want to invite them to the wedding?*

Although I wondered why they wanted people they didn't know well enough to invite to their wedding *at* their wedding, I agreed to ask Jennifer and Marc.

This wasn't the first time I had invited them to hang out with Tom and Katie; the couple had asked me to bring Marc and Jennifer over for dinner previously. Although I wasn't sure why, Katie wanted to meet Jen. I just assumed she was a fan of J-Lo.

Angelo and I knew Marc way before he was with Jen. Our friendship started when the comedian Sinbad invited me to a Marc Anthony concert where I hung out afterward until four in the morning. (Angelo, who didn't come with me, kept on texting me to come home. "It's not like that," I texted back. Angelo texted in return, "Get your ass home.")

I loved Marc like a brother, and so was protective when he had Angelo and me meet his new girlfriend, Jennifer. "I want to punch you in your face," I said when I first met her, "because you are even prettier in person. I was kind of hoping you would be uglier." Jen, who has a good sense of humor about herself, laughed and we hit it off. We had a lot in common. She was from the Bronx, which if we were back in New York would be like a different country from Brooklyn, but in L.A. it basically made us from the same neighborhood. And although Jen is Catholic, her father is a Scientologist, so she knew all about the church. I thought it would be fun to take a trip with her and Marc to Tom and Katie's wedding.

So I called Jennifer the next day and said, "Hey, you want to go to Italy?"

"For what? What are you talking about?"

"Tom and Katie's wedding."

"I'm invited? . . . Are there invitations coming?"

"They're chartering a jet for everybody."

"Let me ask Marc," she said, "but why not?"

While I was happy to have my friend joining me at the wedding, I was uncomfortable with being asked to play the role of the intermediary, but I felt like I just couldn't say no to the request.

Chapter Thirteen

⁓

Tom and Katie's wedding was to take place in Rome in November of 2006. I was very excited—and scared, as I had never been out of the country before, and this was going to be a star-studded affair covered by media outlets from all over the globe. The paparazzi would be mobbing us from the minute we stepped off the plane until we returned home. I needed a get-off-the-plane outfit, complete with sunglasses, a shopping-in-Rome outfit, and a sit-in-a-café-and-have-a-cappuccino outfit, not to mention the gowns and dresses for the rehearsal dinner and the wedding. I was going to need some professional help.

Jennifer and I decided to hire a stylist to work with the both of us, which was great for me because the Jennifer Lopezes of the world get free shit from Gucci and YSL, whereas people like me get Sudafed. That's not true—I don't even get Sudafed.

The stylist filled the empty room where Angelo and I were building a home library with racks and racks of clothes and used the shelves to display bags, hats, and shoes. It was the ultimate girl fun when Jen, the stylist, and I assembled outfits for every possible scenario in Italy. I mean, I'm half Italian, so they could be planning a homecoming parade for me.

When we got off the plane, the paps were there waiting for us, just as I knew they'd be.

"Jennifer! Jennifer!" they screamed as they photographed her.

Not a single "Leah!"

No one had stopped me for a shot of my fabulous get-off-the-plane outfit. And the only "image" of me getting off the plane is a corner of my forehead, behind Jennifer. But to be fair, it was chaotic with all the fans, security, and camera flashes. Maybe they had just missed me. I *had* been standing behind Jennifer, who towers over me. No problem. There were plenty more outfits where this one came from.

The next ensemble I chose, for a little stroll up the Spanish Steps, was my shop-in-Rome outfit: a ruffled white turtleneck, black slacks capped off by a Chanel coat and four-inch Gucci heels. After three hours of preparation, I was finally ready to grab Angelo and leave the secured hotel right near the steps, where the wedding party was staying.

"We are going to be swarmed by reporters and photographers," I predicted to Angelo.

I steeled myself to face the crowd of hundreds who had lined up behind velvet ropes set up around the perimeter of the hotel in hopes of catching a glimpse in real life of the celebrities who were attending the wedding, including of course, me and Angelo. After putting on my very expensive sunglasses and taking Angelo's arm, I walked out of the lobby and bravely waited for the firestorm of fans and paps clamoring for me.

Silence.

I took off my sunglasses.

More silence.

"I guess your show doesn't air in Italy," Angelo said.

Angelo, who wanted to go to the Coliseum, grabbed a cab for us. When we got out, there was a large group of tourists waiting to get into the ruin. My time to step in. I walked past the group and up to the man standing at the front of the gate. I asked him if he ever watched the show *The King of Queens.* He said he did not and told us to get back in line. (Playing hardball, the Italians!) Apparently my street cred as a celebrity did not travel. My feet were killing me. So after Angelo took a picture of us (the only one from the whole trip), we went back to the hotel to get ready for the welcome dinner, the first event of the weekend.

Almost all of the 150 guests invited to Tom and Katie's wedding, which included some of the biggest names in all areas of the business—actors and actresses, of course, but also the heads of the major talent agencies, top entertainment lawyers, and well-known producers in Hollywood—piled into Nino, a classic, cozy Roman restaurant about an hour from the hotel. Old Italian waiters in starched white jackets and black bow ties hustled around the bride and groom's famous friends like Will and Jada Pinkett Smith, Victoria and David Beckham, Jim Carrey and Jenny McCarthy (who were dating at the time), and Brooke Shields and her husband, Chris Henchy.

I had been totally shocked when I saw Brooke Shields on the chartered plane to Italy that we shared. After the whole brouhaha when Tom attacked her on *Today* for taking antidepressants, I thought she was our enemy and had even said some shit about her in defense of Tom and my church. "I wouldn't trust someone who had those feelings with a baby," I remarked on *Entertainment Tonight*. "Do I think she needs help? Yes. Can you take a pill for something that deep? That dark? The answer is no. I got through it, but I didn't get through it by taking a pill." Then I had the pleasure of being on a private plane with her for eight hours. To my mind, it was clearly a PR move on the part of Tom's team. And then there were forced photo ops for the press to capture which celebrities and Hollywood big shots were attending the wedding. Thus it looked like they were associating themselves with Scientology and Scientologists. Although the restaurant was located on a street where it was easy for cars to drive right up and drop people off at the entrance, the wedding planners chose instead to have the street roped off, so we all had to get out of our cars on the main avenue and walk down the street to the restaurant with camera flashes going off the entire way. The church, in a very calculating way, could point to this photo or that photo and say Posh and Becks or Jennifer Lopez and Marc Anthony are associating themselves with this wedding, and therefore with Scientology. It was a smart way of legitimizing the church to the public and an attempt to recover from the bad PR of recent years. It also promoted the illusion of "look how powerful Scientology is in this business."

AT DINNER THAT NIGHT, I saw everyone who was from the church for the first time. I spotted a young Sea Org member who worked for David Miscavige, drinking red wine. I was more shocked at the sight of a Sea Org member drinking—something that I'd never seen before and something that was completely against policy. "What are you doing?" I said to the kid. "You know Sea Org members are not supposed to drink." He responded, "You know what they say—when in Rome . . ."

Someone who was representing the church at such a high-profile moment was completely flouting its rules. Most Scientologists, even just parishioners, don't really drink because they are always on course, and the rule is no drinking twenty-four hours before you are on course or going into session. Sea Org members are held to an even higher standard as they are the ones who deliver Scientology to its parishioners. To see one drinking would be as weird as seeing a priest doing a tequila shot. It's just not done.

Jessica Feshbach and Tommy Davis, the Sea Org members who had become constant fixtures at Tom and Katie's house in L.A., were in Italy, without their respective spouses, and had their hands all over each other at the restaurant—another major taboo. Sea Org members are absolutely forbidden from touching members of the opposite sex aside from their spouses. So at dinner, when Marc and Jen, having no idea who Tommy and Jessica were, asked if they were married, my face went red with embarrassment. But then Jessica took it to a whole other level.

"No, I'm married to a beaner," she said, using a racial slur for her Mexican husband.

"Jessica!" I interjected.

"What? I can say it. I mean I'm married to a Mexican."

"I'm telling you it's offensive."

She was married to a high-ranking Sea Org member. I wanted her to stop embarrassing herself and get her shit together.

Back in L.A. a few weeks before the wedding, I had asked my assistant at the time to call ahead to the hotel to check on the rooms. I asked her to make sure I was in a big enough room so that Jennifer and I could get ready together. She upgraded the smaller room I had been assigned and verified that the new room wasn't one from the block reserved for the wedding party and that it was charged to my credit card, not to the wedding party.

The next thing I got was a nasty call from Jessica: "Who are you to be changing rooms?"

I couldn't believe I had a Sea Org member calling me about rooms. It was like a rabbi calling you about why you switched the mimosa for a Bloody Mary at brunch.

"You're ungrateful," she said.

"Why should I be grateful? I'm going to a wedding."

"Because you're going to the wedding of the century."

So WHILE I MIGHT HAVE come off as "ungrateful" to them, Jessica and Tommy still pulled me in as the church's unofficial liaison to Jennifer and Marc. I had to answer tons of questions. (What kind of car does she need? What does she like to have in her hotel room? What kind of security does she need?) *Why is this of concern to them?* I wondered.

I found it odd that top church officials, Sea Org members, were so involved in the planning of Tom and Katie's wedding. This was unprecedented and off policy, to my mind.

Not only were these high-ranking executives involved in orchestrating the event, they were also all in attendance at the event. To me it could only be viewed as Tom and Katie's wedding now being re-garded as "official church business." I could not shed the thought that Tom must be an unofficial executive of the church. When I brought this up to church officials later on, they went to great lengths to deny it.

"All parishioners, including Tom Cruise, are considered equals and treated accordingly" was their pat response.

My confusion and anxiety about what was going on with my church only increased that night at Nino, where David Miscavige was one of the guests. The bizarre part about him that evening was that his female assistant Laurisse Stuckenbrock was sitting next to him like she was his date. It would have been okay if she had stood off to the side, ready to assist him when needed. But this was just weird. She was in the seat that should have been reserved for his wife, Shelly. Where was she, anyway? Strange not to have your wife, who was also COB Assistant, at an event like this.

Suri was also there that night. I heard a baby crying from the direction of the bathroom. She was a seven-month-old up late in a loud, crowded, dark restaurant, so what else was she going to do? The crying kept up, and Katie didn't seem to notice. Other people took notice, though, and started to look around to figure out what was going on with the baby. I too kept looking around. *Is anyone going to do anything?* I thought.

After about five minutes I headed to the bathroom to offer some help. When I opened the door, I found three women, including Tom's sister and his assistant, standing over the baby, who was lying on the tile floor. I didn't know if they were changing her diaper or what, but the three women were looking at her like they thought she was L. Ron Hubbard incarnate. Rather than talking to her in a soothing voice, they kept saying, "Suri! Suri!" in a tone that sounded like they were telling an adult to get her shit together.

"What are you guys doing?" I asked, but I didn't wait for an an-swer. "She's a baby. Pick her up!"

I'm hardly mother of the year, but even I knew that she was probably hungry and tired. But when I asked where her bottle was, they said it was outside, in the main part of the restaurant. It had to be heated up and they seemed helpless. "Oh, my God, you guys. We're in a restaurant, where typically there's a kitchen," I said. "I'll handle it."

I grabbed the bottle from Suri's diaper bag, went into the kitchen, asked someone to warm it up, which of course was no problem, and returned to the bathroom, where Suri was still on the floor and still crying! "Pick her up!" I yelled. They picked her up, gave her the bottle, and finally she stopped crying. Then Tom's sister turned to me and said, "Thank you," as if I were being dismissed.

I came out, and from his table, David Miscavige mouthed to me the words "Is she okay?" To which I silently replied, "Yes."

When I got back to my seat next to Jennifer, however, I found that Jessica had taken it. I didn't care so much about my seat, but I wanted my phone, which I had left on my seat. I wanted to call home and check on Sofia. I hovered near her and looked for the phone but didn't see it by my place setting. "Did anybody see my phone?" I asked. But no one had. I started to get hysterical as people either shrugged no or ignored me altogether.

I turned to Jessica, the very last person I felt like dealing with, and said, "Excuse me," as I started to feel around the chair for my phone.

"What's next, chick?" she said with a laugh. "You want to fuck me?"

"No, what's next, Jess, is I'm going to punch you in your fucking face."

The weirdness of the night was starting to get to me. When tears started to form in the corners of my eyes, it was Brooke Shields, of all people, who asked me if everything was all right. She was sitting nearby and was witnessing what was going on. She helped me look for my phone, but we still couldn't find it.

I walked outside the restaurant to take a moment, but Jessica followed me. She held my phone up in one hand. "You still want to punch me in the fucking face?" she asked.

"Now more than ever."

Just then Marc Anthony appeared. "Lee, don't be mad at her," he said. "It was me. I took your phone. I am so sorry. I was just playing with you."

I didn't believe it was him at all. I was pretty sure he was just trying to defuse the extremely tense situation.

The next few days leading up to the wedding didn't get any easier. I felt like Jessica and Tommy were watching my every move and every move I made was wrong. Even on the afternoon of the wedding Jessica was on my ass. We still had a few hours before we needed to be at Odescalchi Castle on Lake Bracciano, an hour outside of Rome, where Tom and Katie were getting married, but Jessica kept texting me that I needed to get down to the lobby of the hotel right away. When I texted back that I was going with Jennifer, and we would leave when Jen's security team gave us the okay (they were in communication with the security team at the venue), she kept insisting that I go now with the Scientology group, not with a guest of the wedding—as if my role at this wedding was to publicly show my affiliation to the church, rather than to my close friend. Then Jessica told me if I didn't come now that I would be late.

Jennifer, whom I was getting ready with, per our original plan, finally asked, "Who keeps texting you?"

"Oh, nobody."

Now I was acting weird too.

"Who's texting you?"

"Oh, no one. It's just the—they were just wondering if we were ready."

"Tell whoever that is that we'll go when my team gives us the okay, and not before." And with that I stopped responding to Jessica's texts. We left a bit later and did arrive late, but Tom's sister and assistant were arriving at the same time, so I wondered how late could we actually be? I was trying my best to keep my behind-the-scenes drama with the church to myself—it would have been bad PR to do otherwise—but I was on edge as we pulled into the beautiful courtyard of the medieval castle, where trumpeters announced our arrival.

The guests had to hike up the hill to the entrance, and in doing so I stepped on my gown and ripped it. I was immediately taken up to a room where one of the ten in-house seamstresses from Armani, booked for the wedding, sewed it right up.

I then joined the rest of the guests, who were being served champagne in a room with a fireplace that was as big as my living room. It was here, standing among Tom's assistants, that I casually asked them, "Where's Shelly? She should be here." Again, I thought it so odd that she was not there. Total bad PR. In the past Shelly was *always* by David's side.

They responded with "I don't want to be part of this conversation," and walked away.

Afterward I saw Tommy Davis and asked him the same question. I hadn't seen Shelly for a few years now. I had heard she was on some type of special assignment, but I had my suspicions that the truth was far worse.

"I mean, wherever she is, you could have dusted her off, cleaned her up, and gotten her here," I said.

Tommy replied, "I think it's odd that you're asking."

"No, it's odd being that you are the spokesperson for the church that you didn't have enough sense to realize that not having her here is a bigger PR blunder than anything."

"You don't have the rank to be asking about Shelly Miscavige," he replied, and with that he shut down the conversation.

We filed into the chapel where the ceremony was to take place. Everybody took their seats. Then Norman Starkey and Tom entered and took their places at the front of the chapel, and, inexplicably, for the next twenty minutes (but what seemed like an eternity) Tom stood there with that everything-is-great look plastered on his face even as the crowd grew uncomfortable. Finally Jennifer leaned over and whispered in my ear, "Do you think Katie's coming?"

Eventually she did walk down the aisle. Tom and Katie wed in a Scientology ceremony, where they vowed "to never close their eyes in sleep on a disagreement or an upset." David Miscavige acted as Tom's best man, and Jessica was by Katie's side most of the time. Then we all headed to the receiving line to greet the newlyweds. Tom and Katie hugged and said hello warmly to everyone—except Angelo and me. They bypassed us completely and moved on to kiss Jennifer and Marc.

"What did we do?" Angelo said as we walked into the reception. I just shrugged, because I really didn't know. Was it the fact that we were late that set them off, and if so, why weren't they mad at Jen and Marc too? Or the fact that I asked for a different room? I didn't think either of those things warranted their flat-out dismissal of us.

Along with the rest of the guests, who were talking and mingling, we filed into the castle's grand Hall of the Caesars to find our tables and take our seats for dinner. The opera singer Andrea Bocelli filled the dark hall with Italian love songs in his booming voice. Jennifer, who had picked up our table assignment cards, realized we weren't at the same table and asked what was going on. When I said I didn't know, she replied, "Well, I don't want to sit with people I don't know."

I wasn't sure what was going on either, except that church members had been trying to separate me from Jen ever since we had arrived in Italy. The only explanation I could come up with was that they viewed me as just a springboard for Tom and Katie to get to Jennifer and Marc and for the church to get to them for recruitment. The day before the ceremony, when we were leaving for the rehearsal dinner at the Villa Aurelia, Jessica and Tommy had wanted me to go in a van with other church people even though I told them I was driving with Jen and Marc, who had their own car and security. In the hotel lobby, Tommy tried to pull me aside. "Leah," he said, motioning for me to go toward the van. But Jen, who didn't know what was going on, said, "She's with us."

"Oh, yeah. No problem," he replied.

The same thing happened at the dinner hosted by Katie's parents, who had very little presence at the wedding. As the four of us sat down at a table, Tommy called over to me: "Leah and Angelo, you're over here." But again, Jennifer said, "No, she's with us." And again, Tommy backpedaled. "Oh, yeah," he said. "I think there was a mistake on the tables. Let me just change some things around." Although we returned to the hotel at four in the morning after a long night out with some of the other wedding guests, as soon as Angelo and I left Jen and Marc, Tom and Katie knocked on their door to see if they wanted to take a walk on the beach with them alone. I thought, *It's almost like someone has been watching and knew the moment we left, but I'm sure I'm being paranoid. . . .*

When it turned out that Jennifer and I weren't at the same table at the wedding reception, she asked me to talk to the wedding coordinator to see if we could sit together. I felt responsible for Jennifer, since I had invited her and Marc to the wedding on Tom and Katie's behalf. I'm sure she thought that I could communicate more easily with other Scientologists since I was one. For me to say to her otherwise would have been bad PR. What I failed to realize at the time, and what would later go down as a transgression, was the fact that me sitting with Jen meant that I was not placed at an assigned table where I could be used effectively by the church to promote Scientology among non-Scientology guests at the wedding. They viewed this as a hostile act.

So, knowing I was already in trouble I approached the wedding planner with a very light touch. "Um, is there any way we can add two chairs to our table? Or is that too much? I don't want to make a big deal about this." She assured me it was no problem, and I breathed a sigh of relief.

The reception made my stomach turn as a Scientologist. I watched Jessica openly flirting with Tommy, which was nothing compared to the sight of Norman Starkey, the Scientology minister who had performed the wedding ceremony, getting handsy and inappropriately dancing with Brooke Shields. Starkey was a church leader who had captained one of the original Sea Org ships when LRH was still alive and who was close to Scientology's founder.

I kept my mouth shut, though, through the whole night, which included the traditional cake cutting with, of course, Tom making out with Katie; fireworks set to classical music; a party after the reception at another castle hall that turned into a nightclub with superstar DJ Mark Ronson spinning. With all eyes on Tom, he put on quite a performance reprising his famous *Top Gun* moment by singing "You've Lost That Lovin' Feelin'" (an odd choice of song for a groom to be serenading his new bride with, but okay) directly to Katie, who played the part of the perfect bride. So I was relieved when at some point the hall seemed to empty out of A-listers. Angelo, Marc, Jennifer, and I climbed into her car and headed back toward the hotel. But about halfway through the drive home, I got a call on my cell phone from one of Tom's lackeys, Michael Doven.

"Hey, where are you guys?" he asked.

I explained that we were in the car, on the way to the hotel.

"Right," he said. "And I'm telling you, you need to come back."

Not knowing what else to do—this was beyond crazy—I said, "Here, talk to Jennifer," and I handed the phone over.

"Hey!" I could hear him say on the cell to Jennifer, sounding loud and nervous. "So, Tom and Katie really want you to come back!"

"We're already forty-five minutes into the drive and really tired. We didn't know where you guys were," she said.

"We just went in the kitchen with a bunch of people to make pizza. Everybody was hungry."

"Oh, well. You know, I loved the wedding. It was great."

"You sure you don't want to come back? Tom really, really wants you to come back."

"No, sweetie. We're going to go back to the hotel."

"Are you sure?"

What the fuck? Leave it alone.

Had everyone in my church lost their minds? This was all just too weird. Top officials were here and going against everything I was taught and believed to be right. I had seen behind the curtain. There, in the role of the great and powerful Oz, was not LRH, as I had come to believe, but instead, it seemed to be Tom Cruise. All of these rules appeared to have been broken because of or in relation to him and his standing in the church. Was my church falling apart? Was Tom in charge?

As soon as I got back to the room, I called my mom and in between sobs I told her everything that had been going on.

"I think Jessica's cheating on her husband with Tommy," I ranted. "Norman Starkey is drinking and humping Brooke Shields on the dance floor! I think I saw David Miscavige's assistant touching him inappropriately at the welcome dinner. And Suri was on the floor and these women were talking to her like she was LRH!"

She was in total disbelief and agreed that I had to write it up in Knowledge Reports.

I then called my assistant back home (who was also a Scientologist) and relayed the details of what I had witnessed to her. She was as devastated as I was.

"I need the facts. Give me the facts," she kept saying over and over. "I'm writing it up for the Watchdog Committee"—the highest management group in the church, charged with overseeing Scientology activity worldwide. "Give me the details."

"This is our church," I said. "How can the highest members of our church, the most so-called devout and esteemed members, just ignore policy and operate so outside the lines of what is expected of them, and of us? How did Tom amass all of this power and why is he treated like a church official? Doesn't anyone else care that this is happening?"

"Let's get it handled," she replied.

I agreed with her that we needed to handle things by solving the problem, which in my view was Tom Cruise and David Miscavige. I was still LRH's girl and I remained confident that if I operated within his world, by his policies, writing up everything I had witnessed these last few days, that I was going to be the one to solve the church's problems, and that my friends would stand by me in this important work.

I COULDN'T WAIT TO LEAVE Italy and get back home. But when Jennifer invited Angelo and me to return on the jet she decided to charter on her own (Jenny McCarthy and Jim Carrey, Will and Jada Smith, and the Beckhams all chartered their own jets home instead of taking the one provided by Tom and Katie), I declined. I would have liked nothing more than to go home with her, but if we did that, it would mean another whole day of not seeing Sofia, which I definitely didn't want to do. The chartered jet that Tom and Katie had provided was going back earlier, so I thanked her but explained that I had to get back.

On the way to the airport from the wedding, Angelo and I found ourselves in the same van as Bella and Connor Cruise.

Over the years at the Celebrity Centre I had watched Tom and Nicole Kidman's children grow up, but more recently I'd gotten to know them better by spending time with them at Tom's house. The siblings, who were supervised by Sea Org members, often had their computers taken by the security force at CC to make sure they weren't up to anything and to keep filters on so they couldn't go on any websites that might get them asking questions. Still, Connor was a bit of a rebel. He would show up to course a little disheveled from whatever "fun" he was able to steal.

I had always wondered why they didn't have a relationship with their mom, but I could never ask them, because there was always someone else around. Driving to the airport alone with them, I had my chance.

"Hey, guys. How's your mom? Do you see her a lot?" I asked.

"Not if I have a choice," Bella said. "Our mom is a fucking SP."

I was shocked by her answer.

"I've never seen her do anything publicly to give her that label—and she is your mom."

Bella scoffed and said, "Well, she is."

Connor just looked out the window. There was something more

human about his silence and the sadness I felt in it. My heart broke for him, his sister, and their mother as we rode the rest of the way to the airport without saying another word.

When he and I arrived at the private part of the airport where everyone from the chartered flight was already lined up to get on the shuttle to depart, people ignored us and acted as though we had the plague. After we got on the plane I settled into my seat next to Angelo and didn't really say much to anyone else for the rest of the trip back to the States.

I felt terrible—confused, angry, betrayed, and without friends. But I didn't want to let anyone—not even Angelo—see how upset this whole experience had made me. I was a Scientologist and I knew how to lean on my training and get my TRs in so that I didn't show any reaction. I didn't know who I was going to turn to for this, but I knew that I was on a mission at this point to save Scientology.

Chapter Fourteen

A FTER I RETURNED FROM ITALY, I HAD PLANNED ON GOING down to Flag for a six-to-eight-week upper-level course. The timing worked out perfectly, since I had hiatus from *The King of Queens*. However, right after I got home from the wedding, my auditor, Todd Woodruff, my handler Shane's brother, called to tell me I was wanted down at Flag earlier than planned. I questioned if this directive had anything to do with what had happened at the wedding. If it did, I was not going to go. Todd downplayed the request, telling me that it was just a little Ethics cycle that I had to do and that afterward I would get onto OT VII, no problem. This didn't seem like anything too terrible, so I agreed and dutifully packed up myself, Angelo, and Sofia and headed to Flag.

But almost as soon as I arrived in Clearwater, I was routed to Ethics, where I was confronted with all the Knowledge Reports that had been written about me from the wedding. There were so many, it's hard to know where to begin. I guess I'll start with the plane ride *to* Italy, where someone I didn't know accused me of being drunk and disorderly—on a plane trip where I didn't touch alcohol. I hate flying, since it's the ultimate loss of power. There was no way I was going to relinquish my last vestige of control by drinking. And if I was going to die, I wanted to be alert enough to strangle my husband while we plunged to our deaths. Another report detailed how I had tried to steal Brooke Shields's hotel room from her, which was, as earlier noted, a strange twist on the truth.

According to these reports, I was the rudest person ever to walk the face of the earth. All my crimes were on the spectrum of things that you have immature fights about in your teenage years. Apparently the delay of the wedding ceremony, which started forty-five minutes behind schedule, was my fault because I showed up late to the castle. As if Tom Cruise was waiting for me to arrive to get married. (I had heard that the delay was caused by a reporter who had snuck onto Jenna and Bodhi's van to the wedding location and was trying to get access.)

Jasmine, the MAA conducting the interrogation, showed me the Knowledge Report written by Katie Holmes, in which she referred to my behavior during the wedding weekend as "very upsetting," and accused me of disrupting the party, which she claimed was a "poor example to others." She went on to say, "[She] made the party all about her," and concluded the report with reference to the fact that all of this so-called bad behavior "disturbed me greatly." Jasmine told me I was a bad example for Scientologists and then asked me, "What do you say about this report?"

"What do I say about this childish report that looks like it was written by a seventh grader with all the exclamation marks?"

After that she showed me Jessica Feshbach's Knowledge Report, where she went on and on about how she had to defend my actions to numerous people at various wedding events (including but not limited to CAA president Kevin Huvane and film producer Kathleen Kennedy). She wrote that I was perceived as "loud," "late," and "rude," and that while I may have been trying to "solve a certain problem," the way that I had apparently handled it was "BPR [bad PR] for TC and Scn." She claimed to have successfully managed and "handled" all of these complaints because she knew the "real me."

Both of these Knowledge Reports, like all that are written and submitted to the church, are signed "This is True" or "This is Okay," meaning the person who wrote the report acknowledges that it is accurate in its reporting.

Jasmine continued, "I just need to know what's true about it and what isn't true."

We went through each report that way, because I wasn't about to back down. At this point, I felt LRH was on my side. It wasn't that I thought something was wrong with my faith. It was that there was something wrong with the people at the top, like Jessica and Tommy. Look, I copped to some shit; yes, I'm rude and I shouldn't have been late to the wedding and shouldn't have asked to change seats. But there was something way more alarming going on in our church.

It was naive to think that I was saving my church when I filed Knowledge Reports on top officials in Italy like Norman Starkey for humping Brooke Shields; Jessica and Tommy for being inappropriate with each other; and none other than COB himself, David Miscavige, for letting his assistant treat him more like her date. While technically it's acceptable to write reports on people above you in the church, no one writes reports on senior executives and certainly not on COB. Although I didn't know it at the time, those who write up top officials are usually intimidated into recanting or wind up being declared Suppressive Persons.

As a result of these Knowledge Reports, rather than partake in an Ethics cycle as Todd had mentioned, I was instead sent into a sec-check. With those reports I had written in Italy in her hand, my auditor went at me for hours, days, weeks, and then months. It was relentless—absolutely relentless—as we went around and around on the same questions:

What have you done to Tom?
Do you have evil intentions toward Tom?
Do you have sexual intentions toward Tom?
What have you done to Katie?

Do you have evil intentions toward Katie?
What have you done to David Miscavige?
Do you have evil intentions toward David Miscavige?

It was understood that the only reason I was saying those things about such high-level Scientologists was because I myself was guilty of those same crimes. "You're a cheater, a liar, a home wrecker," I was told over and over. Well, yes, this was true. All true. I was a liar, a cheater . . . but that didn't change the facts that so were they, and they were violating Sea Org policy and LRH policy.

The only way I could be done with it and leave Clearwater was if I retracted everything I said. They wanted me to say I didn't see David's assistant tap his ass affectionately or the young Sea Org member he brought along getting drunk.

When I wasn't in session or Ethics I was up in my room, crying and writing reports. Angelo, who felt so bad about seeing me so upset, thought the whole thing was nuts. He knew I was being put through the wringer but I wasn't allowed to share with him the details of my sessions or what sec-check questions they were asking me. "Babe," he said, "just say the word and we are out of here." He wasn't attached to Scientology in the way I was. For him it was simply a tool to better your life, and if it wasn't doing that, it was time to leave the church. He never got to Clear, despite spending more than $100,000 trying to get there.

But for me, leaving was way too much to contemplate. As my mom explained, if I kept causing trouble it was just going to result in more problems for her, George, Shannon, and Shannon's boyfriend, William, who were all auditing. "Just get through it," Mom said. "Answer their questions."

I was completely responsible for the fate of so many people. There were no good choices before me. As I explained it to Angelo, "Either I decide that I'm going to drastically change everyone's life and we leave, or I have to say what they want me to say."

Still, I continued to fight, thinking that at any point David Miscavige was going to barge into my auditing room and give me life protection from Ethics for the way I had stood up for policy. Instead, my auditor, Irit, and my MAA, Jasmine, did a Truth Rundown—an interrogation process typically reserved for Sea Org members.

In a Truth Rundown, the auditor looks at all the reports you have written, all the reports written by others about you, and all of the notes from your auditing sessions, Ethics Officer interviews, and any other material collected by the church to find critical reports or remarks about LRH, David Miscavige, or any person or policy of importance. Everything is fair game. So for example, if I said, "Tom Cruise is an asshole and I think he is damaging Scientology," the auditor would say, "Let's go to the earliest time you saw Tom being an asshole."

"In 2004 when I saw him at a party and he ignored the guy who handed him a water."

"Okay, so that was the earliest time you saw Tom being an asshole?"

"Yes."

"Right before you saw Tom being an asshole, what overt did you commit?"

In response to that question you have to find something that *you* did wrong. When that is answered, the auditor moves on to the next question.

"Was there an evil purpose or destructive intention that prompted you to commit that overt?"

You keep doing this until you get to the earliest time you can recall—and that's just for one report or remark. Then the auditor goes on to the next report. When the reports are done, they go the main part of the sec-check, which is two hundred different questions like "Have you ever said anything derogatory about Scientology?"

The Truth Rundown worked; I started to crack. I begged Irit to stop, and when that didn't work, I looked into the camera in the wall of the auditing room and directly at the person watching the sessions. "This is not LRH," I pleaded. "You are destroying my and your own faith."

Irit announced we were taking a break, and when she opened the door of the room, which automatically stops the camera from recording, she broke every policy in the church by whispering to me, "Answer the fucking questions and let's finish this shit." In that moment, Irit didn't care about the truth or the technology; she just wanted me to get through it.

Soon I started to question what I saw.

Maybe it is *me? I have so many overts. I upset people. I did something to pull all this in.*

Exhausted after a long day of auditing, I lay down with Sofia, who was sleeping in one of the large hotel room beds. I stroked her beautiful hair and studied her innocent little face. The last thing I thought before I fell asleep next to her was, *What did you do to deserve such an evil person as a mother?*

After weeks and weeks of twelve hours a day in auditing, they broke me and I retracted almost everything. I admitted that I caused a problem at the wedding. I admitted that I shouldn't have asked to change seats. And I held seats that caused upsets to people at the wedding. I guess that was true. Then I started in on the process of creating "good effects" to offset my transgressions at the wedding that caused "bad effects." So in the this-equals-that cosmology of Scientology, because I had bad manners I had to purchase Emily Post books for the library at Flag. I was making up the damage everywhere. I sent gift baskets accompanied by letters of apology to wedding guests like J. J. Abrams, who I was told I also upset. I bought everybody staying in the Fort Harrison a Christmas gift, and lastly I spent $2,000 on framing the invitation and other mementos from the Cruise wedding in a picture box for Katie, which I sent along with a note that said, "I'm so sorry that I destroyed your wedding." Katie responded with a text: "Just handle it with your MAA."

So after I recanted, admitted to what they wanted me to admit to, said I didn't see what I saw, and created "good effects," the church took away my ability to move up to the next OT level (even though I had already been made to do the first course of OT VI at night until midnight for four weeks). When I returned home I would no longer continue to move up the auditing side of the Bridge to the highest OT levels, but would be required to train as an auditor on the other side of the Bridge—the training side. It wasn't just a change of direction but also a major slap on the wrist, a demotion of sorts. Training—as much as eight to twelve hours per day of drilling the data and delivering Scientology to others—was a clear punishment. They basically said, *She's trouble, so let's punish her.* I fully believed that this directive came from specific individuals, not LRH policy.

After staying at Flag for four months, spending $300,000 on auditing to get reprogrammed, and making up damage, I was finally told I could go.

My return coincided with the end of our hiatus from *The King of Queens,* and not long after I got home, I was back on set, where everyone was talking about their amazing vacations in Hawaii and how relaxed they were. "Leah, how was your hiatus?" Kevin asked me.

"Oh, yeah, it was great," I said.

I was in Florida getting my ass handed to me for changing a fucking seat.

"What did you do?"

"I was in Florida for a while."

When it came to talking about my role and required activities in the church, I would often lie to people. When a non-Scientologist girlfriend asked me how things were going with Angelo, I never admitted to the usual marital problems that couples have, because that would have been revealing something less than the perfect image demanded of Scientologists. The list of workarounds to keep up appearances goes on and on.

Being a Scientologist was like having a double life. When Jennifer asked me, "Oh, so you're going to Florida?" after we returned from the wedding, like it was a casual trip to Disney with Sofia, I wanted to scream, "I'm going to Florida after Katie and Tom and everyone else wrote five thousand reports on me because I asked to change a seat at the wedding." But I couldn't say anything other than an equally casual "I've got to do some auditing," unless I wanted to be in deeper trouble with my church. I couldn't even tell Angelo about the full extent of what I was doing at Flag every day while he hung out with Sofia by the pool, since it would discourage him from being on course. So I kept it all to myself, which was the loneliest feeling in the world.

Just because I had made up the damage from my time in Italy in Scientology didn't mean that everything was fine in the real world. I heard through a few different people that Tom's agent, Kevin Huvane, was going around town telling people how disgusting I was at the wedding and how much he hated me. Anybody allied with Tom felt they had to jump on the bandwagon. I didn't blame Kevin for his attitude. If my friend told me that someone had ruined his wedding, I would think she was a bitch too.

But I didn't want Kevin, who also represented the likes of Jennifer Aniston, Julia Roberts, Sarah Jessica Parker, and Meryl Streep, hating me. So I picked up the phone and called his office to apologize. (Naturally, he didn't take my call or call me back, so I kept calling until finally I got him on the phone.)

"Hey, I heard you wanted to represent me," I joked.

"Not in a million years," he said.

"I was kidding. Anyway, I'm sorry if you thought I caused a scene at the wedding . . ."

"Did you just say the word 'if'?"

"Somebody must have told you something incorrect, because—"

"Nobody told me anything."

"Well, I just wanted to say I didn't make a scene . . ."

"So are you calling to apologize, or are you calling to lie to me?"

Now, this is Tom's agent, the last person I need to be out PR with. I couldn't afford to have another report written on me.

"I am sorry that I upset you."

"You are probably one of the most classless people I have ever met."

"And you're an agent, so that's saying something."

Nothing. Zero. Silence.

"Okay, Kevin," I said. "I hope you can forgive me."

As it turned out, I wasn't quite out of the woods with the church either. I certainly was persona non grata with Tom Cruise and his inner sanctum. However, there were also issues with my spiritual development. After all the time and money I spent in Florida, I was not getting on OT VII. Back home in L.A., I accepted my fate and started auditor training. Still I wondered if I was ever really going to be accepted by my church again, despite the countless commendations and rewards I had received from different members of the church and Sea Org.

Or perhaps it wasn't so much that I wondered if I was going to be accepted; rather, I thought, *Who the fuck are Tom and Katie? What kind of religion is this, that my spiritual path is being dictated by actors?* I wasn't there to be doing shit about Tom and Katie. I was there to get to the next OT level.

So when in 2007 Tommy Davis and Mike Rinder (at the time the executive director of the Office of Special Affairs, which oversees a wide range of the church's activities all over the world, from corporate issues to legal affairs to PR to investigations, including secret ones) asked me to join Anne Archer, Kirstie Alley, and Juliette Lewis in defending Scientology for a documentary the BBC was making on the subject, I agreed to do it.

Inside the Hollywood Guaranty Building—the center for the church's secretive Office of Special Affairs, a place that most Scientologists never get to enter—we were briefed about the BBC reporter John Sweeney, who was working on the documentary. According to the files we read, he was essentially a liar with mental problems, a classic Suppressive Person. Tommy, leading the charge in discrediting Sweeney, said, "This guy is crazy. He's going to ask you all kinds of things. You know what to do: Dead agent all his questions."

Scientologists are often prepared to respond with what's called dead agenting—a method of shutting down any criticism of the church by disproving the veracity of the source of information. A common dead agenting strategy is to sidestep any questions from outsiders that could hurt the church, and focus instead on exposing supposed lies the source told or attempt to undermine his or her credibility with *ad hominem* attacks.

We learned to first ask questions like "Do you still beat your wife?" Then only offer partial truths in response to their questions, and finally, try and deflect by referring to positive things the church has done.

When I was younger, I had to dead agent questions during interviews all the time about why I quit school in eighth grade. As stated earlier, formal education is not important in the church, which prefers that all people, even children, focus their studies and life on Scientology. But of course to the outside world that would reflect poorly on my faith, so I told all sorts of half-truths, if not outright lies, from my mother homeschooling me (she did open a school later) to my going to a private school (the Sea Org, not really a school but still an education).

Even though Scientology sees itself as the authority on ethics and responsibility, obscuring the truth is built into its core. You can't give up the details of what's involved on the OT levels because, you are told, those who are not on them aren't ready to receive that kind of information. They might die if I told them. No kidding. That meant if I were directly questioned about the upper levels of Scientology, I *had* to lie. It wasn't really a lie if it was for the betterment of the church.

The day after our briefing, Juliette, Kirstie, Anne, and I went to the Celebrity Centre for our interviews with John Sweeney. A bald British man with glasses, he was already on edge when he arrived, but Tommy and Mike ridiculed and intimidated him in a way that embarrassed me. It was one thing to avoid a question and another to berate someone into not asking it.

When I sat down with Mr. Sweeney I prepared myself for the usual assaults against Scientology. [Question: "Doesn't it cost people hundreds of thousands of dollars to practice Scientology?" Answer: "There are plenty of courses that cost as little as thirty-five dollars." (partial truth) Question: "Do you really believe that an alien Xenu came to earth millions of years ago?" Answer: "How about what Scientologists are doing for the planet today—like the New York detoxification program that has rid thousands of 9/11 rescuers and workers of harmful toxins they got at Ground Zero, a fact backed up by science." (deflect)] Instead, he asked me point-blank, "Does David Miscavige hit people?"

"What?"

I wasn't expecting that. Maybe Tommy was right about this guy—that was certainly a crazy question.

"There are allegations that David Miscavige beats people."

I had never heard them. I could have answered just that, but instead I decided to employ my favorite defense: making a joke.

"Well, I've never been hit by him. Should I be insulted?"

Okay, maybe it wasn't the best joke. Still I think it was better dead agenting than what Kirstie said, answering the same accusation about David by saying to Mr. Sweeney, "I wouldn't ask you if you're still molesting children." Classic church tool.

It was Tommy and Mike, however, who heaped the most abuse on the BBC reporter, bringing up dirt they had on mistakes he'd made throughout his career and ridiculing him for being stupid and nothing but a failed reporter. At one point during the interviews he had to excuse himself and go to the bathroom because he was so upset. I couldn't take it; there's nothing I hate more than seeing someone be humiliated, whether a Scientologist or not. I followed him to the bathroom, where I asked through the door if he was okay. He responded, "I just need a minute."

I was more than aware of the Fair Game policy, which stipulates that anyone against Scientology "may be deprived of property or injured by any means by any Scientologist without any discipline of the Scientologist. May be tricked, sued or lied to or destroyed." This policy essentially allows Scientologists to punish and harass "enemies" using any and all means necessary. The church has stated that this policy was canceled, but there is an exception: "If the person is an SP, this applies."

In this way, Tommy and Mike were just following policy, as I always stated I was. But this made my stomach turn.

I went back to talk to Tommy and Mike, who were still laughing about this poor man being in the bathroom. "What are you guys doing to him?" I said. "What you're doing is wrong. He's in your house. You should treat him with respect. I don't think we're doing ourselves any favors."

Of course they didn't listen to me. In fact, during the journalist's stay in Los Angeles, Tommy bullied him far worse than I could have imagined. He had people follow the reporter—even showing up at his hotel room, though he didn't think anyone knew where he was staying. Eventually Tommy egged him on enough that he broke the guy, who had succumbed to a screaming fit that was cleverly caught on video by the church, which posted the footage on YouTube days before the documentary aired. Mr. Sweeney, who was reprimanded by his bosses for the "unprofessional" outburst, issued his own apology, in which he said he let "the BBC down and I am ashamed." I wish he hadn't done that. The BBC had no idea of what this man had had to endure.

I didn't know about any of that until later, but I didn't need to know it to see what effect doing this documentary had on the journalist. I felt so bad about how he was treated at the Celebrity Centre that I refused to be a part of the project and never signed my release.

Chapter Fifteen

⌒⋙⌒

J OHN SWEENEY'S DOCUMENTARY ON SCIENTOLOGY, WHICH
aired on May 14, 2007, oddly enough coincided with another
major event happening in my life that was hard for me to
handle—the very last episode of *The King of Queens*.

Leaving that show was so difficult; it really was like ending a
marriage in that a lot of history happened in the nine years we
worked on it. When I looked at everything around me, the many
people I knew, the many things I had achieved, they reminded me of
The King of Queens. That was my home, a place where I felt I had finally been accepted somewhat in a business I never felt part of. My
house is *The King of Queens*. My wedding and baby—*King of Queens*.
Kevin's marriage and first two babies—*King of Queens*.

It was also hard to say goodbye to a show that didn't get canceled
but just *ended*. Yes, there were reasons, first and foremost of which
was Kevin's movie career, which took off after he did *Hitch*. Kevin
didn't want to tarnish the series with its being canceled or going out
with low ratings. The show was special to him and he wanted to
honor that.

The show that critics called derivative and not funny enough became the twelfth-longest-running sitcom in all of television history. No matter how many awards we didn't win or how many times the network moved us around, our viewers were as loyal to us as Carrie and Doug were to each other; they were the ones who kept us on air, making us one of only a handful of sitcoms of that period to make it to 207 episodes. So in what was more a collective feeling than a decision, we said, *Okay, this is it, it's time to end the show.*

And although our finale didn't come with the typical fanfare or press coverage, the end of *The King of Queens* was no less dramatic. When Kevin and I looked up at that old piece of wood above the doorway to the set that I promised on our first show we wouldn't see forever (but that we had looked at far longer than either of us ever imagined), we both started crying. We didn't even need to speak; each of us knew exactly what the other was thinking: *That's history. Our history.* I have never recovered. I miss him, our writers, the cast, and the crew every day.

Where do you go from there? I didn't really know what I wanted to do after *The King of Queens* because it was such a big part of me. You don't do a show for that long only to walk right into the next one. My main goal for a few years after the finale was not to go into something else that would be a disgrace to what I had just done for nine years.

In 2010, not long after I ran into CBS head Les Moonves and his wife and television personality, Julie Chen, at a party, my agent received a call about a new chat show for the network called *The Talk,* created by *Roseanne* alum Sara Gilbert as a time-slot replacement for the long-running soap *As the World Turns.* The daytime talk show was pitched to me as six female hosts who would sit around and have candid discussions about our lives as moms, wives, sisters, and working women. We would tell real stories about real relationships and real problems. That idea excited me. It was also something totally different for me, which was appealing, even though I knew that at some point I wanted to return to sitcoms. But CBS, the only network still doing traditional multi-camera sitcoms, offered me a development deal in tandem. I was thrilled to stay in the family and said yes to *The Talk*.

The show—which premiered on October 18, 2010, with Julie, Sara, Sharon Osbourne, Holly Robinson Peete, Marissa Jaret Winokur, and me—turned out to be much more difficult than I had imagined. For the first time on TV I wasn't playing a scripted character; I was just me. And I was scared.

Initially, all of us co-hosts bonded, both on set and off. We went on outings to the zoo with our kids, hung out at one another's houses, and got along well. We shared a lot of moments together. Things started to break down among us when I realized that the producers wanted to script the conversation between the hosts, losing any sense of "realness" to the discussions. I had thought we were going to discuss spontaneous and authentic stories. Instead, this felt manufactured. As a result, I became an "unofficial" producer. The co-hosts and producers would come to me with ideas and I would weigh them and find what I thought was relatable. An example of this came up once in a Monday morning cast and producer meeting. The producers asked us what we did that weekend. Julie mentioned that she and her husband had gone to an event at which the president was speaking. The producers thought this would be of interest. What I found to be relatable and funny was that Holly was at that same event, only her seats were in the nosebleed section, while Julie and her husband Les were somewhere in the first ten rows. Holly kept waving, unsuccessfully, to get Julie's attention. The difference in where they were seated was what was of interest and set up for a better conversation. But while I had what I thought were good ideas and a firm grasp on what our audience could relate to, my opinions and my mouth often got me into trouble.

Celebrities often have a list of what they won't talk about. Understandable. I never wanted to talk about Scientology, ever. But sometimes, when it came to guests on the show, it got to be ridiculous. For example, when Craig Ferguson was a guest on our Valentine's Day show, I thought it would be fun to talk to the late-night host about the worst gift he ever gave his wife on Valentine's Day. The note we got back from his publicist, however, read: "Don't talk about Craig's wife. He doesn't want to talk about his personal life." "Why, is he getting divorced?" "No, they said he just doesn't want to talk about her." This was Craig Ferguson, not Brad Pitt, who I'm sure would have been happy to talk about his wife. As a result I ignored Craig on air because I wasn't allowed to ask him any questions that people could relate to and I could relate to. I got tweets about it that day: "Why are you not talking to Craig?" "Why do you hate Craig?"

I thought the six of us should have real conversations on the kinds of topics that women really talk about, like how sex seriously drops off after marriage. Like, for me, I want to have sex more, but by the time eight o'clock hits, I'm too tired and think I should have done it earlier. But I don't like daylight, so unless blackout curtains are on hand I'm out because I'm trying not to show my husband my cellulite.

That would have been a fun conversation to have on daytime television. That would have been different and a conversation Barbara Walters could *never* have on *The View*.

I would want to hear that conversation. Crass, sure, but that's the kind of thing I'm interested in hearing. Now, I understand that when you're Julie Chen you can't really talk about how your husband does annoying things like scratch his balls. But still . . .

Sharon Osbourne, the resident wacky matriarch of the show, was particularly fond of telling stories about herself on air that stretched the truth. I really loved Sharon's balls. That she could make up a good story and not worry about it.

Sharon, being the grand dame of *The Talk*, was necessary to the show's survival, but her crazy ways and eccentricities that played well on TV were harder to take as a co-worker. One day I might find myself in a fight with her on set (in between the camera rolling), and the next a crazily lavish present of a full-grown tree that must have cost her thousands of dollars shows up at my house with a note that would read, "I'm such a twat!" You just never knew where you stood with Sharon. But when she told me, "I am a true friend to you," I believed her. Having said that, while one day she was your best friend, the next she wasn't. When I would try to ask someone about it, they would reply with, "Oh, that's just Sharon."

As her friend, I knew Sharon had problems with Julie. Wanting respect, not criticism, Sharon started to rail against everything from the eight a.m. planning meetings to the upfronts in New York, which she didn't want to attend because CBS was giving her only one first-class ticket and a coach ticket. If she was going to attend the presentations, which all the networks make to advertisers, Sharon had to bring along her whole crew (hair, makeup, etc.). She also didn't want to stay in the hotel that they were putting her up at. Sharon was so angry she told Holly and me that she was going to quit the show. As difficult as Sharon may have been, I did quite enjoy her, and personally I didn't want anyone leaving the show the first year. She had paid her dues in her career and I felt that she deserved much of what she was asking for. I called a meeting to see if we could work something out among ourselves, pay for the upgrade and share stylists or something. But instead of working things out, Julie and Sharon got into it. I could feel the tension quickly rising between them. Sharon accused CBS of being a cheap network; for *America's Got Talent,* NBC gave her a $50,000 budget for clothes. Julie fought back by boasting about CBS's superior ratings. It was delightful. Our very own *Battle of the Network Stars*! And in this corner . . . I spoke to Julie and persuaded her to give Sharon due respect, let her skip meetings, let her take days off, make her feel important.

Sharon, Holly, and I also decided we were going to go to the network and make some changes on the set so no one individual was running us, but rather we worked as a team. We thought this was the right move. The second season was going to be better. After all it was a tough show and we all had our moments.

Out of all the women on the show, I had the most in common with Holly, as we were in similar situations—we didn't have husbands to pay the bills like Ozzy Osbourne or Les Moonves. Holly and I were the breadwinners of our families, so we had a different perspective that was probably more in line with Sara's. But unlike Sara, Holly and I weren't the type to keep quiet when there was a problem. Sara, although the creator of the show and a producer, had zero power and didn't like to make waves. She worked for the boss's wife. A vital point that one must understand if one wants to keep one's job.

My mother, sitting in my dressing room while we discussed our plan to meet with the CBS heads, wagged her finger no.

"Ma, stop," I said. "We're going to get it all out in the open. It'll be good."

She just shook her head no and said, "You are so stupid if you think this is a great plan."

We had gone through three executive producers before the end of the first season. And to welcome our new EP, we decided to all meet at the Beverly Hills Hotel.

Before the "Go, team!" dinner I had talked to Julie on the phone for an hour about the terrible prospect of Sharon leaving. I knew she was serious about it because she had pitched Holly and me for an NBC show Howie Mandel wanted to do. But CBS really felt like family, so I wanted to make *The Talk* work. "Meet with her an hour before our dinner so that you can massage her a little," I said to Julie. "We really don't want her to quit."

Heartened by the fact that Julie listened to my advice, I decided to send an email out to all the hosts the night before the dinner. I thought this was as good a time as any to kind of clear the air.

"Looking forward to seeing everybody," I wrote. "It's going to be a new wave. It's going to be positive. So, know that."

And I was feeling positive when I walked into the Polo Lounge in the Beverly Hills Hotel the next night to find Sharon and Julie deep in conversation. I went to sit down, but Julie said, "Oh, we need more time."

"Sure, of course. Of course," I said, because I was in on the side deal with Julie. So I went to the bar, where I waited until the rest of the cast and our new executive producer showed up. Then we proceeded to the table, where we made small talk for about five minutes before Sharon answered one of my pleasantries with a serious attack.

"Who do you think you are, sending an email like that to everybody?" she asked, staring me down from across the table.

"What do you mean?"

"Oh, come on, you know, sending that positive email when you're the most negative person on the show."

"I'm negative, or I care? Because I love how everybody asks me in the morning meetings what they should say, because they know I'll tell you if you're going to look like a complete asshole or not. So, yeah, I am harsh, but it's because I want this show to be *good*. So when I say to the producers, 'What are we doing that's a little bit more interesting than *The View*?' it's not to be a bitch but to do better. Meanwhile, you saunter in when you feel like it, and give everyone a hard time. So if you think caring means a bad attitude, then, yes, I have one."

"The only reason you care is because you're a loser, and you have nothing else going on in your life."

"Oh, did everybody hear that?" I said, looking around at the table, where everyone else was dead quiet. "Honestly, Sharon, it would be in your best interest to just back it down."

"Or what?"

"Or what?" I said incredulously.

"Or you're going to get your low-life Mafia family after me?"

"No. I'm going to take this iced tea that I'm holding in my hand and I'm going to crack it over your fucking head."

And with that, I got up from the table before anyone could see the tears in my eyes and went outside to pull myself together. Holly quickly joined me, trying to console me. I was confused and hurt. *Yes,* I thought, *I'm a pain in the ass,* but weren't we a team? Clearly Holly was the only one who took my side and stuck up for me. That's why she and I have remained friends to this day.

DESPITE ALL THE UPS AND downs I went through on *The Talk,* I really did think things were going to turn out okay. It might sound absurd for someone who almost got into a fistfight with her co-host to say that, but TV is a high-stakes business where passions run high. Having been on a sitcom for nine years, where there were periods when Kevin and I weren't talking to each other or the writers weren't talking to either of us, I thought we would get through this, because to me a show is a family and all families fight but they eventually get past their rough moments.

I was so convinced that I had a future with *The Talk* that I hosted a wrap party with Holly at her house after our first season when CBS didn't want to pay for one. We even bought wrap gifts (mugs that said "I survived Season 1").

Cut to the summer of 2011. Not long after the wrap party, I got a call from my agent: "Your and Holly's options are not getting picked up for Season Two." This was a new version of "It's not going any further." I could only believe that Sharon was behind it. So apparently my mom was right again. You know, they say when you get older you learn that your parents might actually know what they're talking about.

At the time, not getting cast for a second season hurt—a lot— because Holly and I helped launch this show. Our blood, sweat, and tears went into it, so to be discarded in the way that we were felt horrible. Not to mention that Holly and I had gone to bat for Sharon, who I blamed for what had happened to us (of course Sharon denied having anything to do with it). Our ex–co-hosts then added insult to injury by going on every program they could to talk about us, and say we were fired because we weren't authentic. Every time they needed a ratings bump, they discussed us on *The Howard Stern Show* and said things about us like that we were "ghetto," or that they'd heard "there's a catering job that opened up on the set— maybe Leah can get that."

I was shocked that they would pull such a childish and vindictive publicity stunt. Coming from *The King of Queens* I wasn't used to all the power games and backstabbing. It was the depressing but real side of Hollywood where everyone is so worried about their own job that they'll do anything to keep it. While we had plenty of opportunity to respond to the attacks, Holly and I took the high road and didn't comment in return. It would have just added fuel to the fire.

I'm not blaming anyone else for the way I acted (my "humor" can come off as abrasive or degrading, so much so that I was actually called into Human Resources while I worked on *The Talk,* where I got reprimanded for how I spoke to people)—and I don't even blame myself. Certain environments don't bring out the best in you, and I can say with full confidence that although I don't have any regrets, *The Talk* wasn't my finest moment.

A few years later, as fate would have it, I took a recurring guest role on *The Exes,* which filmed on a stage upstairs from *The Talk.* So while working on the TV Land sitcom I could actually hear the hosts of the talk show below me. I saw my old dressing room, all the guest rooms I personally shopped for and decorated . . . I felt it was my baby too. I helped launch it. What I should have known was this: The show was going to be on air regardless of my fighting for it to be better.

One day, while I was sitting outside my *Exes* dressing room, who should walk by but Julie Chen. I was angry for a long, long time after leaving that show, but in that moment there was something in my heart that said, "Let it go."

My outlook in life as a Scientologist caused me to ask what responsibility I had for the place I found myself in. So with all those things and more running through my head, I made a quick decision.

I stood up, grabbed Julie, and hugged her.

"I'm sorry for my part," I said.

While hugging me, she was also trying to pull back and get away, but I said, "It's not going to happen. I'm not disengaging. So this uncomfortable moment's going to go a little bit longer, Julie," which made her laugh.

I let her go and she smiled broadly at me and said, "I hope everybody's well, and that you're well. And I wish you nothing but the best."

Her reply was poised and polite. I felt like I had done my work and I was ready to move on, regardless of whether she or the rest of the co-hosts had.

EVEN NOW, AFTER DECADES IN this business, I still have moments where I am trying to fit in as an actress in Hollywood, as if I were somehow an imposter. For so long, I looked for acceptance from everyone from my dad to the people in this town. What I have slowly come to realize, and often still have to remind myself of, is this: There is no "right" way to be. I am flawed and imperfect, but am uniquely me. I don't fit in and probably never will. And I don't have to try to anymore. That other person was a lie. And let's face it, normal is boring. We all have something to offer the world in some way, but by not being our authentic selves, we are robbing the world of something different, something special.

My time at *The Talk* was a lesson in learning who my true friends were. If there is one thing I can brag about and be proud of in my life, it's my dedication to friendship. If I call you a friend, I mean it. You are now on par with being a family member. Friendships are not made overnight; it takes time, effort, and energy. For me, friendships are tested not in the best of times, but in the worst of times. You don't always get a second chance to be there for someone when they really need you. So when I say I will be there, I mean it. And when I need you, you better be there. Everyone has deal breakers and this is one of mine.

If real friends are hard to come by in life, you can imagine what it's like in Hollywood. I have said I can count on one hand the number of real men I have met in this town. Finding real friends, who will step up and say or do the right thing on your behalf, is almost impossible as well. Most are just looking to save their asses or their jobs, loudmouths who will say anything to anyone but secretly apologize behind closed doors. Leading actors, big executives, and powerful people talk a big game until they realize their jobs might be on the line, and they instantly become complete and utter pussies.

Stupidly perhaps, and sometimes at the cost of my own job, or being labeled "difficult," I'm willing to say shit to people no matter who they are and what the consequences may be. And yes, in the end, I'm probably cutting off my nose to spite my face. But that's who I am.

When I started to write this chapter, I had planned to spill all of the details behind why Holly and I were not asked back to season two but then as I read it over, I thought I would just be doing what they wanted. I would be no better than them.

So yes, I was an asshole when it came to defending myself, the other hosts, and the show as a whole. Rather than kiss everyone's ass, I brazenly (and oftentimes obnoxiously) spoke my mind, and as a result lost my job. But I stood by what I thought was right and I was a friend to those who I felt deserved my friendship. While I am able to forgive those who spoke out against me at *The Talk*, I have learned a valuable lesson in Hollywood and in life; by their actions, they will show you who they are.

Chapter Sixteen

N 2012, SIX YEARS INTO THEIR MARRIAGE, TOM CRUISE AN-
nounced that he and Katie Holmes were getting a divorce.

Katie and her team of lawyers initiated the proceedings with her formal filing of divorce. Rumors started flying immediately speculating that there would be an explosive showdown over custody for Suri and fears of revelations of secret facts about Tom's life. While Katie's team denied any of the rumors, the divorce was settled in less than two weeks and Katie ended up with primary custody. Tom seemed to acknowledge that Katie left because she wanted to protect Suri from Scientology. It made me wonder whether protecting his church was more important to him than his own daughter.

Katie's action, of filing for divorce in such a public way (it had quickly been picked up by the media), would definitely get her declared a Suppressive Person by the church. It had always been my understanding that as a Scientologist you have the right to request that any Knowledge Reports written by an SP be removed from your files. I had been fighting for years to get the Cruise wedding fallout expunged from my files. So as soon as I heard news of the divorce, I picked up the phone and called my auditor, Todd, and said, "What do you have to say to me now?"

"I guess you can expect to have that report taken out of your folder," he replied.

We met shortly thereafter and Todd basically admitted that they had screwed up about moving me off my OT levels and onto the training track after speaking up about everything I had seen in Italy.

"Look," he said, "you got some bad auditing the last time you were at Flag. Putting you into training was not the right thing to do. In fact, it was all wrong. Go back to Flag and go back into auditing." (This would, of course, be at my expense.)

Now that my church seemingly had realized that it had fucked up, and was starting to apply LRH policies again, I wondered where were the apologies to me from everyone involved in the wedding debacle? After I reported on what I saw in Italy, I was made to feel like I was crazy and that I was the only one to witness these things. Yet Norman Starkey was sent home early from Italy in disgrace. And guess who got divorced and remarried? Less than a year after the wedding, Jessica and Tommy, who were all over each other at the wedding, both took extensive leaves from the Sea Org—and later wound up married to each other after divorcing their spouses. So did I get a plaque that said, "You were right"? Nope. And I never got an answer about Shelly Miscavige's whereabouts. I made up for the damage that they had accused me of doing. What about the damage they did to me?

"Well, if it was all wrong, are you going to give me back my money? Because, as a Scientologist, when I'm reprimanded I'm asked what I'm going to do to make up the damage. So now I'm asking you, what are you going to do to make up the damage?"

"What do you mean?" Todd said. "Are you asking for a refund?"

Although the church publicly claims that it will simply return funds to anyone who is dissatisfied, the reality of this policy is quite different. In fact, requesting a return of money from the church is classified as a Scientology "High Crime" or "Suppressive Act," which qualifies one to be declared a Suppressive Person. And in an even more bizarre twist, once the church declares you an SP, according to its policy you are no longer eligible for a return of your money. It is the perfect catch-22—if you ask for your money back, you will be Declared and thereby no longer qualify to get your money back.

"No, I'm not asking for a refund," I responded. "What I'm saying is, what does the church do to take responsibility for its actions? When I fucked up I spent my hiatus from *King of Queens* in Florida, in session twelve hours a day, having my ass handed to me. And so I want to know what you people do when you fuck up?"

Eventually, after some time, Todd came back to me and said, "It's done," and that I would get the $300,000 credited to my account. I believed him, never bothering to check my accounts. Why would I? To me Todd's word was that of my church.

Todd went on to encourage me to get back onto my OT levels, but I decided that I wanted to continue pursuing the auditor training path because I liked the idea of helping people, working with preclears, counseling them. With the church's seeming admission of having messed up the wedding fallout, and its agreeing to return my money, I began to re-engage, dedicating myself in the weeks that followed to moving ahead in my training as an auditor. But one thing still nagged at me: the fact that *no one* would tell me where Shelly Miscavige was. When I would ask Todd during our sessions, he would take me outside where there were no recording devices and say, "Shelly is a Sea Org member and you're asking about the leader's wife. How do you expect people to react? I can't call COB and ask him." When I flat out asked if she was dead, he responded, "I'm sure she's not dead, but you and I are not in a position to ask where the leader's wife is. I think it would be in your best interest to stop asking."

In requesting my $300,000 back, I couldn't stop thinking about the fact that if this kind of problem with money happened to me, an outspoken celebrity in the church, similar things must be happening to so many others who suffered in silence. That just wasn't right. Having grown up a Scientologist, I knew firsthand the financial sacrifice that the church demands of its ordinary practitioners. I had met one man who said he was in foreclosure because of a sec-check—and a mom who told me she had drained her daughter's college fund after she was sent to Flag. On a more personal level, I had watched my whole family struggle to move up the Bridge. They were $250,000 in debt at this point. The fact that people making average salaries of $50,000 a year somehow find a way to pay the $500,000 necessary to get on their OT levels—frankly, it's a superhuman task. The level of dedication is astonishing and admirable, but over the long term it means financial destruction for a lot of people and families.

When anyone arrives at Flag, one of the first places he or she is sent is to the IAS (International Association of Scientologists). It's one of the various wings in charge of getting donations out of parishioners. But the IAS is the eight-hundred-pound gorilla of extracting money from Scientologists for the church's monumentally important causes. Before you've even had time to go to your hotel room, they've looked up how much money you've donated to the church and immediately started to question it: "Do you really think you're going to get onto OT VII with this donation?" No matter what you say about the state of your finances, the fund-raisers of the IAS can always find a way for you to give more. They'll ask for your credit card number and its limit. Then they "help" you call Visa or Amex and they know exactly what to say to get your limit upped. And once they've helped you get that $10,000 or $25,000 credit limit increase, you end up charging that amount to your card as a donation. Either you're an able being, or you're not. Able beings make major donations. And of course, any "good" Scientologist is expected to be able.

I wondered how many Scientologists with far fewer resources than I had were in debt to the church because they had spoken out about something they saw that wasn't right and were punished with a costly security check or a course of reprogramming. I also continued to wonder why parishioners had to pay for the same things over and over again. Why we had to keep purchasing new or revised textbook editions and CDs of the same policies/courses we had already bought. Forced to repeat courses if we wanted to move up the Bridge. Redo auditing actions over and over again, all at our expense. If we were made to abide by the same rules of "you are responsible for all," why didn't the church say, "Hey, we fucked up on that process, so we are going to have you do it again at our expense"? Instead, there was just no end to what was required of a parishioner.

The response I would get whenever I voiced my concerns to someone in the church was, "We just have to do it," or some other runaround excuse. No one was willing to challenge these financial practices, instead just accepting them as the status quo. Even more infuriating was my original complaint that as parishioners we had to make financial and spiritual amends for our wrongs, but the leaders of our faith took no responsibility for anything ever. How could that be?

Here was Tom Cruise, being rewarded for being the most dedicated Scientologist on the planet, but you know who should actually get that reward? The guy who makes $75,000 a year and donates $250,000.

Soon after my various conversations with Todd, I got a call from my handler, Shane, who worked with Todd on my service. "You know what, Leah? I'm looking at things in your folder from over the years, and there have definitely been some issues in regards to your speaking up. Why don't I come over and I can help you write up some Standard Request for Withdrawal Reports." (Apparently the previous ones I had submitted to have earlier Knowledge Reports on me from people like Katie Holmes pulled from my file had been rejected due to the fact that I showed too much emotion in the language I used. I had found out that the requests were essentially ignored for years.) I agreed to meet with Shane, and together we worked on the new requests.

As we were working I once again broached the subject of Shelly. I told Shane that I found it surprising and concerning that I hadn't gotten a holiday card or thank-you note from her after I sent her a gift that past Christmas, something she had always been diligent about in the past. It wasn't like her. Shane, like Todd, responded with "I don't know, I can't ask where the leader's wife is."

I figured as long as Shane was here trying to help me with the requests for withdrawal, why not have him help me try to get a letter to Shelly, to which he agreed. I wrote the following note and gave it to him for delivery:

Dear Shelly,

It has been some time that I have seen or heard from you. I have sent you a few Christmas cards and gifts. It was not like you to not write back right away. I had asked about you and was told you were on project. Out of respect I didn't want to say "Are they (meaning you and Dave) not together?" or "Is she on the RPF?" I let it go for a bit. But, it has been way too long now that I have not seen or heard from you.

I have come across some letters from you to me, my family, my daughter and I just feel as someone who I considered a friend, I needed to know that you were indeed ok.

I get it that you might be busy and might very well be on project, but you were there for me when I needed you and I don't take that lightly. Further, you were always in comm. with us.

I am sure you can understand why I would write.

My cell is XXX-XXX-XXXX.

With Love,

Leah

A week or so passed and I called Shane to see if he had been able to get the note to Shelly or if he had gotten any response. He told me, "Honestly, Leah, I never sent the note. It was inappropriate the way you referred to COB's relationship." He told me to write a new note with a more appropriate tone and language. And so I did:

Dear Shelly,

It has been a while since we have spoken or seen each other. I came across a few letters that you had written to me and my daughter and I thought "I really love & miss Shelly." What better way to show someone you love them than to not write them for 6 years! (That's a joke.) So, I decided to write! ☺ I think of you often, Shelly—you were really there for me when I needed you and I will always consider you a friend.

I would love to hear from you and have a coffee with you!

Call me.

With Love,

Leah

XXX-XXX-XXXX

Once again, I received no response. I later received word back that my letter to her was considered "entheta," meaning bad energy, sarcastic, angering, upsetting, and was basically thrown away. By this point Shelly had been missing for more than six years.

A few more weeks passed and I'd yet to hear any responses from the MAA about the requests for Knowledge Report withdrawals that Shane and I had submitted. I asked Shane about it, and he responded with "Let me check on it."

When a request for withdrawal of a Knowledge Report is reviewed and accepted, formal paperwork and documentation accompany the agreed-upon withdrawal so that the parishioner knows the request has been granted. When I asked Shane to provide me with the formal paperwork, he instead forwarded an unofficial email from an MAA stating that the requests had been accepted. I knew this wasn't on policy. I was getting the runaround. And now I was starting to get pissed.

I asked Shane for a full review of all of my accounting with the church as I had not yet received the $300,000 credit I had been promised. Shane in turn accused me of asking for a refund. I once again told him, "This is *not* a refund. This is a *credit*. A credit for all of the shit you guys have screwed up. When will you accept accountability?"

And with that, I received a personal call from none other than

Hanging out with my stepsons: Nico, Alex, and Angelo.

I actually thought I looked pretty skinny here and wondered if people knew I was pregnant. Meanwhile I'm big as a house, and wearing white.

Sofia, don't be mad at Mommy, but I had to share that cute butt.

One of the rare moments our daughter wasn't crying.

Me and my girl.

Blowing out the candles and making a wish at Sofia's fifth birthday party.

Here I am with Jennifer and Marc in Italy. Look to the right of Jennifer. That's my white sleeve.

The view from our hotel room in Rome, where we stayed for Tom and Katie's wedding, with paparazzi waiting below.

This is one of the only photos Angelo and I took the entire wedding weekend. All I could say about the Colosseum is, it's not like in the movies. Where's the part where the gladiator comes out? Boring, as far as I was concerned.

Supporting my girl at *American Idol.*

Jen supporting me at *Dancing with the Stars.*

Cuteness all around.

Sofia, hanging with the
boys—Angelo and Marc.

Early on, I was excited about doing something different at *The Talk*. Pictured here with Sara Gilbert, Sharon Osbourne, Holly Robinson Peete, and Julie Chen.

Me and the ladies of *The Talk* on the Sony private jet on our way to the television upfronts to promote our first season.

Backstage at an Ozzy Osbourne concert for my mother's birthday. Sharon not only had a cake for my mom, but had Ozzy surprise her and pull her onstage. He literally had to kick her offstage because she wouldn't leave.

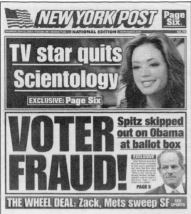

Finally made the cover of the *New York Post*!

My partner, Tony Dovolani, always had my back on *Dancing with the Stars*.

A great friendship that came out of *DWTS*. Here with Tony and his beautiful wife, Lina.

It's become a Christmas tradition for me to buy all the girls in my family matching PJs. Here we are in a cabin we rented in Big Bear: Shannon, Nicole, Mom, me, my niece Brianna, and Sofia. The ladies in red.

A publicity photo for my reality show *It's All Relative*. Although working with family can be difficult, we were all so appreciative of the experience.

COB, David Miscavige, asking if we could meet. I told him there was no point, but he insisted, offering to clear out the Celebrity Centre for me, Tom Cruise style. I declined but agreed to see him that night so I could confront this issue once and for all.

Angelo, who was worried, said, "Babe, do you want me to go with you?" I refused. The last thing I wanted COB to think was that I needed backup. I was after all, taller than David Miscavige.

David Miscavige, the leader of Scientology, greeted me. His longtime assistant Laurisse (whom I had seen with him at Tom and Katie's wedding) was also there. He immediately told me he had been traveling and was not aware of what was going on with my situation.

I repeated everything I had already said to others many, many times, plus I went on to ask why wasn't anyone seeing Tom Cruise the way I saw him? Why with his three failed marriages and couch-jumping antics was he considered to be the epitome of a great Scientologist? Why was he not treated as an SP who should be in session twenty-four hours a day? And why couldn't I get an answer as to where David's wife, Shelly, was? He told me that Shelly was okay and that he had to keep her away because SPs are constantly trying to have her subpoenaed. It was so out of left field that I didn't know how to respond.

We talked a bit more, and all the while he continued saying he knew nothing about my problems but that he would look into things for me. I agreed to have him investigate further and get back to me.

I wasn't sure that I believed his offer to look into things. So, frustrated with the constant runaround I was getting, I started making phone calls. I broke another one of the cardinal rules of Scientology and began reaching out to those who had been deemed Suppressive Persons. I knew I was yet again stepping outside the bounds of what was acceptable to my church, but given my recent experiences, I couldn't help but wonder what had happened to these people, who had been very high up on the Org board, to make them give up everything and everyone in their lives.

I reached out to Mike Rinder, who had left the church in 2007.

I was honest with him that I wasn't a big fan of his because of the way he had acted toward John Sweeney during the BBC documentary fiasco and a famous interview he gave to *Dateline* in which he blatantly lied to all of America when he said there was no policy of disconnection in Scientology. But for the man who was head of OSA for twenty-five years, a Sea Org member for forty years, and a Scientologist for fifty years to leave? Something must have happened to him. I listened to what he and another former top executive had said, that Scientology's management—themselves included—was continually subjected to, and inflicted physical beatings on, other Sea Org members. I questioned him how this could possibly be. What about LRH policy?

"What you don't understand is that we *were* backed up by policy," Mike said to me.

I was stunned.

There were seemingly some secret flag orders and dispatches that Mike said he had seen that permit hitting and abusing people if it is in the course of getting someone to comply with policy, which would make it acceptable. According to several eyewitness accounts, in the Hole—a set of trailers on Gold Base (International Base), a remote 500-acre compound in Southern California—fallen executives are kept separated, humiliated, and often beaten. Mike said that at the direction of and by the hand of David Miscavige, leaders of my church, including Mike, were subjected to punishments like being made to lick bathroom floors or being doused in cold water, punishments that were so bad they felt they had no other choice but to flee. Mike decided enough was enough, choosing to leave the church and speak out; as a result he lost contact with his son, his daughter, and his wife of thirty-plus years, his mother and brother and sister and everyone else in his family.

My assumption up to this point—that terrible things like what was happening in the Hole were not an indictment of my church but bad Scientologists misusing policy—was wrong. Mike was saying that if David Miscavige was beating people, he wasn't misguided; he was following LRH policy—which is what all good Scientologists are taught to do. "That's why at the time I thought it was okay," he told me.

Of course, the Church of Scientology has always denied that any of this is true—the church says there is no Hole, no abuse, no beatings, at least not by David Miscaviage. But then why were so many former executives leaving Scientology and telling consistent stories of abuse?

I also reached out to Debbie Cook, the woman who was the captain of the Flag Service Organization (FSO), which meant she ran Flag, which she did for seventeen years. She had also been in the Hole, but she wouldn't talk to me. The church was suing her for violation of a contract after the famous New Year's Eve email that she wrote and disseminated on December 31, 2012. In it, she described herself as "dedicated to the technology of Dianetics and Scientology and the works of LRH . . . and I absolutely know it is worth fighting to keep it pure and unadulterated." But she went on to say, "I do have some very serious concerns." Those concerns could be summed up in two words: David Miscavige. "There never was supposed to be a 'leader' other than LRH," she wrote.

The church charged that the email violated the terms of the agreement she made back in 2007 after spending seven weeks in the Hole. But as Debbie testified in court, after the abuse she experienced in the Hole, "I would have signed that I stabbed babies over and over again and loved it."

Scientology made the mistake of suing Debbie Cook, and in a Texas courtroom under oath, she described her experience in the Hole, stating that she had watched David Miscavige punch people, and that for twelve hours she was made to stand in a trash can with a sign that read "Lesbo" hung around her neck. During this twelve-hour period, cold water was periodically poured over her head while people screamed at her to admit she was gay. (In *Dianetics*, LRH explicitly called homosexuality a "perversion." Then later, he put being gay on the Tone Scale as "Covert Hostility," which registers at

1.1 on the scale of human emotions, which is considered by Scientologists to be a person avoided at all costs.)

Reading Debbie's email started me on an Internet search. In Scientology you are told to stay away from the Internet or other forms of media or intelligence that might be against Scientology. I broke away from this long-held rule and looked at hundreds of stories about my church and just sat there and cried. Not just for me, but for the many who believed in something that they thought was bigger than themselves and dedicated their whole lives to sustaining it. How could I have been blind to the stories that the rest of the world knew? Scientologists are hardworking, dedicated, and caring people, albeit misinformed people, and I was no exception. The reason for their blind faith lies in their core belief that they alone have the answers to eradicate the ills of humanity. You run back to the safety of the group that shares your mentality, and in this way your world becomes very insular.

During my crisis of faith I did what most people do in similar circumstances—I relied on my friends and family as a sounding board. But when I brought up my discoveries of abuse with John and Val Futris, my dear friends, former employer, and closest confidants for the last twenty-five years, I was surprised by the reaction my concerns elicited.

After confessing that I had read Debbie Cook's email and tried to contact her, I asked them why no Scientologists would read it.

"Why would I read entheta?" Valerie said.

"How do you know that it's entheta?" I asked.

"Because it's from somebody who's against our group."

"It was somebody *in* our group, Valerie. And not just a somebody but a trusted member. Debbie Cook was the captain of the FSO, on the front lines of Scientology, for a very long time. Why wouldn't you give her the time of day, to even look at what she has to say?"

Debbie and many of the others whose information and statements I was looking at were considered to be among the chiefs of our church. These weren't just some ex-parishioners, bitter apostates, kicked-out members, looking for fame or a quick payout. These were men and women who were respected leaders in our church, who dedicated their lives not only to our church but also to the Sea Org, signing billion-year contracts. They essentially gave up their lives for the church.

"Why would I go out of my way to read an enemy's email?"

"It makes me wonder what you would do if *I* wrote an email like that."

"I wouldn't read it."

"That kills me inside. I mean, you wouldn't read an email from me? Are you kidding me, Val? You've known me since I was fucking sixteen."

Once I opened myself up to the outside world, I heard so many terrible things. I learned what had happened to Sherry's brother, Stefan, years after he came to me for help in getting his wife, Tanja, back from Gold Base, where she was kept for two years. At one point she was even put into isolation after she scaled an eight-foot wall topped by razor wire and jumped to freedom, only to be returned by Scientologists who found her walking along the highway.

Stefan never gave up on getting Tanja back. Eventually he came up with a plan that included sending her a Victoria's Secret box, which he knew the security guards wouldn't open because they wouldn't want to risk being caught going through lingerie, which would certainly be considered aberrated behavior. In the box Tanja found a letter from Stefan and a cell phone so they could communicate. In 2006, seven years after they were first separated, Stefan pulled up at Gold Base in a car, and in the middle of the night Tanja jumped the wall again and the pair drove off to freedom.

Not long after I spoke to John and Val, Shane called me into the Celebrity Centre, but when I arrived at my course room, I found him standing with two men I had never heard of or met before. Shane introduced me. "This is Mike Sutter and Hansuli Stahli. They are executives from the church. They were sent here to talk to you." The two of them, I later found out, were infamously referred to as David Miscavige's "henchmen."

"We wanted to sit down and answer any questions you might have," they said.

"Great. Where's Shelly?"

Rather than answer my question, they responded by showing me some policies they had on hand. I quickly dismissed them.

They then went on to say, "We got a report that you're asking about Shelly and hooking up with the Debbie Cooks of the world."

"Well, let me see the reports, because as per LRH policies you just showed me, I should have gotten a copy of the reports."

"Well, it was a verbal report."

"A verbal report? Why don't you show me the LRH policy that says that's okay? You can't, because you know it's not policy."

They stared at me. I turned my attention to Shane.

"Shane, did you not know that I asked about Shelly? Did you not know that I was questioning what was going on?" Shane nodded that he did. "You're all acting like I'm hiding something that I've been asking about for years. What the fuck kind of bullshit is this?"

Sutter and Stahli started in on a presentation of the expansion of Scientology and all the buildings the church had recently purchased. Pointing to images of millions of dollars' worth of Scientology's real estate holdings, Stahli said, "This is what we're doing, Leah."

"When you connect up with a Debbie Cook or a Mike Rinder," Sutter said to me, "you're cutting across the survival of mankind and impeding what we're trying to do here."

That's right—according to Sutter, just talking with an SP means you're trying to destroy Scientology by proxy. And if Scientology is humanity's only hope for salvation, well, I was on the wrong side.

"Listen, guys, I really appreciate the eighth-grade presentation, but I could give a shit about buildings," I said. "What I care about is myself, my family, and the people who are getting fucked by a church that doesn't give a shit about the truth but rather buildings, which represent not only my millions of dollars but the millions of people who don't have that kind of money but continue to remain dedicated and contribute."

As I went on and on and on, it was clear they had no idea what to do. They weren't prepared for this.

"I want answers as to why Tom Cruise seems to be running our church; I think he's an SP. I want answers on why we have to spend hours and hours in session for minor transgressions, but you people, the embodiment of ethics and morals, don't have to take responsibility for anything. I mean, what the fuck is going on here? . . . I want answers about Shelly Miscavige. So, do you have answers to where she is or anything else I'm asking about?"

No answers. They just "acknowledged" me, like every Scientologist learns in the introductory communication course. There were no human qualities to any of this.

"You're going to acknowledge me, and I'm going to want to throw you out that window," I said. "I don't know who you think you're talking to. But you only acknowledging me is *not* the way you're going to handle me. So if you want to handle me, come straight, and come with some fucking answers. Other than that, we're done." I then turned my attention to Shane. "You honestly thought having these guys work on me would be a good idea? Well, it wasn't. And as I asked before, I want a full accounting of all of my finances within the church. How much money have I spent in total on Scientology?" I honestly had no idea up until that point. "How much has my family spent? I want all of it."

And with that I walked out the door and left.

Two days later Shane and the Commanding Officer of the Celebrity Centre, Dave Petit, showed up at my house unannounced. Angelo answered the door even though I said not to let them in, because I knew this was just going to amount to more bullshit.

"Do you have answers as to where Shelly Miscavige is?" I said to Dave. "Otherwise I'm going to slam this door in your face."

"I do," he replied.

So the four of us went into my office, where Dave and Shane began taking out all these LRH policies from Dave's briefcase.

"Oh no. I'm not going to read policy," I said.

"You're refusing to read LRH policy?" Shane said.

"Shane, I have read more policy than you. I'm higher than you on the Bridge; I'm also higher trained. You're not going to school me on LRH. Okay? So back to my original question: Where's Shelly?"

"I just need you to read this policy before we start," Dave said, sliding the paper across the table to me as if it was too much trouble for him to stand up and hand it to me. I slid it right back and stood up myself.

"Listen to me, Dave Petit. You can take that policy and shove it up your ass. Where's Shelly?"

"She's at Gold."

"Get her on the phone," I said.

"We don't have the number."

"You don't have the number, Shane? Really, you want to play games?" I walked over to the phone near my computer. "Okay, let's call Tom De Vocht. Maybe he has the number?"

Tom, a former Sea Org officer who dealt intimately with David Miscavige, would have the number to Gold.

"Leah, Leah," Shane said, "what's happening to you?"

"You're playing games with me," I said, then turned to Angelo. "You see what is going on here? Didn't they say they had answers about where Shelly was, and now he doesn't even know the number to Gold?"

Then I turned to Shane and said, "If I don't get answers, an apology, and the money I'm owed, I'm going to call the cops and the FBI. I know you've known me to make empty threats in the past, but mark my words, Shane: This one will happen. So I'd better get some fucking answers."

"Leah, Leah, Leah," Shane continued.

Angelo interrupted him. "Actually, stop. Just give her the answer you said you had. Where is Shelly?"

"Leah," David said, ignoring Angelo, "what's happening? Why are you talking to Debbie Cook?"

"Why don't you make Tom Cruise disconnect from Nicole Kidman and Katie Holmes, both of whom you declared to be SPs? Everybody else in the world has to suffer and cut ties, but when it's Tom Cruise, your god, policy doesn't apply to him. Families are being destroyed every day by this. But not Tom Cruise. Never Tom . . . So you're bullshit. And the church is bullshit."

"You're a fucking bitch," Shane said.

Angelo jumped up out of his seat, slammed the door to the office shut so Shane couldn't escape, and cocked his fist.

"Listen, man," Shane stammered.

"You don't call my wife a fucking bitch in front of me in our house," Angelo seethed.

Like a trapped animal, Shane didn't know what to do.

"Apologize to my wife," Angelo said.

"Angelo, please . . . ," he said.

I didn't lift a finger to stop Angelo. I wanted him to bust Shane's ass no matter what the consequences were. I mean, I was full on ready to be arrested; you know, I'd just put on a little lipstick, mug shot ready. I'd take that bullet to see this asshole go down. I was so hyped up I wondered if I could take Dave Petit. But my fantasy was interrupted when Shane said, "Sorry, Leah." Then he ran out of the house with Dave not far behind.

Shortly thereafter I was called in to meet with David Miscavige again.

We talked about what I knew to be my bad auditing at Flag. He was trying to justify what had happened to me and claimed that it was Jessica who was the one who had sent a written communication on his behalf to get me handled. That Jessica called the code red on me, not him.

"Dave, it's not just about me. It's about the whole thing. Families are being destroyed, people are in debt, OTs are leaving, highly trained auditors are leaving. Something is not right."

He asked me to give him names.

"Dave, come on. How about at the next event you ask to see a show of hands from all the people who are in debt because of this church."

He laughed as if I was being ridiculous, but I wasn't kidding.

"My whole family is in financial ruin. I mean, it's happening every day."

He questioned the fact that I had reached out to people like Debbie Cook and Mike Rinder, referring to them as his enemies.

"I don't know that they're your enemies. I know that they left the church and I know that they're claiming to have been abused by other Sea Org members."

He dismissed what I was saying and tried to move the conversation along and "focus on the good."

Sick of the many dismissals and runaround I was getting, I refused to focus on the good. Instead I started talking to him about my concerns with Tom Cruise and what I perceived to be his overwhelming role in the church.

"Tom needs to shut his fucking mouth and stop representing Scientology," I said.

Miscavige then directed the conversation toward getting me onto my OT levels. Not what I wanted to hear.

I was surprised when I got a call shortly thereafter from Laurisse informing me that after nearly six long years, the $300,000 due to me was finally going to be credited to my account. I in turn asked for it to be provided to me in the form of a check, which she agreed to. I had Angelo pick it up at the Celebrity Centre and it was deposited into my bank account.

The church had finally done right by me. But my newly restored faith was quickly squashed when Susan Watson, the president of the Celebrity Centre, called a week later and ordered me to come in right away with my mom and Angelo. The "mother of the church," the woman who hugged me whenever I came in for auditing, who married Angelo and me, who loved my daughter, now treated me like I was a criminal. As I walked through those doors, it was like all of a sudden this place where I had spent most of my life—on course, helping others move up the Bridge, fundraising, catching up with friends—was no longer my home, my refuge, my sanctuary.

I was taken upstairs to my former auditing room, another space in which I had spent countless hours and gone through all kinds of

emotions and experiences, but waiting there for me was not my auditor, but the MAA Julian Swartz and Cassie Woodruff, Shane's wife.
They were both glaring at me when I walked in.

David Miscavige made the call, and now I, like those before me
who had questioned what was going on, was an enemy of the church.

Looking at Cassie, I hostilely said, "You don't speak now? What
are you even doing here anyway?"

"I'm here to chaperone," she said and then I was shown the
policy that states there must be a witness on hand when a parishioner is going to be severely reprimanded. Okay, I was ready for it. It
was at this point that Julian started showing me more than a dozen
reports that my so-called "friends" had written up about me. I later
learned that as a result of my association with SPs like Debbie
Cook and Mike Rinder and my speaking out against David Miscavige and Tom Cruise, Julian had reached out to all of my closest
friends in the church and requested that they write Knowledge
Reports on me regarding any disaffection toward the church that I
might have expressed, or anything negative I might have said about
COB, or any mentions I had made about reaching out to SPs and
Squirrel groups. Squirrel groups are those who collectively practice
Scientology beliefs and techniques independently of the Church of
Scientology.

He showed me a few examples of the Knowledge Reports my
friends had written, including those from John and Val Futris. Their
reports pretty much just recapped what I had already said or expressed, including that after Tom and Katie's wedding I thought I
was "unjustly sec-checked and investigated," that I was talking to
John about Sea Org members being "held against their will" in the
"Hole," and that I was continually asking people where Shelly was.
Also that I had read Debbie Cook's New Year's Eve email. They went
on to reveal that I felt that too many people doing their OT levels
were "completely broke and in debt," and that I "disagreed" with all
of the money being spent on new buildings and design, as this was
"not what LRH would want," and instead suggested that it should be
spent "getting people up the Bridge and paying staff."

Michelle Workman, a friend of twenty years, wrote about what I had revealed to her in my meetings with COB. That I thought the denials coming from COB about his knowledge of what was going on was "bullshit," and that I "might have said" that Tom Cruise was an SP and "running the church."

"What's all this?" I fired back.

"You tell me," Julian said.

"What do you mean, me tell you? The fact that other people regurgitated my own story and wrote it in a report is meaningless. I reported it myself! Are you crazy?"

They might have been crazy, but I was stupid. Despite everything that had happened over the past weeks, I still didn't think I was leaving Scientology. Even while making a stink about subjects that most Scientologists wouldn't dare address; while confronting the church's leader, who was said to administer beatings; while personally declaring Tom Cruise, a pillar of the community, to be an SP; and while facing down Julian Swartz and the many reports of condemnation—I still naively hoped that someone would step up and prove me wrong. I prayed that this belief system I had submitted to for most of my and my family's life wasn't, at best, a waste of time and, at worst, evil.

Make it right. Please, make it right, I thought. *Get Shelly, who has now been missing for more than six years, on the phone for me. Do something.*

I was actually naive enough to believe that all my carrying on, all my "fuck you"s and threats would lead to resolution. That David Miscavige would say, "You were right!" That all my friends who wrote reports on me would apologize. Or at least that somebody would see the truth.

But of course that never happened.

All Julian—and the church—focused on at this point was for me and my family to do a sec-check, an interrogation by an Ethics Officer to make sure a person hasn't thought or acted in a hostile way toward the church. But I refused to bend. I wasn't going to submit to more scrutiny, more fines, and more punishment when I wasn't the one who did anything wrong.

"I'm not going to do it," I told Julian.

Instead, for four weeks, I went in every day, reading every policy Julian wanted me to read. He wanted to break me, to have me recant what I had said, to admit that I was wrong to have done any investigating on my own. But I refused to acknowledge this. He also wanted to know which other celebrity parishioners were disaffected, a term Scientologists use to describe someone who is no longer willing to support certain church initiatives. Again, I refused to tell him. Finally, he asked me who I considered my friends to be. When I refused to include David Miscavige's name in the few names I had given, he tried to insist that I include it. I told him what he was asking was off policy, as this was not my realization, but rather something they were trying to force upon me.

"COB is not my friend by the very actions he's taken against me. And why does he even care if I like him?" I said, calling his bluff.

"You should be able to produce policy on this and you can't," I went on. "So I can only surmise that you're taking your orders from COB, because I know you don't have the balls to talk to me that way unless you're being told to from above."

And speaking of friends, during this time, many of my friends in the church started calling me, crying, "I'm not going to disconnect from you. I know that your heart's in the right place," and then, little by little, after hearing from Julian, they would write me emails that read, "You have to get yourself handled."

I was devastated when my friend Michelle Workman told me that after speaking with Julian she believed that I was a liar.

"By calling me a liar, what you're about to do is destroy a thirty-five-year friendship," I responded. "Our children, who were born and raised together, will not know each other because you don't have the balls to stick up for what's right."

After I revealed to another longtime Scientology friend what I had found out from my investigating, she replied that she was on my side, claiming, "You were on the right side of the tech. I know you're not an SP."

"You're saying that now, but your whole family is in the church," I said. "I understand if you need to disconnect."

"There's no way I would ever do that," she said.

A few days later she called me hysterically crying.

"I was with Julian. . . ." she sobbed.

"You don't have to say another word," I said, sensing what was coming next. "I love you and understand why you're calling me. If circumstances change, I'm here." We both said I love you once more and hung up, knowing we would probably never speak again.

These types of exchanges became too heartbreaking for me. In response I blocked everybody in the church from writing, texting, or calling me. To be potentially branded a Suppressive Person by a whole group I dedicated my life to and have all its adherents turn their backs on me was incredibly sad, but not at all unique. It's something that happens to Scientologists every day. I wrote counterreports on all of them and told them not to contact me.

Julian continued to press me about doing a sec-check and I continued to refuse. Then he ordered sec-checks for my mother and George, which they agreed to. My mother didn't want to believe me about what was going on. That this was a witch hunt. "I'm telling you; it's all leading up to me," I said to her. "So if you want to submit yourself to a sec-check, Mom, you're going to be really fucking sad when you've realized that they just want intel on me. But go ahead and do it."

She did just that, and in the process, Julian pulled the wool over her eyes to get her to doubt me. He said that David Miscavige offered to get me onto OT VII in L.A. instead of Flag—which is unheard of. I mean, everyone spends huge sums of money and up to six months to get onto OT VII at Flag, and Julian was claiming that I would get to magically do it in L.A.? He also told her that I basically told him to go to hell. "Leah needs help. We need *you* to help her," Julian said to my mother. "She's connected up with some pretty heavy SPs. She's making mistakes. She's making bad decisions."

Anyone who has spent more than five minutes with my mother knows she can't keep a secret. Anything she is feeling shows immediately on her face. So as soon as Julian fed her that lie, she began acting weird. And anyone who knows me knows that I'm going to call you out on it the minute you are acting weird. "Mom, you're doing that thing. What's up?"

"What thing?" she said.

My mom's resistance didn't last long. She finally let it out. I told her immediately that this invitation to do OT VII in L.A. wasn't true, but I knew I had to prove it to her or she would always have doubts.

I wrote David Miscavige a letter right away, asking about his offer for me to do OT VII in L.A. and not in Florida, and I had the letter messengered to his office, where it was rejected. So I brought it to Julian directly and taunted him by saying, "David Miscavige's offer was so gracious. I misunderstood you. I'd love to get onto OT VII here in L.A. Let's do it." Julian just glared at me.

I showed my mom the letter I had written saying how I would be thrilled to do OT VII in L.A. and how it was rejected by David Miscavige's office and Julian didn't seem to have anything to say about the offer.

And if that wasn't proof enough, after my mother did her last sec-check, she said, "You were right. It was bullshit." Just like with my stepfather's sec-check, none of the questions were about her. They were all about me: what I knew; what they knew about me and Debbie Cook; what they knew about me and Mike Rinder. As I knew, it was all just to gain intel on me.

On top of all this, Julian had spread the word that my family and I were under investigation, which made us look horrible to everyone in the church. People averted their eyes when we walked by and refused to acknowledge us.

As a last effort to take us down, Julian threatened to take away all of my mom's certs (credits earned, thus she would have to throw away thirty-plus years of training and start at the bottom of the Bridge) and claimed that he had enough evidence of suppressive acts to get my stepfather, George, declared an SP.

I in turn responded with "I'm not going to have a church tell me who I can and cannot talk to. That day is done. Where does it stop? What if my mother was an SP? Should I disconnect from my mother? Do you think I'd disconnect from anyone after the way you and the church have treated me?"

His response was "I'm not telling you to disconnect. LRH is."

And with that, I decided I was done. I decided to sever ties with Scientology permanently.

I could have just let it go. I could have simply walked away, before being declared an SP. Then if I ever wanted to come back to the church, they would have me. But I didn't want to leave that door open. I knew if I filed a police report about Shelly Miscavige, I would be declared an SP and that would be the end. That was the step I had to take. So I called the LAPD and asked, "How do I officially file a missing person report?"

LOS ANGELES POLICE DEPARTMENT	☑ ADULT (DSVD/MPU)	☐ JUV. (INVESTIGATING DIV. _____)

☑ MISSING ☐ FOUND PERSONS INVESTIGATION	MISSING PERSON'S NAME (LAST, FIRST, MIDDLE)	DR NO.
*If missing, DR No. shall be obtained within 2 hours.	**Miscavige, Michele Diane**	

INC #

DESCRIPTION OF MISSING PERSON:	SEX	DESCENT	HAIR	EYES
	F	W	BRN	BRN

RESIDENCE ADDRESS (If unknown, general locale) — CITY **Los Angeles** — ZIP — RD — RESIDENCE PHONE

HEIGHT	WEIGHT	AGE	BUILD	COMPLEXION
503	100	52	Thin	Fair

DOB	DATE/TIME M.P. LEFT HOME (if unknown, approximate)	DATE/TIME OF FORMAL REPORT TO POLICE
01/18/1961	08/01/2006	08/05/2013 19:00

IDENTIFYING MARKS & CHARACTERISTICS (False Teeth, tattoos, visible dental work, etc.) **Very long hair**

LOCATION LAST SEEN (if applicable)	CITY	DATE/TIME LAST SEEN
Same as above		08/01/2007

POSSIBLE CAUSE OF ABSENCE (Despondent over debt, etc.)	PROBABLE OR POSSIBLE DESTINATION
Unknown	San Bernardino County

MENTAL CONDITION (Good, poor, etc. If poor, explain.)	REPORTED MISSING BEFORE (Even if no report taken)
Fearful, Distant	☑ NO ☐ YES DATE:

CLOTHING WORN ☐ GLASSES ☐ CONTACTS	LAST PRIOR ADDRESS OF MISSING PERSON	DOES THE M/P USE THE INTERNET? ☐ YES IF YES, EXPLAIN IN THE NARRATIVE. ☑ NO
Unknown		

ALIAS, MAIDEN NAME, OR ADDITIONAL SURNAME	NICKNAME	MARITAL STATUS
Barnett	Shelly	Married

JEWELRY, PAPERS AND OTHER ARTICLES CARRIED	BIRTHPLACE	FINGER PRINTED (When/Where)
Unknown	Dallas, Texas	Unknown

PERSONAL HABITS (Drinker, gambler, etc.)	WHERE FIRST HEARD FROM OR KNOWN TO HAVE GONE ON PRIOR OCCASION
Smoker	CST compound, San Bernardino County

REL RPTS #

BUSINESS ADDRESS OF MISSING PERSON	BUSINESS PHONE	OCCUPATION/UNION	SCHOOL (Name, City, State)	GRADE
None				

VEHICLE DRIVEN (if applicable) ☐ MP ☐ SUSP	YEAR	MAKE	MODEL/STYLE	COLOR	LICENSE NUMBER	STATE	LIC. YEAR	VIN #

OFFICERS SHALL QUERY THE MASTER INQUIRY FUNCTION OF NECS

SOURCES CHECKED: Include Name/Serial No.	☑ MI CHECKED	☑ MISSING PERSONS (ADULTS ONLY) (213) 996-1800 Guevara 26210	☑ MENTAL EVALUATION (213) 996-1300 Fernandez 27770	☑ LOCAL HOSPITAL(S) CHECKED	☑ CORONER - (323) 343-0714 Natalie

IF JUVENILE, ALSO CHECK: Include Name/Serial No.	☐ PROBATION INTAKE DETENTION CONTROL (323) 226-8516	☐ AREA JUVENILE DETECTIVES (if available)	☐ DCFS (800) 540-4000 Option 4

CODE: R - PERSON REPORTING ABSENCE   L - PERSON LAST SEEING MISSING PERSON   P - PARENTS OR GUARDIAN (Juvenile only)   F - FRIENDS/RELATIVES   S - SUSPECT (DOB)

CII #

NAME	DOB	CODE	RESIDENCE ADDRESS	CITY	ZIP	RES. PHONE	X	BUS. PHONE	X
Remini, Leah	06/15/1970	R					☐		☑
							☐		☐
							☐		☐

DENTIST NAME	ADDRESS	PHONE
Robert Horn	Unknown	

KNOWN ASSOCIATES	IF OUTSIDE AGENCY INVESTIGATING, FAX NO.		
	DATE FAXED	OFFICER NOTIFIED	SERIAL NO.

AGENCY OF RESIDENCE	EMPLOYEE NOTIFIED NAME #	☐ YES ☐ NO	AGENCY LAST SEEN	EMPLOYEE NOTIFIED NAME #	☐ YES ☐ NO

SS #

SUPERVISOR APPROVING RPT.	SERIAL NO.	INTERVIEWING OFCR(S)	SERIAL NO.	AREA/DIV.	DETAIL	PERSON REPORTING DISAPPEARANCE (Signature)	RELATIONSHIP
J. Hays	22768	K. Becker	25941	HWD	6W70	X	Friend

DATE/TIME REPRODUCED	DIVISION CLERK	☐ PHOTO X-RAY WAIVER RELEASE (DOJ SS8567 or BCIA - 4048) PROVIDED BY OFFICERS COMPLETE NARRATIVE ON PAGE 2	BDCST/TTY NO.	DATE	NCIC NO.

☐ FOLLOW-UP REPORT	TO BE COMPLETED BY DETECTIVE	FCN NO.

CLEARED:	UNFOUNDED ☐	ARREST ☐	OTHER ☐	DATE	REPORTING OFFICER	SERIAL NO.	DIV.	DISPOSITION

COMMENTS (For Investigating Detective Only)

CAL OP/ID #

FCN/MUPS CLEARED? ☐ YES ☐ NO   VEHICLE CLEARED? ☐ YES ☐ NO   (ATTACH PRINT OUT)   DETECTIVE CASE TRACKING CLEARED? ☐ YES ☐ NO

CANCELLATION BDCST. 4, 5, 6 BY: TT R&I ADV'D BY:	DATE	IF MISSING MORE THAN 30 DAYS	☐ 03.15.00 SENT TO DOJ BY DATE	☐ PHOTO ☐ DNA	☐ DENTAL RECORDS SENT TO DOJ	☐ DENTAL RECORDS NOT OBTAINED

INVESTIGATING OFFICER	SERIAL NO.	ADULT PRESENT AT INTERVIEW	DET. SUPERVISOR APPROVING	DATE/TIME REPRODUCED	DIVISION CLERK

03.15.00 (08/10)   **MISSING/FOUND PERSONS INVESTIGATION**   INT. CASE NO.

| PAGE NO. **2** | | TO BE COMPLETED BY DETECTIVE | | | |

| TYPE MP:
(CHECK **ONE**) | ☐ RUNAWAY JUVENILE
☐ PARENTAL/FAMILY ABDUCTION | ☐ NON-FAMILY ABDUCTION
☐ STRANGER ABDUCTION | ☐ VOLUNTARY MISSING ADULT
☐ DEPENDENT ADULT | ☑ UNKNOWN CIRCUMSTANCES
☐ CATASTROPHE ☐ LOST |

| CATEGORY: | ☐ AT RISK | ☐ PRIOR MISSING | ☐ SEXUAL EXPLOITATION SUSPECTED |

PHOTO AVAILABLE: ☐ YES ☐ NO	DNA AVAILABLE: ☐ YES ☐ NO	PHOTO/X-RAY WAIVER RELEASE (DOJ FORM SS8567) SIGNED? ☐ YES ☐ NO
(AGE IN PHOTO) PHOTO SENT TO DOJ? ☐ YES ☐ NO		SAMPLE OR PARENTAL APPROVAL: ☐ YES ☐ NO

| SKELETAL X-RAYS AVAILABLE: ☐ YES ☐ NO | BROKEN BONES/
MISSING ORGANS: | DENTAL X-RAYS AVAILABLE:
(ATTACH CHART AND X-RAYS) ☐ YES ☐ NO | DENTURES: ☐ UPPER ☐ FULL
☐ LOWER ☐ PARTIAL |

ABDUCTION INVOLVING MOVEMENT OF MISSING PERSON IN THE COMMISSION OF A CRIME: ☐ YES ☐ NO	SUSPECT NAME	DOB
	RESIDENCE	RESIDENCE PHONE BUSINESS PHONE
	RELATIONSHIP TO VICTIM	WARRANT #

IF JUVENILE, WRITTEN NOTIFICATION AND PHOTO SENT TO MISSING PERSON'S SCHOOL WITHIN 10 DAYS OF REPORTED DISAPPEARANCE, IF JUVENILE IS STILL MISSING (LAPD Form 09.29.00).

☐ _____   _____

NAME   SERIAL NO.

NARRATIVE - RECONSTRUCT THE CIRCUMSTANCES SURROUNDING THE DISAPPEARANCE:

CONTINUATION SHEET

Los Angeles Police Department

PAGE NO. 3	TYPE OF REPORT		Missing			BOOKING NO.		DR NO. 1306
ITEM NO.	QU AN	ARTICLE	SERIAL NO	BRAND	MODEL NO.	MISC DESCRIPTION (EG. COLOR, SIZE, INSCRIPTIONS, CALIBER, REVOLVER, ETC)		DOLLAR VALUE

Missing Person (MP): Michele "Shelly" Miscavige

Person Reporting (PR): Leah Remini

Background: MP is married to Church of Scientology leader, David Miscavige. PR is a well-known celebrity and until recently, a 30-year member of the Church. MP is the subject of ongoing news reports due to her sudden and unexplained disappearance several years ago.

On 8/5/13, the PR reported that she has been a long-time personal friend of the MP, who has not been seen nor heard from in public, to her knowledge, since August of 2007 when the MP attended a funeral in Las Vegas. The PR last saw and had personal contact with the MP in August of 2006 while attending a large yearly event at the Church of Scientology's Celebrity Center, located at 5930 Franklin Avenue in Hollywood, which is also the last known residence for the MP. The PR stated that she and the MP have exchanged cards, phone calls and gifts numerous times each year, since 2004, especially on special occasions and it is totally out of character for the MP not to contact or communicate with her.

PR stated that while helping the MP get ready for the event in 2006, the MP seemed happy, talkative and behaved normally until her husband would appear, causing the MP to become nervous, fearful, withdrawn and timid. PR recalled attending an event in 2005 with the MP during which the MP seemed fine until her husband would come near and then the MP would become fearful and quiet. It was obvious to the PR that the MP was in fear of her husband but refused to talk about it.

In November of 2006, the PR attended the wedding of celebrity Tom Cruise in Italy and noticed that the MP was not in attendance. The PR asked the MP's husband where she was and was immediately chastised for asking. The PR was shocked and alarmed by the angry reaction to her inquiry about the absence of her friend and asked another member of the Church why the MP was not at the wedding and again she was warned not to ask any questions about the MP. Shortly after returning to the United States, the PR was sent to a Church location in Florida and subjected to intense "thought-modification" counseling by Church members for having questioned why the MP was not at the wedding.

The PR said that as a long-time member of the Church, it is well known that members become "controlled" by the Church and are conditioned to believe that they cannot leave the Church once they have joined nor can they communicate or talk about Church dealings or workings with outsiders. If members disobey or run afoul of the Church rules, teachings, or question authority, they are separated from their friends and family and made to do menial hard labor. In essence, the members are "brain-washed" and begin to believe that they must obey and follow the Church leaders and they become distrustful of outsiders and refrain from speaking against their treatment by the Church out of fear of recrimination by Church leaders.

The PR believes, as do other ex-members of the Church, that the MP is being secreted against her will and not allowed to communicate with anyone on orders by her husband. Given the PR's intimate knowledge of the Church and their harsh response to any criticism, the PR is in fear for the MP's safety. The PR provided contact information for other ex-members who can verify these concerns: Mark and Claire Headley can be reached at ▓▓▓▓▓▓▓▓▓

Recent rumors report the MP is being held at a Church location in the community of Running Springs in San Bernardino County called CST.

Chapter Seventeen

THE CHURCH OF SCIENTOLOGY IS KNOWN NOT ONLY TO PAY big money to off-duty LAPD officers who work as security at the Celebrity Centre and its other locations, it also employs a practice known as "safe pointing," meaning inviting members of various police and sheriff's departments that surround its churches to speak at events, presenting them with awards, or donating money to their charities. So you never quite know who is in tight with the church.

I met Detective Kevin Becker when he worked security on the set of *The King of Queens,* and we became fast friends. When I had brought Kevin to a Celebrity Centre event as my date about a decade earlier, he was already familiar with the building's security systems. His precinct was located nearby and one time when they were trying to find surveillance footage of the surrounding area for a recent crime that had been committed, they came to the church and asked to see their video feed. "They have a better surveillance system than the police department does," Kevin remarked.

When I decided I wanted to file a missing person report for Shelly, thus officially severing my ties with the church, I asked Kevin to help me, but I was concerned that it might put him in a bad position with the LAPD. If he took the report, he would be labeled an SP and therefore might not be able to cover church events for the force or work there in an off-duty capacity.

Fully aware of the risk he was taking, Kevin stood by me all the way. No questions asked. He came to my house to take down the information for the missing person report (knowing that if I had gone into the police department, there might have been a person there who would alert the church). I explained to Kevin where I thought Shelly had been held for all of these years, but of course I couldn't confirm it. I also asked that if they did find Shelly in Hemet, California, at Gold (where she was rumored to be), they try to pull her away from her handlers and give her a letter from me. Then I gave Kevin my letter.

August 5, 2013

Dear Shelly,

It is NOT normal for you to be so out of communication. It is NOT normal for you to not be with your husband at the wedding. For years, I have been trying to get confirmation that you were okay. I was met with such resistance that it has caused me enough concern to go to extreme measures to make sure you were in fact, OK. My letters were not sent to you and I was told that I "did not have the fucking rank to ask about Shelly."

That is not human.

Shelly, this is not right. I don't care what you think you are doing; this is NOT LRH. And you need to do something about it. You need to go with this gentleman now. I will take care of you, I will give you a home and the protection you need. From there, you can do what you need to do, but you need to leave right now. Do not worry about clothes, money, lawyers and what this will do; this will all get worked out later.

All you need to say to this person who has come to get you is, "I want to leave with you now."

If you don't do it now, you probably won't have another

chance to get out. So I beg you to take this step, for you. It is the right thing to do.

Leah

Kevin went directly to the head of his division, Deputy Chief Beatrice Girmala, and asked if he could handle my missing person report himself. But his boss ordered him to send the report on Shelly over to LAPD's Missing Persons Unit. Despite Kevin's protests, Chief Girmala, who didn't want to make waves, wouldn't budge on her original decision.

After a few days, Kevin called over to Missing Persons to check on the status of the report. That's when a detective told him that someone from the unit had spoken to the church's lawyer, who said Shelly was fine and didn't want to be found. Kevin asked the detective if anyone had spoken directly to Shelly. "No," the detective answered. "We spoke to the attorney." Then she cut the conversation short and said she couldn't answer any more of his questions. "We're done here," she said.

The LAPD didn't find Shelly, but it did release a statement on August 8, 2013, that the case was closed and my report had been "unfounded," which the Church of Scientology used to discredit the reason for my report in the first place. I called Lieutenant Andre Dawson, who oversaw the "investigation" as the person in charge of the Detective Support and Vice Division, which encompasses Missing Persons.

"Hi, Lieutenant. I was wondering why you guys did nothing about this case but still took the time to say that my report was unfounded."

"I am sorry, but I can't discuss it with you," he said.

"You can't discuss the friggin' report *I* filed?"

"We looked into it and she doesn't want to be found."

"Did you see her with your eyes? Did anyone see her? Did you pull her aside and give her my note when you were alone like I asked?

I mean, I told you the only way to do this was to get to her first, pull her aside, and give her my note. Did you do that?"

"Ma'am, I am sorry, but the case is closed and I can't disclose any information to you."

And there you have it. Case closed.

Later on, a friend of Shelly's explained to me that on numerous occasions Shelly told her that she believed that when you get to the top of Scientology, you forgo your right to escape. Her friend was convinced that Shelly truly believed this. That same friend had seen several high-up people try to leave, only to be tracked down and brought back to the church. She thought that even if someone reached Shelly, she would not want to leave. Typical for this situation, she likely had been indoctrinated since early childhood to believe that whatever circumstances she finds herself in are her doing. That she is responsible for being sent away to live in isolation from her family for years, and that only when she has resolved her own transgressions will all be well.

All the people that I had considered my extended family—like John Futris, Susan Watson, and so many more—turned their backs on me. Even those who at first said they would stand by me eventually disconnected. Stacy Francis, the woman whom I had introduced to Scientology and taken into my home when she needed a place to stay, whose daughter I witnessed being born and was Godmother to, wrote me around the time of my problems with the church: "You have been the only family I have ever known and I don't give a fuck what these motherfuckers have to tell me."

But I never heard from Stacy again.

A couple of years back, when I turned forty, I had a big birthday party that all my good friends from the church came to, people I had known since I was a teenager. Each person gave me a letter to commemorate the milestone. When I looked back over the thirty-five letters I received on that birthday I realized that I had lost every single Scientology friend who had written me a letter.

As much as I tried to shield Sofia from what was happening to me, one day she saw me crying. "Mommy, I know you're done with psychology"—ironically she confused the word "Scientology" with "psychology"—"in here," she said, pointing to my head. "But you have to be over psychology in here." And then she touched my heart with her finger.

I couldn't have loved my daughter more in that moment. How she knew what she was saying, I have no idea, but her words were wise way beyond her years.

While my so-called "friends" had turned on me, my family, amazingly, showed me nothing but support. Whatever I had felt I might have lacked in a "traditional" family during my upbringing, my ideas profoundly changed when the chips were down and my immediate family had to make a decision between the church and me.

There was no discussion. It was not something they had to consider—they simply chose me. To some people that may sound like a no-brainer, but where this particular church is concerned, it was in no way the norm. A simple search on the Internet will reveal the thousands of stories of disconnection, where mothers, fathers, children, husbands, wives, and more have been torn apart because they were convinced they had to choose the church over their families, that their "eternity" was at stake if they failed to do so.

So for me, knowing that my family was willing to "lose it all," including their eternity, and everything they had dedicated themselves to for more than thirty years, by choosing family instead, was enough for me to feel overwhelmingly grateful and loved.

My husband, whom I sheltered from many of the truths of what I believed to be the real practices of Scientology, had to deal with most of the fallout from my decision. For months after leaving the church, every day and every night I unburdened myself to him, revealing more than thirty years worth of complaints and heartbreak. He, like my family, put aside his own concerns to take care of me. While I doubted many decisions in my life, it was in these moments with Angelo that I realized I, in fact, had made one really good one. He is my Prince Charming.

My team that keeps me going (nanny, assistant, housekeeper, makeup artist, handyman) are not Scientologists. Some would consider them just employees, but to me they are everything. They too had to deal with the repercussions of my choice to publicly leave the church. But rather than hold this decision against me, they stood alongside me, always concerned with how I was doing and if I was okay. Everyone lost something in this fallout. My assistant Raffy, who was recommended to me by a former assistant and a Scientologist, was disconnected from half of his family because he refused to abandon me after I was declared a Suppressive Person by the church. This group supported me and were protective, loving, and caring, not only to me, but to my whole family. Without them I don't think we would have made it out as well as we did.

So while my team and my immediate family supported me, there were, however, some other family members who did disconnect from me. I had no good answers for Sofia, who at nine years old asked me: "Mommy, why doesn't Auntie Catherine talk to me anymore?" Shannon, my sister, and her husband, William, were constantly giving money to his sister Catherine, who was broke and without a job. One night they even drove to Portland, where Catherine lived, to get a dog she could no longer care for and bring it back home with them. This was a woman who when she got pregnant didn't have food or blankets for her bed. I called her father, a Scientologist on the upper levels, to tell him the situation his daughter was in, and he didn't care. "She got herself pregnant," he said. To me that's not how family acts, but our being there for Catherine in her time of need meant nothing now that we were all SPs.

"She can't talk to us because we left the church," I told Sofia.

"I don't understand that," she said.

"And you're exactly right not to. You shouldn't understand it, because it doesn't make sense, and it's not okay."

That sums up my problem with Scientology—despite its claims to the contrary, the practice doesn't help you better the world or even yourself; it only helps you be a better Scientologist. "Scientology works 100 percent of the time when it is properly applied to a person who sincerely desires to improve his life," the church states. "As Scientologists in all walks of life will attest, they have enjoyed greater success in their relationships, family life, jobs and professions." Well, it didn't work for me or anyone I knew. All those years of applying LRH didn't make me any less flawed, hurt, aggressive, or insecure. And that was only the emotional part. The economics of Scientology often seemed to come at the expense of its parishioners.

Once when the church wanted me to donate a million dollars, my business manager, who was a Scientologist, advised me against it because he didn't think I had the money. Trying to put a stop to the donation was not looked at kindly. He was immediately pulled into a sec-check by church officials and quit working for me. He appeared to be punished for simply doing his job.

Most Scientologists are in the church because their hearts are in the right place and they really believe they're helping the planet. That was certainly the case with Tom Cruise's longtime assistant when she decided after more than a decade of working with the star that she wanted to move on to spend more time with her husband and newborn child. Who knows whether Tom complained about her leaving or the church decided on its own to put her through the wringer. Someone decided that she had done something wrong, and she had to undergo a sec-check that she says cost her so much that she lost her house. Instead of viewing this process surrounding her leaving her job as cruel injustice, she felt a huge sense of accomplishment when she finished her sec-check. She took pride in the fact that she left Tom in good standing with the church.

I was once a big fan of Tom's—before I got to know him. I'm sure many people could say the same thing about me or any other celebrity. But this is different; most actors are not in charge of your faith.

I don't doubt that Tom is in Scientology because he believes in it, but to me he has simply been given too much power by his church.

My disaffection wasn't a result of Tom receiving preferential treatment, it was a response to what I saw as church rules being broken for him and, as a result, families were torn apart, and people's lives were altered forever.

Tom didn't just use his position within the church to hold sway with parishioners who worked for him, he also flexed his muscle with fellow Scientology celebrities. One former Sea Org member, Marc Headley, told me about an encounter with David Miscavige in which David had been thrilled that Tom was urging other Scientology celebrities to become more active in the field and use their celebrity to disseminate Scientology in the press. Tom had even called a meeting essentially preaching Scientology to his fellow Scientology celebrities, reading LRH policies to them and even suggesting that it would not be good for their careers in Hollywood if they did not start actively promoting Scientology. Marc recalls that David specifically told him that he did not ask Tom to make this strong push. He did it on his own. He did not ask permission. He just did it. Dave told him that if he could, he would make Tom Cruise the number two in Scientology. He said that Tom Cruise was a more dedicated Scientologist than anyone else he knew.

There was seemingly nothing the church wouldn't do to keep its most dedicated Scientologist happy. They were even said to be involved in finding him a girlfriend. The unlucky girl chosen after Tom Cruise broke up with Penelope Cruz was Nazanin Boniadi. Naz, as her friends call her, was a beautiful dark-haired actress. She was warm, approachable, and smart. She was also a college graduate, which was unusual for a Scientologist. She had just graduated from the University of California, Irvine, in 2003, with Honors in Biological Sciences, and was about to apply to medical school.

Her mom had joined Scientology when Naz was seventeen, and Naz had quickly moved up the Bridge herself. We first met in 2003. We were both working on our OT levels when we became friends. We would find time to talk before courses or during breaks. Then, in late 2004, she disappeared. I wondered if Naz had gone back to her "real life."

Years later, I found out what had happened to Naz during this time. She underwent a confidential mission for the church where she thought she was being prepared for a special humanitarian project, but ended up with the role of Tom's girlfriend.

The man assigned to preparing Naz for this mission was Greg Wilhere, a senior Sea Org executive (Inspector General RTC) and David Miscavige's right-hand man. His efforts should have been focused more on furthering the aims and goals of Scientology; instead, it seemed his expertise was used for prepping people for the real-life Mission Impossible: putting up with Tom Cruise and David Miscavige.

To get Naz ready for Tom, he needed to get rid of her current boyfriend. He tried to convince her that her boyfriend was only a distraction to her mission in the church. "No," Naz said, "I love my boyfriend; he is my best friend and I won't do that." The next angle Greg tried was telling Naz that her boyfriend was "not qualified to associate with the dignitaries and world leaders Naz would be meeting on the mission," implying that he was committing transgressions against Scientology and wasn't a good person. Naz still refused. Unable to convince Naz, Greg showed Naz parts of her boyfriend's confidential confessional folders in which he admitted to several transgressions against Naz. Still not convinced, Naz confronted her boyfriend without revealing her source. When he admitted to the transgressions against her, she broke up with him.

Once Naz was available, the church did its homework on her, including background checks, culling her personal and confidential PC and ethics folders with a fine-tooth comb, countless sec-checks, and an extensive study program that included reading the policy "The Responsibility of Leaders"—Scientology's indoctrination on how one should act with and around those in a position of power and influence. This screening process also covered physical appearance and included on-camera interviews and photo shoots at the Celebrity Centre in Los Angeles.

After some time, Naz was "approved" to meet Tom. The next step required that her physical appearance met *his* standards. Her orthodontic braces were removed, her hair color was darkened, and Greg took her on a very expensive shopping spree in Beverly Hills to buy a new wardrobe for her mysterious meetings with "dignitaries."

Naz was flown first class to New York for the first step in her secret mission. On the flight Greg randomly asked Naz, "What would your ideal date be like?" Naz wasn't in the mood to think about dating as she'd just ended a five-year relationship and was heartbroken, but after some thought, she said, "Well, I love ice skating and sushi," oblivious to the intent behind Greg's question.

Their first stop for the mission was the New York Org where Naz was to get a special tour and briefing by Greg. Tommy Davis and Tom Cruise happened to walk by. Greg introduced Tom and Naz and then Tommy asked if Greg and Naz would like to accompany them to the Empire State Building (which was closed to the public at that time), followed by sushi at Nobu and then ice skating at the Rockefeller Center ice skating rink (also closed to the public when they got there). And although in that moment she realized that it all could not have been coincidence, who could say no to Tom Cruise? He was not only handsome and hugely successful, he was also revered among Scientologists, and he had chosen her. She overlooked the way in which the church got her there and felt like she had won some kind of lottery. After the wooing process, Naz was in love. (The church was quick to deny that there had been any special project or that any of her boyfriend's auditing materials were shared.)

But her joy was short lived. She dated and lived with Tom for three months. The church appeared to be involved in all aspects of the relationship. She was chaperoned by Tommy and Jessica constantly, who asked Naz to report anything "non-optimum" she observed in Tom so they could help him. "Do you think he is happy?" they would ask her, and Jessica even offered unsolicited advice such as "Why don't you be more aggressive with Tom and just put your hands down his pants when you see him?" Naz quickly discovered that her "mission" was to make Tom happy, even at the expense of her own happiness.

Three months into Naz and Tom's relationship, Jessica was summoned to a closed-door meeting with Tom. Right after the meeting Jessica told Naz to pack a few things and go with her to Celebrity Centre, where Naz was going to be staying for just a few days. She wasn't allowed to talk to Tom, who was said to be "busy" after his meeting with Jessica and was not to be approached. Jessica showed Naz a few policies from the PTS/SP (Potential Trouble Source/Suppressive Person) course and told Naz that she had become a "robot" and that because of this, Naz needed to sign up for the PTS/SP course immediately and not to contact Tom Cruise, because he was busy and didn't need his girlfriend.

"You've lost that certainty you had when we first met you," Jessica told her.

"That is what happens when you are separated and isolated from everyone you know and love and told what to do in every aspect of your life," Naz said. "If I am a robot, it is because you turned me into one."

Next came a meeting with Tommy Davis. Tommy said, "So, how do you think it's going with Tom?"

Naz replied, "Not good?"

Tommy agreed, "Yup, not good."

Naz wanted answers as to why her boyfriend wasn't doing his own breaking up and asked to talk to Tom directly, to no avail.

Naz then went back to Greg and told him she was aware that this had all been a setup and he had misled her from the start. He responded, "Of course, how else is he going to meet someone qualified? At a club? Look, I can lead a horse to water, but I can't make it drink."

Not surprisingly, Tom, through his lawyers, has denied all of this—the church never helped find him a girlfriend, Naz never moved in with him.

Almost as some sort of consolation prize, Naz was sent to Flag to get onto OT VII and was put up in a suite. Even though this stay was all expenses paid, it did nothing to remove the hurt she felt.

Devastated by her experience, Naz confided in a friend who seemed to want to help her. The friend then immediately wrote up a nine-page report on Naz.

Tommy told Naz that he briefed Tom and told him that Naz was being handled. She was then quickly demoted to living in a cheaper motel, away from Cruise's environment, and subjected to doing four months of menial labor, including tasks such as digging ditches and cleaning public toilets with a toothbrush. Eventually she was promoted to selling *Dianetics* books on the streets of Tampa. Better, but still humiliating. All the while she was being deprogrammed with security checks and the PTS/SP course. She wasn't allowed to talk to anyone, particularly her Scientology friends, since she was considered a traitor. She was not allowed to go anywhere alone unless escorted by either church security, ethics staff, or a representative of Flag's President's Office.

And if you ask the church, they will deny that these practices exist or that people are punished at all.

One day, while being escorted to do amends, Naz saw a friend and fellow actress, Marisol Nichols. Naz smiled and said hello, but Marisol turned her back to Naz and walked off. Naz asked her escort why she would do something like that, and the woman's response was "Why wouldn't she? You just got done scrubbing toilets. What makes you think you have anything to talk about with a successful Scientologist like that? You have nothing in common."

Naz had started to believe that perhaps she was as evil as they were suggesting. After all, this was her religion and they were telling her she had committed the ultimate sin of betraying Tom. Naz found her faith being tested because she couldn't reconcile any of these practices her church had appeared to be behind.

But she mainly complied because her mother was still a Scientologist at the time and would have been forced to disconnect if she didn't remain in good standing with the church. Naz's mom, like many Scientologists, said to her daughter, "Naz, please just do what they ask and get through your punishment."

Naz's house, as well as her mother's house, were visited by church officials and anything Tom had ever given her—pictures of the two of them together, gifts given to her by Bella and Connor, anything of their lives together—was removed.

Months later, Tom was engaged to Katie Holmes. That's when Naz and her mother left Scientology, and everyone they knew from it, behind.

I certainly felt sorry for Naz, who reached out to me after I was declared an SP, because she also had left the church. But I was afraid that she was actually a double agent (she had never publicly spoken out against Scientology), so I would meet in person only if it was in a public place—more specifically, the restaurant where I was having dinner with my *Dancing with the Stars* partner, Tony Dovolani, and our respective families. In the fall of 2013, I was one of the celebrity contestants on the ABC dance competition show. Since I had just left Scientology, it was a very emotional time for me, and sometimes I seemed to break down for no reason at all. Without asking too many questions about my story, Tony, who remains a good friend, immediately started to defend me, which got him and Cheryl Burke (another friend) un-followed and un-friended by Kirstie Alley, who actually tried to convince the *DWTS* producers not to have me on the show when she heard I was going to be a contestant.

I hadn't seen Naz since she fell out with Tom, but in the lounge of a Beverly Hills hotel, with my family and Tony's surrounding us, she fell into my arms and wept. It didn't matter that we were in public, she had finally found someone who was sympathetic to what she had been through and who *understood*. I held her, because I, unlike most people, understood her pain and what they had put her through. To explain it to someone outside the church would take months, and if you were to explain it to someone inside the church they probably wouldn't care, wouldn't want to hear about it, and would most likely write you up in a Knowledge Report for even discussing it.

Naz had been manipulated and lied to, all in an effort to keep

Tom Cruise happy. Who knows whether Tom was aware of all that was done to her, but for him to have dismissed her without saying goodbye or speaking directly to her seemed beyond cruel.

"I know, baby. It wasn't you," I kept saying to her while she cried. "What you were put through was evil."

Like me, Naz just wanted assurance that she wasn't crazy and that she wasn't evil.

Every Scientologist personally takes on so much. If it isn't trying to figure out what transgression you've committed, it's going from course to course and auditing until collectively, you're in it for half a million, easy. And for most—those who aren't celebrities, executives, or people who come from wealth—this is money they don't have.

It's all so upside down. Even if you want to give back to the greater world in some way, Scientology provides the venue. It's an all-inclusive religion. "Oh, you want to be a humanitarian? We have just the program for you." But it's always in the church. Always. You are discouraged from giving money to the Red Cross when disaster hits; instead, give it to the church to help disaster victims.

The result is you get to feel like a better person without ever needing to dirty yourself with the outside world. You are under the impression that you and Scientology are doing amazing things for the outside world and for humanity when all you're actually doing is forwarding the church's agenda. Because parishioners are discouraged from checking the facts (online and elsewhere) of what is actually being done and who is actually being helped, you buy into it completely. Even as your own life falls apart before your eyes, you don't notice because you are too busy receiving all these awards and certificates from your church that say you are moving up. It's a satisfaction you don't get in the real world, where doing good things doesn't immediately, or even necessarily, translate into recognition.

Once I realized that about Scientology, I could no longer stay in it. And I never looked back. The big mistake I made, however, was in trying to change the system instead of just changing myself.

I didn't need to fight the machine, make it wrong in order to prove myself right. If Scientologists are happy in the church, I say God bless. Honestly, it's probably better for them to keep getting jerked off in the church, because they will never experience that kind of validation in the real world. Once outside the church, they would be devastated, as my family and I had been, to find out that what they had dedicated their lives (and money) to was not happening. That Scientology was in fact not clearing the planet.

IN TRUTH, I AM LUCKY. Unlike many others whose families disown them after they leave the church, my family chose to leave with me. Despite the fact that the church did everything in its power to break us apart. As much as I'd like to say my family's leaving Scientology was out of pure love for and solidarity with me, it wasn't *just* that. They were disillusioned with the church as well.

My mother had been on OT VII for twenty-five years, meaning that she was required to audit herself six times a day, seven days a week, 365 days a year. Additionally, my mother was asked to do more and more sec-checks, auditing, and trips to Flag (all of which, of course, cost more and more money), and finally she began to lose faith. Even someone like my mother, a woman who devoted her entire life and her family's lives to Scientology, had the nagging feeling that she was going around in circles. But she had come so far (and spent so much money), to give up at that point would have been really depressing. "I just want to get through it," she used to say. "I've been doing it this long; I just want to get through it."

After my mom achieved OT VIII, the highest level on the auditing side of the Bridge and became a class VI auditor, the highest-classed auditor that she could become as a parishioner, she admitted it wasn't everything she'd thought it was going to be. All those missed birthdays, vacations, and anniversaries, only to find out that Scientology's secret to the universe hadn't been worth it for her. She couldn't move objects with her mind or cure cancer by the force of her will. She was still just herself. So after I proved to her that everything I was saying about the church's leadership was true—that they don't apply policy and will do anything, including lie to the parishioners who pay their bills, to get their way—she was really done.

I too was done, but as Sofia said, it takes longer to be done inside. You can take the girl out of Scientology, but it's much, much harder to take the Scientology out of the girl.

Chapter Eighteen

~≈~

S O WHILE THOSE IN THE CHURCH KNEW I HAD LEFT SCIEN-
tology, those outside the church found out courtesy of the
front page of the *New York Post*. It was picked up by hundreds of news outlets around the world. The headline read:

EXCLUSIVE: ACTRESS LEAH REMINI QUITS SCIENTOLOGY
AFTER YEARS OF "INTERROGATIONS"

As a response, in a statement to *The Hollywood Reporter*, I said, "I
wish to share my sincere and heartfelt appreciation for the overwhelming positive response I have received from the media, my col-
leagues and fans from around the world. I am truly grateful and
thankful for all your support."

And with that, it was confirmed that I had, indeed, left.

Everywhere I looked I now realized that my world was *not* being
helped by Scientology. Previously I had blinders on. Because I had
to. If I didn't, I would have had to make a decision that would affect
not just me, but also my entire family.

Unlike most people who grew up in the church, I always maintained friendships outside of the church. I guess in a way I was always disaffected. My Scientology friends didn't really have non-Scientology friends. And if it appeared that they did, it was merely to eventually, over time, recruit them into the church.

It was a good thing that I insisted on keeping friends outside the church, because once they found out I had left, they immediately reached out with their support and kindness.

Kevin James called me and said, "How's your family? Are you guys all intact?" He said he was proud of me, that we were brave, and told me whatever I needed he was there.

Chelsea Handler texted me from out of the country when she heard the news. "Hey Twat, be home in a few days, hope you are okay and if you are not, let me know what you need and I will be there."

Michelle Visage, a friend I had met and grown close to during my *King of Queens* days, called me right away: "Are you home, I am coming over." And she did. Michelle also publicly came to my defense, which is a lot, knowing how the church deals with anyone defending someone who attacks Scientology.

My longtime friend Lucille from Brooklyn was crying when I picked up her phone call. She said, "Lee, do you have your family with you? I just need to know they left the church with you."

"Yes, Lu, they are with me," I said, consoling her.

My ex-boyfriend's mother texted me: "Lee, I loved you before, but I don't think I ever respected you and your family more than today."

I had a community of people supporting me and my family on social media, in the press, in emails—small gestures that meant everything. But my publicist instructed me not to talk to the media because she didn't want me to be known as "the person who left the church." But I also didn't want to be known as "the person who said 'no comment.'" I was definitely caught between being the girl who speaks out and the girl who just wants to work and be known for that work.

I did a few interviews where I tried to explain my position while not going into too much detail. But anything I said was blown out of proportion to make a headline. The church's dismissals and bullying of those who had left before me and spoken out made it harder and harder to remain silent. I called my publicist daily to ask, "Please, can I tell the media the truth and have the church challenge and debate me, instead of defenseless people?"

"Of course you could," my publicist always responded. "But why?"

The *why* was—somebody needs to stand up for those who can't. But I understood what my rep was saying; I was still angry, confused, and experiencing myriad emotions I couldn't make sense of. I didn't yet know how to tell my story from a place of strength as opposed to one of just pain and anger.

Certainly, I couldn't do that on a five-minute segment on *Ellen*. But while I was promoting the seventeenth season of *Dancing with the Stars,* which I competed in right after I left the church, that's all people wanted to talk to me about. Instead of fighting it, I chose to deal with it in a way that sent a message but wasn't too in-your-face.

In the first week of the ABC show, during a filmed rehearsal with my partner, Tony Dovolani, I made the following statement, which was picked up by various media outlets all over the world. "I'm going through a personal and big change for me and my family," I said. "The church is looking for me to fail so they can say to their parishioners, 'See what happens when you leave the church?' They're waiting for me to fail."

In response to my comment, the church issued its own to *Good Morning America*: "We know this may come as a surprise to someone as self-absorbed as Ms. Remini, but we could care less if she wins or loses on *Dancing with the Stars*."

That was the on-air drama. There was so much more going on, however, off camera, including Tony being surveilled and followed by a car for two weeks. Maksim Chmerkovskiy, Kirstie's dance partner and friend from when she was on the show, was given the cold shoulder by Kirstie when she found out he had been at my house. Maks didn't take it too hard. "I'm Jewish," Maks said. "I don't really believe in science fiction, but whatever. It's sad that we've gone through so much together, and I feel like I've helped her. And this is where we're at now. But I think the world of her, and I wish her the best."

Kirstie also went on *The Howard Stern Show,* where she said that I "was very critical" after leaving Scientology. Then she made a completely disingenuous comment: "There's nothing going on, and there was nothing going on for years," she said. "I didn't shun her, but if a lot of people are rejecting you, at some point you gotta ask, 'What am I doing?' I mean, that's what I would have asked myself."

When actor and former Scientologist Jason Beghe, whom I had met and befriended in acting class, was asked in an interview if he thought Scientology wanted me to fail, he responded, "It's not just that they want you to fail. It's kind of like they want you to die."

Tony Dovolani had no idea what he was getting himself into when he found out that he was getting me as a partner for *Dancing with the Stars.*

With only few exceptions, over the seasons, Tony was known for getting the short end of the stick when it came to dancing partners. Perhaps for this very reason I had requested him as a partner (that and the fact that Angelo approved of him); I just knew he would be right for me. I couldn't see myself dancing with anyone else. When they paired us, I remember thinking, *This poor guy, he is in for a shitstorm.*

Tony wasn't familiar with the Church of Scientology. So I filled him in a little. But he learned more by observing me than by what I shared with him. My family and I had just left the church and I was dealing with the fallout, including the media attention that came with it. It was a lot to cope with. Our lives had changed in an instant. But I had made the decision to do this show and I didn't want to fail, despite the fact that I had NO prior dance experience. Not even *The Nutcracker* as a kid.

Tony's job is difficult. He has to become all things to a perfect stranger from day one. In a normal season, all he might have to deal with is a person's insecurities with dancing, but with me, he not only had to hold my hand through dances, but he had to deal with a whole other set of issues. He had to maneuver through my defenses, through my tears, my anxieties and insecurities on a daily basis. He was there for me when I needed him, when my friends from the church had deserted my family and me. If a workday was supposed to be four hours, Tony gave me twelve. He never said, "No, I can't rehearse any more" or "No, I can't talk to you anymore about this." I never once heard him say, "No, and I can't listen to one more story about your former life." It was always and still is, "Whatever you need" and "I am here for you." And he and his family continue to be there for me and my family.

After every show, competitors were required go through a press line with more than a dozen media outlets. Tony literally and figuratively held my hand through the first weeks of the show. He knew how I was always on the verge of tears when I was asked a question about Scientology and he would always say, "Come on, man, this woman just danced her ass off, talk about that." He did this repeatedly.

When the producers pushed him to get me to talk about leaving the church during televised rehearsals, he turned them down. He stood up to everyone on my behalf. No matter who it was or what it was for.

I wish they awarded mirror balls for being an extraordinarily loyal friend, protector, and therapist. Because Tony would certainly win it, all while attempting to teaching me a cha-cha. For that I will always be indebted to him.

A few weeks into *Dancing with the Stars,* Tony came to me and said, "Look, the producers would like you to at least consider doing something with the Scientology subject." Up until this point, Tony and the show's producer had done a great job of protecting me from the constant questions from the press line as well as on the show. But for the Most Memorable Year show, where contestants create dances out of the biggest moments in their lives, the producers wanted to get what was really going on in my life, and that was a big part of it.

They asked if I would consider the subject of leaving Scientology as the inspiration for the dance. I didn't want to keep saying no to them. It was show business, after all, and I felt I had to give them something. So I chose to dance to Katy Perry's "Roar."

Looking at the pop song's lyrics, I thought, *Yes, this is how I felt so many times in the church.*

You held me down, but I got up
Get ready 'cause I've had enough
I see it all, I see it now . . .

I shared my idea with Tony, who loved it, as did the producers. Tony worked overtime choreographing a dance that showed me as a puppet and him as the "Church of Hypocrisy" pulling my strings, controlling me. I broke down several times during the rehearsal. I was plagued by doubt. Were people going to see this as a sad attempt for publicity? Would they get the pain involved in this? Each time I started to cry, Tony would pull me outside, away from the cameras (which was against the rules) to shield me from being filmed. Everyone on the show knew how difficult this was for me and offered me nothing but support. Sometimes the producers stopped the cameras on their own. Cheryl Burke would leave her rehearsal room with Jack Osbourne anytime they saw me and Tony go outside to talk. They gave up precious time from their own rehearsal just to be there for me. That is why I fell in love with Tony, Cheryl, Jack, and the show as a whole. It comforted me and took care of me in ways that I had never imagined.

The day of the Most Memorable Year show, I was nervous. But I told myself that people would understand what I was doing and the world would see it as my "roar."

That night, in front of the audience and my family, Tony and I danced our hearts out. Unfortunately, the judges didn't think much of the dance, giving Tony and me the low score of the evening. Upon hearing this I started to cry, but Tony grabbed my shoulders and said, "Don't you do that. Don't let them see you like that. You were great." As always, Tony had my back.

I couldn't have gotten as far as I did in *DWTS* if I hadn't had the guts to do the show in the first place. I had been asked to do the show in a previous season and had declined. I eventually agreed to do *DWTS* because I didn't want to be scared to go out of my comfort zone; I didn't want to care about what people thought of me anymore; I didn't want to be judged for my decisions. The truth is I was scared to do a live show—a live show that I had to dance in! But I didn't want to shrink from the public eye. I wanted to get myself out there, and that's exactly what I did.

Chapter Nineteen

RIGHT AFTER I LEFT THE CHURCH, MY FIRST THOUGHT WAS: *Bad things are going to happen to me.* Even though bad things had been happening to me *in* the church—and for a long time—I still couldn't shake a thought process of personal cause and effect that had been hammered into me ever since my mother sat Nicole and me down at our kitchen table in Bensonhurst as kids and talked to us about the precepts from her communication course.

As an antidote to my ruminating, I actively filled my head with a different kind of idea. I looked at everything I used, from Post-its to shampoo, and reasoned that somehow these companies have found a way to be successful *without* Scientology. People—happy, well-off, fulfilled people—walked by me every day who didn't use LRH technology.

After thinking a certain way, and being told what to think based on strict policy for more than thirty years, learning to think for myself and make my own choices did not come easily, nor did it happen overnight. Now, more than two years after cutting ties with the church, I'm still trying to figure things out. This mindset, which had been drilled into me for decades, is not an easy thing to "unlearn." With practically every decision I made when I first left (and still even now), I had to ask myself *Is that what* you *really think, or what a Sci-entologist would think?*

During this confusing early period, I sometimes felt adrift, but I had one figure I kept front and center in my mind to keep from going crazy: Nicole Kidman.

That's right, Tom Cruise's ex was my guardian angel. Although I never met her or attempted to meet her, I thought about her a lot. While I stared at the dark ceiling at night, unable to sleep, I would say to myself, "Remember Nicole Kidman. She was declared an SP and left the church, and she's doing okay. Her career is still going, and she has a husband and family . . . Just remember Nicole Kidman. She left and she's okay . . ."

And while the many friends I had in the church turned their backs on me, a number of those who had already left offered me comfort and solace.

My friend Paul Haggis, the movie director and former longtime Scientologist, sent me a note, part of which read:

But here is what I want you to know; I will do anything for you—anything you need. Privately or very publicly. Decide what that is, what you need of me, and ask and I will just say yes.

The fact that you refused to disconnect [from me] truly touched me. You were the only one. Which says a lot about you and even more about the good people who used to be our mutual friends. You are a better example of a scientologist than they ever were, because you truly applied your code of honor, and the danger formula, both of which they are afraid to do honestly.

Over the past few years I've read this letter hundreds of times to remind myself that I could just possibly be a good person at times. When Paul left the church and became the subject of a *New Yorker* magazine article and Lawrence Wright's book *Going Clear,* he took and continues to take a lot of heat from the church and its members. It was very public. One of the reasons Paul left the church was because of the offensive manner in which they view homosexuality. Two of Paul's daughters are gay, and he knew that he could no longer participate in a religion that discounted his own children. I, like him, was disgusted by the church's position and as a result I refused to disconnect from him despite the fact that I had been told to do so. Paul was and remains a friend.

"I'm so happy for you. You're about to experience life for the first time," Jason Beghe said to me a few weeks after I had left. "It's like Christmas when you're a kid, magical and amazing."

The last time I saw Jason was at CC. I said, "Hi, baby, whatcha doin'?" Naturally, I meant course-wise or auditing-wise, but he answered: "Leaving." I was confused, so I asked him what he meant.

"Leaving the church," he said.

I still didn't get it.

"CC?"

"No, the whole thing, Kitten."

The news came as a complete shock. Jason was so dedicated.

"What happened? What can I do to help?" I said. He just smiled his movie star smile and said, "No, baby doll, it's done, but I love you."

Now that I had left the church, Jason was trying to show me what he had already experienced. His comment about it being like Christmas reminded me of the movie *The Nightmare Before Christmas*, where everyone lives in Halloween Town, and all they know from is a world related to Halloween. One day the main character Jack Skellington wanders into the forest and finds seven holiday doors and opens a portal to Christmas Town. Here, for the first time, he finds that there is a world outside of Halloween. He begins to question all he sees when he continually asks "What's this?" It was the same thing for me and I imagine for anyone else who has left a cult-like community. Worlds open up to you that you were previously cut off from. I now realize that there are plenty of people in the universe doing good things. Not just Scientologists, as I was falsely led to believe.

———

MOST SCIENTOLOGISTS WILL NEVER MEET Tom Cruise or David Miscavige. They will never experience seeing behind the curtain like I and a handful of others have. And that is why most of my friends found what I went through unbelievable.

On the other side of things, sitting down and talking to my non-Scientology friends for the first time about the "double life" I had been leading and unburdening myself to them with the truth was scary but ultimately cathartic.

I was nervous to tell Jennifer that not only had I left the church but her father, David Lopez, a longtime Scientologist, might have pressure put on him to disconnect from his daughter or to have Jennifer disconnect from me.

I called her and told her I needed to come over and talk to her. Her first response was "Is everyone okay?"

"Yes, it's about the church."

I drove to her house, going over in my mind if it would be the last time I would see or talk to her, if our friendship would be over. Much like it had been with my friends in the church who had chosen to disconnect from me.

Upon my arrival at Jennifer's, she was waiting for me with my favorite coffee.

I started with "So the church has this policy . . ." And I explained disconnection to her. "If you stay friends with me, your dad will have to choose between you and the church and in more cases than not, people choose the church. So I am telling you that I understand your choice to disconnect from me."

Jennifer is a family girl, 100 percent. And although we are close, I assumed she would unequivocally choose her family, which I respected and was totally prepared for. Although I would have to mourn the loss of yet another friendship, I wouldn't want her to make any other decision. As I sat there with my head down and tears welling in my eyes, she said, "That is the most ridiculous thing I have ever heard."

"I know, Jen, but it's the policy of the church."

She rolled her eyes and said, "That's my dad, he would never. And you are my friend. I don't want to ever talk about this bullshit again." And with that she offered me a chocolate chip cookie.

As the press rolled out the news in subsequent weeks, Jen often reminded me not to get caught up in the game of it, but to remember that good things happened to me while I was in the church and to take what positive experiences I had and move on with love from there. To find my peace with it, not to hate them.

I am grateful to have Jennifer in my life. And while she may be known as J-Lo to most, at the same time she is a person who continues to improve who she is as a mother, a daughter, a sister, a woman. Once people reach a certain level in this business, they stop trying. And my friend hasn't. And for that, I admire her and am most impressed.

Jen is open to different paths, which is one of the many things I love about her. She doesn't judge and is truly about self-love. She introduced me to therapy and she helped me to open up my mind to the idea that "there is more than one way." For the last thirty-plus years, I was taught that there *is* only one way and that way is Scientology.

So while it's been a little more than two years now since I left the organization, for the first time it's like I'm living a real and authentic life—everything from sitting and enjoying a glass of wine with non-Scientologist girlfriends without secretly judging them as they speak about their lives and thinking Scientology could help them with that, to worrying that I am wasting my time finding enjoyment in my child or family when I should be on course or in session instead. I put so much time, energy, and resources into the church that it left little room for anything else.

In an attempt to further explore the world outside Scientology, I have been learning, or at least trying to learn, how to deal with my emotions in therapy (any form of psychoanalysis or therapy is completely frowned upon by the church).

My therapist has opened my eyes to so much information and knowledge that has helped me understand myself and other people.

We also worked on trying to alleviate the massive guilt I felt not only for abandoning a church that I was part of for my whole life but also for leading my whole family out of it as well. I was responsible for the fact that my mother, stepfather, sister, and brother-in-law lost their entire social network. My brother-in-law also lost his dad, his sisters, and his nephew. The damaging domino effect started with me. It has occurred to me more than I like to admit that maybe I was a Suppressive Person, who did the wrong thing.

"Did you ever think that maybe you've saved their lives?" my therapist once asked. "You all learned what you learned from Scientology. Now you're out, and your new job could be something else because you went through it."

Instead of bashing Scientology, she asked me what worked about it. Her point was that in life there are "knowledges." You can take a little bit from this and a little bit from that. Use what works for you and leave the rest.

"Leah, it doesn't need to be all right or all wrong. Take what worked. Don't try to throw away everything from Scientology."

But that was the policy of the church. You were either all in or all out. It is an extremist religion. There is no middle ground. And there within its structure lies the danger.

It was as if she were giving me permission to find resolution in my past. With that I felt such relief. Once I started to encounter testimonies of abuse at the hands of the church, I also started to doubt all of the technology and practices that I had learned and applied over the decades as well. Today, I'm able to ascertain which concepts and precepts were helpful to me and am able to still apply them. And I am now comfortable with the idea that even if I could find things the church offered me that feel "right," that didn't mean my leaving it was wrong. And although I thought the problem with the church was David Miscavige and Tom Cruise, now I realize that if both of them left the church tomorrow I wouldn't necessarily feel differently about Scientology. To me, it's a structural flaw of the faith that its adherents are forbidden from challenging the leader (and its policies) at all costs. And right behind the current leader is another of the same kind.

PEOPLE ARE SURPRISED WHEN THEY hear that I don't feel any anger toward my mother for getting us into Scientology in the first place. She stood by me when it mattered the most, after I left the church, and I know she always had my best interests at heart. She didn't want her daughters growing up in a bad environment; she wanted more for us, and yet she didn't have any other options for getting us out of Brooklyn. My mom—aspiring, hardworking, but without resources or a safety net—was the perfect candidate for Scientology. So she took us to Florida on a leap of faith, believing in what she was doing, just as I believe in what I'm doing now.

And just as my mother fought for Nicole and me to have a better life, now I am looking out for my own daughter, and I'm very grateful that I never indoctrinated her in any way before I left the church. As long as I was a Scientologist, the church told me what to do and what not to do in almost every aspect of my life. If I had any doubts about leaving my faith, they vanished when I thought of Sofia growing up with that same kind of dependency. I didn't want her to grow up thinking her connection to the church was the measure of her success in life. I wanted her to be an individual. Belief and faith are great, but very few people have been led astray by thinking for themselves.

In the end, change is never easy. Living with a core set of beliefs that completely unravel is unsettling, to say the least. We all have to decide, do we want to live in regret, suffer pain, and demonize ourselves for believing in and carrying out the tenets of the church, or do we want to look at what we gained? The "bad" had to happen. If it didn't, we would still be walking around with blinders on, not seeing the world at large. We wouldn't have been given the gift to explore new ideas, new ways of being, thinking, open to the possibilities that there are other beliefs, different paths that can bring us closer to others. We would not be able to be more solid than ever in our belief that "what is true for you is true because you yourself have observed it to be true."

We all have a newfound strength, in that we will never again "believe" just because.

For most of my childhood and adult life, I thought I had the answers and most of the world was just lost. As I've grown, I've learned that I know almost nothing. And so, in that I feel reborn in a sense. I am reading, I go to therapy, I do things that bring me joy, learning to love the one person I didn't like very much—myself.

I am a combative, inquisitive, argumentative person, and I will never allow anyone to change that. I still have anger, but I'm okay with that because it fuels me to continue to right any wrongs I may see. And it's because of that and the support of my true friends and family that I was able to fight my way out of Scientology and see the world for the first time. Without judgment or pressure not to think the way I do or to have a different faith. Our lives have begun. Lessons are being learned, and we are healing. It's never too late to begin again. Better, stronger, more evolved.

And to all my fellow troublemakers, I say, "Carry on."

Acknowledgments

I would like to thank my publisher, Ballantine Books, for having the balls to say yes to this book. Not everyone (regardless of how much "in the headlines" the subject may be) has the courage to publish a book knowing how litigious the Church of Scientology is toward people and groups who simply want to tell their story. My editor, Pam Cannon, worked morning, noon, and night to get this book right. (If I heard "Mommy is on the phone" once during this process, I heard it a thousand times.) You kept your promise to me to hold my hand the entire time, and I will be forever grateful to you and your team.

To Rebecca Paley, you spent so many hours listening to me go on and on; you laughed at my dumb jokes and stories that I swore were vital to this book. You did a beautiful job of editing some real nasty crap I wanted to say about myself and others, always keeping the bigger picture in mind.

To all the people I pissed off, personally and professionally: Forgive me. But I'm sure not much will change.

To APA's Jim Gosnell, Hayden Meyer, Brian Speiser, Steve Fisher, Lee Dinstman, and Jonathan Perry: Thank you for putting up with me, probably the most irritating client in APA history.

To Carol Bodie and Oren Segal: How brave you were to take me on as a client even after I told you how many managers I had fired!

To Kelly Bush and Rachel Karten at ID: I am lucky to have you both.

To Tony Biancosino, Mike Odair, and the crew of *It's All Relative*: Thank you for hanging in there.

To *The King of Queens* creators, writers, cast, and crew: Thank you for making our show so great that audiences still find it entertaining today.

To Kevin James: Thank you for being my leading man. Even now, you are leading me by teaching me about forgiveness. And I love you for that.

To Harry Gold: Although we have parted ways professionally, I will always love you for what you have done for me.

To Jessica Paster: You are a wonderful and caring person in a jaded business. You go far and beyond for me and my family.

To my support team—Celia Reyes, Trish Sereka, Louie Barbusca, Raffy Ganimian: You are more than employees. You are there for me in ways that go far beyond the call of duty. Without you, I would fall apart. I love you all.

To Corina Duran Rabichuck: Despite your being rude, obnoxious, and unprofessional as my makeup artist, you have been one of my most dedicated and loyal friends.

To Jennifer "Jai" Jordan, Henry Byalikov, Yaron and Colby Abraham, Loren Ridinger, Nilda Rodriguez, Addie Markowitz, Lucille Chuiasano, Brendan Johnston, Laney Ziv, Andrea Martin, Nazanin Boniadi, Anna Maria Orzano, Maria Savoy, Sinbad, and Debbie Barbusca: I love you and I cherish our friendship.

To Cheryl Burke: You are family now and I love you.

To Mark Feuerstein: You are the mensch of all mensches.

To Marc Anthony: Thank you for singing to us. Always.

To Chelsea Handler: Thank you for trying to force drugs on me after I left the church. I may just take you up on it. You make jokes for a living, but there are no jokes when it comes to your loyalty as a friend. Your love and compassion know no bounds. Thank you for always being ready to come to my defense. I adore you.

To Jennifer Lopez: I'm hoping as we grow old together, you get fat and ugly.

To Sandy Campanella, friend for life: Thank you for your words of love and support. Thank you for your belief in me.

To Sherry Lewis Ollins, Chantel Dodson, and Trisha Conley: Ladies, you are courageous. Wear your necklaces proudly. And although we are all SPs, you are fearless. To us, "the Fearless Four."

To Michelle Visage: Thank you for the love, laughs, and your continued courage to stand by my side, regardless of what might come your way. You are a champion for your friends, your family, and the LBGT community. I am proud to know you.

To Kevin Becker: Thank you for going up against the machine for me and doing it with a lot of comedy. For a detective, you are pretty damn funny. You are always ready to "Protect and Serve" our family. We are eternally grateful.

Alice Whitfield, my soul sister: I wish we were related for real. You have taught me so much. You always thought I was better than I allowed myself to be. Thank you for always being the one to speak the truth to me even when I don't want to hear it. I love you madly.

Jocelyn Jones: You said to me, "I love the Brooklyn stuff and it will get you far in this business, but I know you are a sweet, vulnerable teddy bear inside and I want to see her once in a while." Thank you for seeing that side of me. And thank you for being the beautiful, insightful woman you are.

To those who follow me on social media: You have supported and loved me in ways I couldn't have imagined. Thank you for being with me all these years and embracing my crazy ass. You lift me up when I need you.

To Stephanie, my therapist: You have the patience of a saint. Thank you for helping me on my road to recovery. You have your work cut out for you.

To Debbie Cook and Wayne Baumgarten, Mike Rinder, Marty and Monique Rathbun, Marc and Claire Headley, Tony Ortega, Lawrence Wright, Tom De Vocht, Larry Anderson, Alex Gibney, Jason Beghe, the Garcias, Ron Miscavige, Jenna Miscavige Hill, Karen de la Carriere, Amy Skobee, and Paul Haggis:

You all have had the courage to expose the Church of Scientology for the harmful effects it has had on you personally and in general. You have told stories for those who didn't have a voice; you continue to be harassed and yet you continue to tell the truth.

To those who continue to write about and speak out against Scientology, and what it does to destroy families: I applaud you. You are strong; the church did not defeat you. It taught you to know what is true for you. And you do know that. They do too—which is why they fight you.

To the ex-Scientology kids and the ex–Sea Org children: What was done to you was wrong. You did nothing wrong. You were supposed to be protected and you weren't. Fight for a better life; you are not forgotten.

To my family:

Mary Remini: Grandma, you Sicilian spicy lovely lady, R.I.P. You are the angel by my side.

Dennis and Maryanne: I am glad that our families have remained connected.

My stepsons, Alex, Nico, and Angelito: You have grown into beautiful men, and I am blessed to have you in my life.

The Pagáns: Coco, thank you for being the brother-in-law I always wanted. You make me laugh. Thank God, because your brother doesn't.

To my brother-in-law Mike Wiskow, thank you for putting up with my sister and our crazy family.

My sisters, Elizabeth, Stephanie, Christina: You endured a lot. You are all fighters. Stephanie (R.I.P), our little firecracker—we spent four hours on the phone saying goodbye. Thank you for knowing I needed that.

Brianna and Brandon: I'm constantly inspired by your spirituality. But you could be better at calling me when you don't need something.

My brother, Michael Anthony Divicino: Though you've been incarcerated for twenty-five years, you have been a source of comfort and strength for me nevertheless. One day I hope to hold your hand and walk right out of there with you. I love you. Your li'l sis always.

George: You made my mom a happy woman. And you took on four crazy women, and we thank you for that. You are the only grandfather my daughter and Nicole's children have ever known. You have done your job well. You are a good man, George Marshall. We love you.

Shannon: One of the funniest people I know. And the most disgusting. I love you like you are my own child. You and Willy are always there when I need you. I am sorry that my decisions cost you relationships with friends and family, but your dedication to what is morally right is what I admire the most. You stood up for what you believed in, and for that I love you.

Nicole: You beat the shit out of me when we were younger, but you also beat the shit out of anyone who looked at me sideways. You continue to do so today. You are brave, Nic. You are always willing to fight my battles, and you are much stronger than you believe. If I'm in a fight, I want you by my side. Always.

Dad: I thank you for the life lessons. Your presence and absence make your girls stronger. I forgive it all. And still love you.

Mom: You are my rock. You believed in me and supported me in ways that made me who I am today. Your laugh is infectious, and your love for life is astounding. I know now how you hustled to make a better life for your family. And I can't thank you enough for it. Your decisions led us all here and I am grateful. When the chips were down, you gave up all that you worked for your whole life.

Angelo: You know me inside and out and yet you've stayed with me. You have allowed me to put your stuff out there for the world to see, and although you threatened me with a lawsuit (kidding), I want you to know that I realize how much courage it took for you to allow me to tell our story, good and bad. You are brave, not only for this, but to be with someone as annoying and trying as me. You got involved in something that didn't come naturally to you but embraced it because you thought it would help you to be a better person. Really, though, you did it for me. And you remained in it for me. And you left it for me. You are a beautiful father to your sons and continue to be an amazing daddy to our daughter. Thank you for being the one consistent man in our lives.

Sofia: I hope one day you will read this book and it will inspire you to be a strong, independent woman, who relies on her family. I hope you see that in the end, as much as I may have screwed up your childhood, I, your family, and your real friends will be there when you need us most. I hope you'll be able to see that *not* having the "perfect" childhood could lead you to places that will teach you life's most valuable lessons. I want you to be the person who will lead, not follow. If it weren't for you, I wouldn't be here right now. It is because of you that I wrote this book. You brought me here, and you gave me the strength to make these big changes in my life. You have led me. Already.

About the Author

LEAH REMINI is an actor, producer, and writer. A fixture on television since the age of eighteen, Remini is best known for her beloved role of Carrie on the nine-season hit *The King of Queens*. Remini went on to produce and star in one of the earliest and most successful comedic web series, *In the Motherhood*, and appeared in the movie *Old School* alongside Will Ferrell and Vince Vaughn. In 2010, Remini helped launch and co-hosted the first season of the CBS daytime hit show *The Talk*, and in 2013 she was seen on the dance floor in *Dancing with the Stars*. She currently co-stars in the TV Land comedy *The Exes* and TLC's reality show *Leah Remini: It's All Relative*, which she also created and executive produces. Remini finds great joy in her philanthropic work with numerous and diverse military, women's, and children's charities. She lives in Los Angeles with her husband and daughter.

About the Type

This book was set in Garamond, a typeface originally designed by the Parisian type cutter Claude Garamond (c. 1500–61). This version of Garamond was modeled on a 1592 specimen sheet from the Egenolff-Berner foundry, which was produced from types assumed to have been brought to Frankfurt by the punch cutter Jacques Sabon (c. 1520–80).

Claude Garamond's distinguished romans and italics first appeared in *Opera Ciceronis* in 1543–44. The Garamond types are clear, open, and elegant.